Teaching Quantitative Methods

'There is much talk and often hype nowadays about the crisis in quantitative research methods in British social science. It is time for a clear-thinking discussion of the underlying issues and how best to address them through teaching in this area. Payne and Williams's book represents a highly significant contribution to such a debate and should be essential reading for all of us who have taught quantitative research methods.'

Alan Bryman, Professor of Organisational and Social Research, University of Leicester

'This is a balanced plea for improving the way we teach social science methods and makes a compelling case for addressing the crisis in quantitative skills and reasoning in contemporary social science education. But this collection does more than make the case. It also provides evidence based approaches to improving the way we teach quantitative social science. This collection is timely and will equip those charged with the task of teaching quantitative methods to deliver.'

David de Vaus, Executive Dean, Faculty of Social & Behavioural Sciences, The University of Queensland

Teaching Quantitative Methods

getting the basics <u>RIGHT</u>

GEOFF PAYNE AND **MALCOLM WILLIAMS**

Los Angeles | London | New Delhi
Singapore | Washington DC

First published 2011

SAGE Publications Ltd
1 Oliver's Yard
55 City Road
London EC1Y 1SP

SAGE Publications Inc.
2455 Teller Road
Thousand Oaks, California 91320

SAGE Publications India Pvt Ltd
B 1/I 1 Mohan Cooperative Industrial Area
Mathura Road, Post Bag 7
New Delhi 110 044

SAGE Publications Asia-Pacific Pte Ltd
33 Pekin Street #02-01
Far East Square
Singapore 048763

Library of Congress Control Number 2010933649

British Library Cataloguing in Publication data

A catalogue record for this book is available from the British Library

ISBN 978-1-84860-000-3
ISBN 978-1-84860-001-0 (pbk)

Typeset by C&M Digitals (P) Ltd, Chennai, India
Printed by MPG Books Group, Bodmin, Cornwall
Printed on paper from sustainable resources

CONTENTS

About the Authors   vii
Preface   xi
Geoff Payne and Malcolm Williams

1   Introduction: The 'Crisis of Number': Informed Citizens,
    Competent Social Scientists   1
    Geoff Payne and Malcolm Williams

2   Mapping the Academic Landscape of Quantitative Methods   9
    Geoff Payne

3   Best Practices in Quantitative Methods Teaching:
    Comparing Social Science Curricula Across Countries   32
    Jonathan Parker

4   The Place of Quantification in the Professional Training
    of Sociologists: Some Career Reflections   49
    Martin Bulmer

5   Challenges and Opportunities for Developing
    Teaching in Quantitative Methods   66
    Malcolm Williams and Carole Sutton

6   How to Teach the Reluctant and Terrified to Love Statistics:
    The Importance of Context in Teaching Quantitative
    Methods in the Social Sciences   85
    Katharine Adeney and Sean Carey

7   Improving the Teaching of Quantitative Methods to
    Undergraduate Social Scientists: Understanding and
    Overcoming the Barriers   99
    Jane Falkingham and Teresa McGowan

8   Increasing Secondary Analysis in Undergraduate
    Dissertations: A Pilot Project   121
    Jo Wathan, Mark Brown and Lee Williamson

9   Mathematics for Economics: Enhancing Teaching and
    Learning   142
    Rebecca Taylor and Angela Scott

10 Jorum: A National Service for Learning and Teaching   157
   Jackie Carter

11 The Problem, Strategies and Resources in Teaching
   Quantitative Methods: The Way Forward   177
   Matthew David

Index   183

ABOUT THE AUTHORS

Katharine Adeney is a Senior Lecturer in the Department of Politics at the University of Sheffield. She is the author of three books, including *Contemporary India* (Palgrave, 2010) and *Federalism and Ethnic Conflict Regulation in India and Pakistan* (Palgrave, 2007). Her principal research interests include: India and Pakistan, ethnic conflict regulation and institutional design; the creation and maintenance of national identities; the politics of federal states, and democratisation in South Asia. Together with Sean Carey she recently completed an ESRC-funded project to develop innovative methods for teaching quantitative research methods at the undergraduate level.

Mark Brown has a background in demography, and over ten years of experience at Manchester University in teaching quantitative methods to undergraduate and postgraduate students in the Social Sciences. His key interests lie in trying to make quantitative approaches more accessible and interesting to students with non-quantitative backgrounds, and he is a strong advocate of teaching with 'real' survey data. To this end he is a regular user of UK Government Survey Data that are made available via the Economic and Social Data Service (ESDS).

Martin Bulmer is a sociologist who took up his first academic appointment in the Department of Social Theory and Institutions at the University of Durham in 1968, and retired in October 2008 from the Department of Sociology at the University of Surrey, where he is now Emeritus Professor of Sociology. For one year during the 1970s he was a statistician in the Office of Population Censuses and Surveys, London, now part of the Office for National Statistics. From 2000 to 2008 he was Director of the ESRC Question Bank, and from 2002 to 2008 he directed the ESRC Survey Link Scheme. Both are now part of the ESRC Survey Resources Network. He edits the journal *Ethnic and Racial Studies*. His most recent publications are *Secondary Analysis of Survey Data* (edited with P. Sturgis and N. Allum, 2009) and *Social Measurement Through Social Surveys: An Applied Approach* (edited with J. Gibbs and L. Hyman, 2010).

Sean Carey is a lecturer in the Department of Politics at the University of Sheffield. His research centres on voting behaviour and public opinion, with a particular focus on the impact that political parties, the media and national identity play on influencing public attitudes towards European integration. With Katharine Adeney he recently completed an ESRC-funded project to develop innovative methods for teaching quantitative research methods at the undergraduate level.

Jackie Carter did a degree in Mathematics with its Applications after which she taught maths to 11–19 year olds. She subsequently obtained a Master's in Computing and PhD (in Geostatistical Methods for Radiation Monitoring data) and has worked with social science data for over fifteen years, primarily aggregate census data and international time series macrodata, with a focus on providing national data services to the academic community from Mimas based at the University of Manchester. Jackie has also worked on delivering national learning and teaching online services, managing an award winning vocational service and co-directing the national learning and teaching repository service, Jorum. She attempts to interweave these two main areas by focusing on how using data can assist in building statistical capacities at the undergraduate and taught post-graduate level.

Matthew David is a lecturer at Brunel University, where he teaches sociology of culture and research methods. He is author (with Carole Sutton) of *Social Research: The Basics* (Sage, 2004) and its expanded second edition – *Social Research: An Introduction* (Sage, 2011). He also edited *Case Study Research* (Sage, 2007) and *Methods of Interpretive Research* (Sage, 2010). His substantive interests are in science, technology and popular culture. He is author of *Knowledge Lost in Information* (with David Zeitlyn and Jane Bex: Office of Humanities Press, 1999), *Science in Society* (Palgrave, 2005) and *Peer to Peer and the Music Industry: The Criminalization of Sharing* (Sage, 2010), along with numerous articles and chapters on power, knowledge and inequality in the digital age.

Jane Falkingham is Professor of Demography and International Social Policy and is currently Director of the ESRC Centre for Population Change and Head of the School of Social Sciences at the University of Southampton. She has taught research methods to undergraduates and post-graduates at Southampton and previously at the LSE. She remains passionate about students acquiring the knowledge base necessary for both understanding and producing the evidence base for informed policy making.

Teresa McGowan is the current Research Programme Manager for the ESRC Centre for Population Change at the University of Southampton. She was previous employed as the Research Fellow on two linked ESRC pilot projects aimed at improving the teaching of quantitative methods to undergraduates in the social sciences. She completed a BSc in Population Sciences and an MSc in Social Statistics from the University of Southampton prior to beginning studying for a PhD.

Jonathan Parker is a Lecturer in American Politics in the School of Politics, International Relations and Philosophy (SPIRE). He received his PhD from the University of North Carolina at Chapel Hill in 1999. His research interests are in public policy, state politics in the USA and education. His is currently the principal investigator for an International Bench-marking

Review of Best Practice in the Provision of Undergraduate Teaching in Quantitative Methods in the Social Sciences for the ESRC. His teaching interests include American government, contemporary America, mass media, research methods, and service learning.

Geoff Payne teaches social research methods at Newcastle University. He is a former BSA President who, as an advocate of methodological pluralism, has made a number of contributions to the debate about research methods in British sociology. The second edition of his *Key Concepts in Social Research* is due shortly from Sage.

Angela Scott's academic background is in English Literature, in which she holds a Master's degree. Angela's extensive experience as project coordinator within the education sector led to her involvement with the METAL project (Mathematics for Economics: Enhancing Teaching and Learning), and to her overseeing the final two years of its development. Angela's contribution ensured that the resource bank was simple to use and visually stimulating, and also reflected the needs of potential users. Angela is now working on a business sustainability project at Nottingham Trent University.

Rebecca Taylor is the Associate Dean of the Nottingham Business School. She has a PhD in Economics and is engaged in research on international trade as well as developments in economics education. Rebecca is an Associate Director of the Economics Network and has directed a number of HEFCE funded teaching and learning projects, including Mathematics for Economics: Enhancing Teaching and Learning (METAL), Teaching Resources for Undergraduate Economics (TRUE), and Depository of Statistics Resources in Social Sciences (De-STRESS).

Jo Wathan supports the secondary use of government microdata as a member of the Samples of Anonymised Records team (funded under ESRC's Census Programme) and the Government specialist function of the Economic and Social Data Service. She completed a PhD using the Labour Force Survey at the Cathie Marsh Centre for Census and Survey Research in 2000 and has since spent most of her time working at the centre on data and teaching projects. She teaches statistics software and secondary analysis practice at Manchester and provides training on using secondary data in research and teaching under the auspices of the data support services.

Malcolm Williams is Professor and Director of the School of Social Sciences at Cardiff University, which he joined in 2010. Prior to this he was Professor of Social Research Methodology at the University of Plymouth. He is the author/editor of several books on method and methodology, including *Science and Social Science* (Routledge, 2000), *Making Sense of Social Research* (Sage, 2003) and *Philosophical Foundations of Social Research* (Sage, four volume collection, 2006). He is the author of many scientific papers in areas such as probability theory, objectivity, representation and empirical work in household transitions, the measurement of homelessness and social research pedagogy. He is joint editor of *Methodological Innovations Online*.

Lee Williamson gained her PhD in statistics and demography from the Cathie Marsh Centre for Census and Survey Research (CCSR) (University of Manchester) where she has also worked on various projects. These included providing user support for large-scale government surveys as part of the Economical and Social Data Service (ESDS) and contributing to the development of the Secondary Analysis for Social Sciences (SASS) pilot project for undergraduate students within the University of Manchester. Lee is currently a researcher at the University of St Andrews working on various longitudinal research projects as part of the Longitudinal Studies Centre, Scotland (LSCS).

PREFACE

In *Teaching Quantitative Methods*, we set out to do three things. First, we explore the nature of 'the crisis of numeracy' in contemporary social science, and in particular how this relates to the way the social sciences are taught. Our second step is to present some well-researched, experimental approaches to tackling this issue in the teaching of undergraduates. Finally we reflect on what further changes in practice and what kinds of resources can be made available, not only for those who are currently teaching social research methods but also for anybody concerned with improving the shape and content of the university curriculum.

In other words, this is a book for anyone interested in how empirical social science is carried out and carried forward, not just the specialist lecturer in social research methods. It is a book about how quantitative methods can be better and more extensively taught, but it is not a narrow-minded or narrowly focused attack on other methods of research. It is about the basic skills we should expect from our graduates, not esoteric specialist knowledge.

Academics are notoriously good at defining problems but less good at coming up with answers. Indeed, two thing that swiftly emerge here are that we are not dealing with a single problem, and there is no quick fix. As editors and as contributors to this collection, we neither offer a set of prescriptive recipes for classroom practice, nor claim to have found a complete solution to the problem of numeracy in the social sciences. But we do not want to exaggerate the challenge we face, or to spread despondency. Change is already taking place (even since starting on this collection), and there is scope for further innovation. The projects reported in the core of this collection are offered as suggestions and sources of ideas, as works in progress, and we hope as encouragement for further innovation.

Prior to the development of what has recently become a substantial area of policy debate, the origin of this collaboration between the editors lies, as with many research studies, in a casual conversation over a cup of coffee more than a decade ago. Our first small-scale contribution (eventually published as Payne et al., 2004), which attempted to identify the methods of social research that were being used in UK sociology, was supported by the Department of Sociology's Research Development Fund at the University of Plymouth. Subsequent project funding was kindly supplied by the *Higher Education Academy* Subject Network for Sociology, Anthropology and Politics (C-SAP), the British Sociological Association, and the Economic and Social Research Council (ESRC). These projects, together with the efforts of many others, provided the foundation for a programme of work funded by the ESRC on a much larger scale, the outcome of which makes up the bulk of this collection. All of the authors gratefully acknowledge the financial support they have received, and the contribution made by the many colleagues and students who took part in the research projects. As editors we must also thank our contributors for their forbearance and cooperation, and Jai Seaman at Sage for her support and for guiding the book through to publication.

However, the teaching of quantitative research methods is never static, nor is the concern about it restricted to the past 10 years. Looking backwards we can find debates, in sociology for example, dating from the 1970s, which were stimulated by leading players such as Bell and Newby, Burgess, Bechhofer, and the former Council for National Academic Awards. Looking forward, the International Benchmarking Exercise, the excellent current work led by the National Centre for Research Methods and by John MacInnes as ESRC Strategic Advisor on undergraduate teaching of quantitative methods (as well as the impact of rapid IT development, Data Archives, and projects such as METAL and Jorum; see Chapters 8–10) will all add to the momentum for continued change. We intend this collection to provide an extra push behind the wheel of enhancing the teaching of quantitative methods and research skills.

Geoff Payne   Malcolm Williams
Newcastle University   Cardiff University

Reference

Payne, G., Williams, M. and Chamberlain, S. (2004) 'Methodological pluralism in British sociology', *Sociology*, 38 (1):153–64.
All *URLs* given in the text were accessed and working at the time of writing.

The 'Crisis of Number': Informed Citizens, Competent Social Scientists

Geoff Payne and Malcolm Williams

Whether we like it or not — and whether our students like it or not — the contemporary world runs on numbers. There is hardly a single issue in public life, in civil society, in the world of employment, business and management, or even within the domestic home, which does not depend on counting, measuring and calculating — and crucially, *reasoning* with number. Both as ordinary members of the public, and as social scientists, we need to acquire better skills in quantitative methods in order to make sense of what a recent Economic and Social Research Council (ESRC) document described as the 'seismic changes' in our modern, diverse and dynamic society, and to tackle the 'increasingly complicated questions about UK economic competitiveness' posed by 'the relentless pressures of globalisation' (ESRC, 2008: 2).

The dramatic demand for greater national capability in quantitative analysis — the 'crisis of number' — can be met in a number of ways by improving education at any point from primary schooling, through to continuing professional development in mid-career. The specially commissioned contributions that make up this collection focus on *basic quantitative methods in undergraduate teaching and learning in the social sciences*, because we see undergraduate education as the pivotal stage for enhancing quantitative skills, and the social sciences are a major source of future analytical expertise. Thus what we offer in this book is an argument, supported by evaluated examples, rather than a 'cookbook' of teaching recipes. Only in the most general sense is this a 'How to Do …' book.

The chapters come from a network of researchers who have recently completed major projects or reviews in response to ESRC initiatives (see ESRC, 2006). The lesson from these studies is that what undergraduates encounter, and how they react to it, determines their numeracy levels when they come to make career decisions and enter the graduate workforce. In an era when over a third of all young people go through higher education, the habits of thought and advanced technical skills acquired during a university education have never been more significant. In particular, it is from this body of students that the next generation of postgraduates and future social scientists are selected.

Our argument for improving skills in quantitative methods is based not only on the vocational needs of 'Great Britain Ltd' for technically proficient professionals – although we do accept that this is important – but also on an ideological vision of active and critical citizens in a democratic society. An additional goal is to see the internal intellectual evolution of each of the social sciences. Of course, there are many ways in which such developments in knowledge and understanding can take place: raising the profile of quantitative methods is but one of them. However, this last theme both broadens and balances our case. Our advocacy is not dependent on a narrow view of mass higher education as primarily utilitarian, or economically functional, unlike those of both major British political parties for some time now (e.g. Department for Education and Science, 1987; Department for Education and Employment, 1999). We do not see the pay-off for quantitative methods as being solely what it offers for the job market or for employers: knowledge and skills have value in their own right, a value that is intrinsic to the disciplines themselves, rather than instrumental, and which does not lie simply in the commodification of learning or reduction in intellectual standards as part of a crude performative conception of the contemporary university (Barnett, 2005; Barnett and Coate, 2004).

As part of our commitment to this wider and deeper model of higher education, the central importance we attach to developing quantitative expertise in research methods training does not ignore or denigrate other methods of research and social analysis. On the contrary, we believe that the contribution of quantitative methods, and the problems currently associated with acquiring the necessary skills, can only be appreciated first as part of how students experience research as a whole, and second by seeing how research fits into the rest of the curriculum. Our intention is that by addressing the problems of teaching and learning quantitative methods encountered by social science undergraduates, we can make a case for seeking, and in some concrete ways, achieving a new *balance* and synthesis of analytical tools for understanding today's world. We do not claim that quantitative methods are sufficient *on their own* but equally, without them, the alternative methods of understanding and analysis available to us are similarly inadequate. The particular strength of a comprehensive quantitative approach is not numeracy *per se* but the rigour it introduces from the philosophy of social science to reasoning, the research process, and the relationship between empirical evidence and theoretical statements.

Nonetheless, even to be active citizens we need to understand a plethora of social phenomena which impinge on our lives: an ageing population or arguments over alternative therapies; benefit payment levels or bullying at school; climate change or crime; devolution or drugs; the environment or education; friendship choices or family sizes; gender discrimination or genetics; health or housing needs; and income, inequality and immigration, let alone religiosity, sexuality, taxation, unemployment, voting, warfare, xenophobia, youth or zealotry. Without resorting to numbers – sizes of groups, frequencies of occurrence, rates of change, distributions across locations – these cannot be fully comprehended. If we have no intellectual tools to measure interactions and effects we cannot explain which 'things' are linked to others, let alone develop interventions aimed at changing complex causal relationships. What do we know about production, productivity, profitability, predicted markets or personnel unless we have the numeracy skills to manage our economy?

While we would eschew a crude recasting of complex human issues into a simplistic numerical form, a lack of basic arithmetic competence is a severe handicap for the individual, and a collective impossibility for a complex technology-based society. If numeracy has become so important for everyday living, how much more so is it vital for today's social scientists at all levels to be competent in the use of quantitative methods which combine number with argumentation and exposition. It has become essential that we possess a critical awareness of the sources and validity of quantitative information, have the capacity to apply statistical analysis to raw data, and can engage and reason with numerical evidence. Without a strong base of quantitative methods in social research, and a further integration of quantitative research skills acquisition into the curriculum, the social sciences in Britain will continue to fail to realise their potential contribution to the common good, and lose their current high standing in the international academic community.

This has recently been dramatically illustrated by the International Benchmarking Review sponsored by the ESRC, the British Sociological Association and the Heads and Professors of Sociology group (ESRC et al., 2010). Although the international panel of independent experts found that UK sociology ranked second in the world (behind the Americans) it raised doubts about the true extent of claims to international reach and influence. The low levels of quantitative numeracy in UK sociology have inevitably isolated British sociologists not just from international collaboration but have also reduced their capacity even to appreciate the extensive quantitative work produced in other countries and reported in other nations' sociology journals. Poor quantitative skills can isolate a discipline from the rest of the world, restrict its development and damage its international standing.

If the more obvious characteristics of numeracy in terms of operational skills with number were the only issue, it might be easier to move forward. However, it is fundamental to our good practice of quantitative methods that we see them not simply as technical dexterities, but as part of a logical system of reasoning. Numbers themselves are not more important than the framework of the philosophy of social science that contains them. In the same way, other forms of data and analysis also have their part to play. The chapters in this collection, being based on the one hand on empirical research studies, and on the other hand, drawing on case studies and qualitative data to sustain our argument, therefore aim to be a more than a technical contribution to the 'crisis of number' debate.

The structure of the book

The contributors to this collection come from a range of social sciences. While the explorations and interventions they have made have chiefly been within their own disciplines, they have also kept in mind the wider ramifications of their work, and some of the chapters, such as Jonathan Parker's comparison of several different countries, or Jackie Carter's updating of the Jorum project, look at the social sciences as a whole. Each of the ESRC-funded projects was free-standing, but the common themes that emerged from them demonstrate the benefit of collecting together the experiences of the project teams. This delivers a wider dissemination of their several 'messages' and opens up the prospect of having a more influential impact than could be achieved by individual reports or articles addressed to and read in separate disciplines.

All of the chapters have been specially written for the book. This introductory chapter and Chapter 2 are intended to give an overview and also to give licence to the editors to express their own personal views – with which not all of the other contributors would necessarily agree! These lead into the next three chapters, each of which is directed at presenting a framework for thinking about teaching quantitative methods.

Jonathan Parker's international survey (Chapter 3) provides breadth, in the form of a comparative international benchmark against which to set our current practices in the UK. He reports on how the Scandinavian/north European model tends towards a more coherent pattern of developing research methods skills, concluding that the key issues are how quantitative skills are integrated with other research methods, and how these methods are spread through the whole of the curriculum. Quantitative methods do not exist in a vacuum. Becoming a graduate who can practise their discipline takes more than that: 'two modules do not turn undergraduates into social scientists'. Disciplines vary, with business studies and economics placing the greatest emphasis on quantitative competence, whereas politics is the social science devoting least time to research methods. In North America, initiatives such as the Integrating Data Analysis project have begun to gain ground, but the issue remains that the individual members of staff who teach methods cannot achieve change on their own: teaching teams as a whole have to be willing to work collectively to introduce changes that will promote student use of research skills. The chapter concludes with some examples and a checklist of questions that anyone teaching or designing modules in research methods should ask of themselves and their colleagues.

Although Chapter 4 is not based on a recent ESRC grant, Martin Bulmer's past involvement with ESRC and other policy projects, major contributions to the research methods literature, and engagement in the teaching of undergraduate and postgraduate quantitative methods give him a unique position to provide a historical perspective. Chapter 4 is thus a personal guide to 'How did we get to where we are now?', providing background depth to contemporary debate by drawing on his 40 years' experience of promoting research methods in social policy and sociology. Apart from its intrinsic interest and careful accounting of events and personalities, it provides a sharp sense to the historical contexts in which our ideas about quantitative methods were formed. The teaching of research methods is not an abstract discussion: it was grounded in institutions, curricula, individual career ambitions and competition for scarce resources in specific locations and times. It is all too easy to forget or misinterpret earlier episodes that shaped today's framework of attitudes. A deep-rooted resistance to, and even resentment towards quantitative methods in particular, and rigorous methods training in general, was an important feature of the development of later academic 'fashions' and current styles of research. Chapter 4 provides a salutary reminder that today's challenges are remarkably similar to those of the 1970s – and are still awaiting resolution.

Chapter 5 draws mainly on sociology, in particular a national study of what students – as against academics – say about the experience of learning research methods. Malcolm Williams and Carole Sutton present data on the maths backgrounds of students, and link this to how 'scientific' they believe their chosen discipline to be. Students' attitudes towards methods and the degrees of difficulty reported with quantitative elements are associated with their assessment performances. The research implies further support for placing students' *experiences* at the centre of thinking about how the subject is taught, while the second part of the chapter illustrates this with a case study of students' reactions to a field(work) trip.

Chapters 6 and 7 describe two experimental projects in curriculum innovation. Katharine Adeney and Sean Carey have developed a new research methods module in politics, which could be adapted for other subjects. Their approach starts with trying to engage student interest by lots of attention being paid to up-to-date examples. They see students as not only having anxieties about number *per se*, but also that their 'reluctance can also come from a denial that quantitative analysis has any place in the study of politics despite the pervasiveness of numerical data in the making of political argument'. It follows that students first need to be shown that this is a misplaced view. Only when students are gaining confidence does the module move on to more conventional statistics. In the light of earlier comments about how methods teaching is presented, an important feature in the success of this innovation has been the strong base of support from politics colleagues.

The two linked projects reported by Jane Falkingham and Teresa McGowan (Chapter 7) were aimed at a more disparate range of social science undergraduates, but with a more focused goal. The first dealt with enhancing the integration of quantitative methods skills in the broader undergraduate curricula, with a focus on first and second year undergraduates and courses. The project used focus groups to explore not only student attitudes, but staff views as well. Having identified a number of difficulties, the team then ran a 'consultancy' service to supply examples to lecturers. This worked in two directions: the methods staff received a flow of substantive social science exemplars, while the other staff were supplied with numeric case studies that they could build into their core topics. The second project aimed at 'increasing the use of quantitative methods in third year undergraduate dissertations in disciplines where use of such methods has been historically low'. The distinctive approach was to offer supplementary tuition in vacations, and to recompense students for the potential loss of earnings this entailed. While this is not a model that can easily be adopted without special funding, the promising outcome was that an increased number of volunteers signed up for the next academic year – when there was no financial incentive!

This attempt to encourage secondary analysis of large datasets is echoed in Chapter 9 by Jo Wathan and colleagues at the Cathie Marsh Centre for Census and Survey Research (CCSR). Again, volunteer groups of students interested in criminology and sociology were offered extra tuition (in the form of practical workshops and specially prepared handbooks) as well as small financial incentives. The fact that these projects felt it was necessary to offer financial rewards is itself an indication of staff perceptions of how resistant many students are to quantitative methods, although as the project developed, it became apparent that continued student involvement did not depend on the financial incentives. The project confirmed initial assumptions about the low awareness among undergraduates of the extensive holdings of datasets by the Economic and Social Data Service, and that there were barriers set up by difficulties in accessing them. The teaching intervention increased student confidence, and a number of dissertations incorporated secondary analysis, involving students in an extra workload commitment which the research team feel may not fully rewarded in most dissertation marking-schemes.

The final three chapters offer some positive responses to the issues raised in the earlier chapters: there is nothing more depressing than 'contributions' that define a problem and then leave readers despairing of any solution. Chapters 9 and 10 concentrate on two specific IT-based resources that are available to staff and/or students to use in teaching and learning quantitative methods. Rebecca Taylor and Angela Scott report on 'METAL' (Mathematics for Economics: Enhancing Teaching and Learning) which originated from a specific academic need encountered by lecturers in economics and related disciplines. This large network project is more directly concerned with basic competence in mathematics than the earlier chapters, but it shares with them the belief that successful teaching requires confidence-building, a demonstration of subject relevance, and the use of examples and case studies from everyday life, which having commonsense meanings for students. The materials that make up METAL are held in the form of downloadable programmes which include tests and self-assessments, video clips and animations showing mathematical issues in real world settings, as well as more conventional information. The keynote is flexible access and application, presented in 'bite-size' units that can either be a resource for module design, or a supplement for the students' independent learning.

As Jackie Carter explains, the other chapter (Chapter 10) about IT resources for teaching is not uniquely aimed at assisting the learning of quantitative methods, nor does the Jorum facility set out to provide content prepared by specialists in the project team. Instead, Jorum is a cooperative venture which offers a means for lending and borrowing teaching resources. The project maintains the infrastructure and works to promote user participation, but its ultimate success can only be judged by the willingness of lecturers to deposit 'their' materials for others to share. This in turn is related to the ease with which this can be accomplished. The potential of Jorum as a means of building enhanced teaching of quantitative methods is tremendous, and at a resource level, is a further indication of positive steps that those teaching the subject can take in their own institutions.

Finally, in what is almost a coda, Matthew David reflects briefly on the ways in which we can respond to 'the problem' that runs through the book. As somebody who has taught research methods to undergraduates, he objects to being labelled as a 'research methods lecturer': he is a *sociologist* or an *academic* (who happens to be able to teach methods). His own preference for mixed methods reflects this stance, and is a useful counter to any tendencies to see quantitative methods in isolation, or inherently superior. He concludes his call for positive action with examples of encouraging recent developments, and provides some points of contact for 'those wanting to get into the loop'.

This introductory summary of the chapters indicates that we now have more up-to-date, evidence-based knowledge about undergraduate attitudes to, and experience of, learning quantitative methods of social research than in earlier times. Much of this evidence has not been assembled or analysed with traditional quantitative methods, and that is no coincidence. Our argument is not that we need *only* quantitative methods, but rather that good social science research needs to draw on 'mixed methods', and to deploy the methods that are most appropriate to the task in hand. *But we cannot have mixed methods or make an informed choice about which are the most appropriate methods unless we include quantitative methods in our toolbox of research techniques.*

The changing context

We hope that the contributions in this collection will amount to a better understanding of what has to be done, not just in terms of a fundamental approach, but also increasingly in more detailed classroom activities. We also have greater resources in the form of IT resource centres, so there can be less excuse for not attempting a root and branch reform, whether we are talking about the research methods lecturers who will carry the torch, or our colleagues who can build quantitative illustration and student practice into their modules across the curriculum. We should not underestimate the conservatism of our colleagues. A key measure of success will be the extent to which the curriculum as a whole changes, rather than just the enhancements in the syllabuses of research methods modules.

Nonetheless, it is reasonable to anticipate that teaching and research across the social sciences will, for a variety of reasons, change markedly in the next few years. Although additional resources would make this easier to achieve, the emergence of a new coalition UK government, which rejects Keynesian economics and is ideologically committed to dismantling the public sector, paradoxically may even hasten change within higher education by the pressures of budget cuts and calls for greater 'relevance'. Any discipline that attempts to opt out is going to be increasing isolated, and left behind when it comes to future access to support funding both for capacity building and the conduct of research. This collection offers some choices for change during a period when research foundations and funding councils are developing new priorities and policies. In the words of a recent ESRC document:

> more needs to be done to improve the teaching of quantitative methods and to persuade students of its value … Without improvements at this level, sustained growth at postgraduate level and beyond will continue to be hampered. (ESRC, 2008: 4)

References

Barnett, R. (ed.) (2005) *Reshaping the University*. Maidenhead: Open University Press/McGraw-Hill Educational.

Barnett, R. and Coate, K. (eds) (2004) *Engaging the Curriculum in Higher Education*. Buckingham: Open University Press.

Becher, T. and Trowler, P. (2001) *Academic Tribes and Territories*, 2nd edn. Buckingham: SRHE/Open University Press.

Department for Education and Science (1987) *Higher Education: Meeting the Challenge*. London: HMSO.

Department for Education and Employment (1999) *Learning to Succeed*. London: HMSO.

Economic and Social Research Council (2006) *Development of Undergraduate Curricula in Quantitative Methods (Call for Proposals)*. Swindon: ESRC.

Economic and Social Research Council (2008) *Strategic Advisor for the Undergraduate Teaching of Quantitative Methods (tender document)*. Swindon: ESRC.

Economics and Social Research Council, British Sociological Association and Heads and Professors of Sociology group (2010) *International Benchmarking Review of UK Sociology*. Available at: www.esrcsocietytoday.ac.uk/ESR CInfoCentre/Images/Sociology IBR Report_tcm6-36279.pdf (accessed April 2010).

Mapping the Academic Landscape of Quantitative Methods

Geoff Payne

Despite great diversity among the social sciences, there are several common features to the learning experiences of their undergraduates when it comes to social research methods. Almost all of the UK's degree programmes in the social sciences contain one or two 'modules' of *general* research training in which basic approaches and techniques are introduced. In some disciplines such as economics, or in certain universities, this is supplemented by a further module intended to remedy any shortfalls in mathematical knowledge arising from inadequate secondary education, or by a final year option/ elective module in quantitative or research methods.

However, the social sciences are also united in an ambiguity towards the formal requirement of *quantitative* research methods. The curricula of British higher education are not externally determined, but rather operate within a framework collectively developed by academics and the funding councils in the form of subject benchmarks. While there are penalties for programmes that do not conform, these benchmarks are not energetically enforced, and indeed, perhaps understandably, the benchmarks are in most cases framed in very general terms that allow great flexibility in their application.

> Many make no specific mention of quantitative methods, or of ability to interpret numerical data or evidence, as opposed to simply citing knowledge of research methods, or interpreting evidence etc. ... a minority of students can graduate without doing any QM training at all, and indeed some may not even have the opportunity to study it as an optional course (MacInnes, 2009: 8)

The worrying result for MacInnes is that whereas graduates have been found to have generally high levels of confidence that they had achieved benchmarks, research shows that this did not extend to quantitative methods (Jary, 2002).

A second shared feature is that almost all programmes, with the possible exceptions of more mathematical subjects such as economics, treat quantitative methods as matters that are learned in a specific module, rather than integrated into the body of the degree. As several of the contributors here show, there are a number of reasons for this, but the unfortunate consequence is that quantitative methods exist in isolation in their 'ghetto' (Payne et al., 1988). This discourages students from seeing the relevance of their methods training.

The one exception to this isolation may be the dissertation. A standard requirement for UK honours degrees is completion of a research-based dissertation, which is usually regarded as the culmination of the degree programme because students are expected to work on their own, researching a topic of their own choice, and practising the wide range of intellectual capabilities that they have acquired during their studies. Expectations about the dissertation will, however, vary even within one single-discipline department, ranging from empirical fieldwork, through secondary analysis of documentary collections or datasets, to more limited forms of desk research, which sceptics say will yield little more than an extended essay, rather than a genuine piece of research. This emphasis on a research-based dissertation is not part of every nation's model of higher education but a number of other countries have recently moved towards increasing the amount of research method training and practice, as Jonathan Parker reports in Chapter 3.

Despite these variations in the emphasis placed on the deployment of research skills, disciplines (and indeed most countries) seem united in perceiving a reluctance among many of their students to engage with quantitative methods, and by the difficulties students report in coping with 'stats' or 'the maths'. The particular techniques that seem to be the site of these difficulties may vary from subject to subject – and of course from student to student – but the sense that a problem exists (and may be getting worse) is shared across the social sciences. This universal feature can only mean that we still have some way to go in delivering an effective undergraduate education in quantitative methods of social research.

Working towards some definitions

At a commonsense level, 'quantitative methods of social research' involve, on the one hand, counting and measuring those human behaviours which are plausibly quantifiable, and on the other hand, applying these data as evidence in the interpretation and analysis of the issues addressed by the various social sciences. Economics and Social Research Council (ESRC) disciplines are: anthropology, area studies, communications and media studies; criminology; development studies; economic and social history; economics; education; human geography; linguistics; management and business studies; politics; psychology; social policy and social work; socio-legal studies;

sociology; and town and country planning. For our purposes here, the word 'social' is shorthand for the sociological, economic, political, policy, demographic, historical and human-geographical topics which comprise the business of these social sciences. While each contributor to this collection comes from a specific discipline background, which naturally influences what they write, the lessons learned from their projects can be readily transferred to other social sciences: none of the chapters has been written solely for one audience in a single discipline.

This apparently simple definitional starting point for quantitative social research, however, soon leads us into a range of further skills. If we are to measure actions and social characteristics – buying, voting, belonging, reproducing, discriminating, or age, gender, health, income or employment – we do indeed have to start with basic arithmetic skills. But in order to collect and analyse data, it is necessary to link these to other kinds of expertise in identifying, gathering and sorting information, which *incidentally* will take a numeric form. For effective deployment of our evidence, we do need to develop not only confidence in processing numbers but also a critical awareness of the reliability and nature of our data (and their sources), a sense of pattern and the inter-connection of the units of what we have measured. In some kinds of analysis, and in particular in disciplines such as economics, this takes us into more complex mathematical techniques, whereas other subjects are likely to be more concerned with the irreducibly complex detail of human existence and direct human contact.

Thus our technical competencies will be highly varied, depending on the discipline we consider. The range of competencies will include mixtures of visual presentation of numerical data in the form of graphs and charts; numeracy and quantitative skills, including data analysis, interpretation and extrapolation; survey design and analysis; experimental design; descriptive statistics; the manipulation, treatment and interpretation of statistical data; the econometric representation of ideas and analyses; psychometrics; and mathematics. Although in the literature the term 'quantitative methods' is sometimes used as a singular noun, in this collection we treat quantitative methods as plural, not least to reflect the complexity and range of these elements (just as we also continue to regard 'data' as plural). However, while the techniques may vary, the common mode of argumentation in which they are applied is basically the same.

This working definition of quantitative methods by exemplars and inclusion not only begins to describe our subject matter, but also serves two other important purposes. First, to repeat, there are different degrees of numeracy. Some research topics are amenable to a direct and straightforward treatment, whereas others call for a more complex or abstract approach. The latter techniques will often depend on a prior familiarity with the basic number skills that conventionally precede them: as school studies taught us, maths is nothing if not an accumulative and progressive discipline. In addressing 'the problem of number' here, we focus more on the difficulties that many early-stage undergraduates encounter with even the more straightforward statistics that they are expected to handle, than on more specialist tools such as those of multivariate analysis or mathematic modelling, which may be included in some disciplines or departmental curricula but for many students in several of the social sciences are not part of the core undergraduate (or indeed, postgraduate) studies.

The identification of levels of number skills (and career stages: see ESRC, 2008) is not intended to imply that some techniques or indeed disciplines have an intrinsic moral or intellectual superiority because they involve more complex numeracy. It may be true that economics involves more maths, but certainly in the UK, politics has a greater grasp of philosophical ideas, psychology draws on strengths in experimental design, social policy and social work arguably provide a closer sense of the day-to-day lives of ordinary people, and sociology has developed a challenging critical scepticism about the nature of social facts. There are distinctive methodological strengths in each of the 17 social sciences recognised by the ESRC. There is little point in sibling rivalry over relative intellectual status between, or indeed within, sister social sciences (however much campus life often feels as if it consists of territorial struggles between the tribes of alien disciplines).

Instead, the second advantage of our definition is that it indicates a more fruitful direction for understanding, through comparing what we have included as 'quantitative' with the alternative research methods that we have left out of our definition. Drawing on Jonathan Parker's positioning statement in Chapter 3, research methods which are not classified as quantitative methods become the 'other'. Non-quantitative methods are likely to include interviewing, narration, projective stimuli, ethnography, grounded theory, interpretivist and cultural studies constructions of meaning, as well as the other research techniques that are usually grouped under the heading of 'qualitative research methods', and which are so influential in sociology, and increasingly in other disciplines (Payne et al., 2004, 2005). Consideration of certain types of epistemology; categorising different types of research and the various ways they can be carried out; deconstructing the traditions of each discipline; and possibly explaining their different methodologies, ethics, and project participation and ownership, would also be at risk of exclusion. However, we would not want the quantitative sphere to lose those key elements of epistemology, formal logic and similar philosophical contributions which frame the research process.

While we can categorise both quantitative and qualitative methods by listing specific activities, this does not mean that a crude division between the two, or between quantitative methods and 'the rest', is the most useful intellectual framework for thinking about social research. While one may sometimes wish to imply a convenient dichotomy (as in the title of this book) so that discussion can be simplified and speeded up, dichotomies of this kind are ultimately self-defeating. Techniques conventionally placed on one or other side of the divide actually depend on elements from the other side, and many a research problem benefits from a mixed methods approach as several of the chapters here show (see also Tashakkori and Teddlie, 2003;

Brewer and Hunter, 2006; Plano Clark and Creswell, 2008). Even quantitative methods can be researched using non-quantitative methods! A resolute determination to deny and denigrate the value of alternative methods too often indicates a narrowness of conception and a self-defeating rigidity of thought.

Of course, the requirements of the social sciences do differ. Disciplines such as social statistics and economics have perhaps lamented 'the crisis of number' the loudest (e.g. see ESRC, 2008: 2). This is entirely reasonable: a basic grasp of mathematics is more important for economics and its related disciplines, than for much of sociology or politics. An understanding of the statistics associated with experimental design is central to psychology but less important in human geography. Social policy has more need of quantification than social work. Even though some disciplines such as economics, accountancy, business studies and psychology 'have better resources for assessment, training and improvement of mathematics, statistics and general quantitative skills' than other social sciences (McVie et al., 2008: 3; Lynch et al., 2007: 4) their subject content equally requires a greater application of quantitative techniques. Even within a discipline, the institutional emphasis on number work will vary. Each subject, and each of its undergraduate programmes, selects particular techniques from the general statistical and mathematical toolkit and/or from non-quantitative methods.

Quantification therefore has to be seen in a wider context of research and analysis. Although 'maths' and 'stats' are legitimate disciplines in their own right, their part in the social sciences takes on its meaning from the interests of each social science, and indeed, the various approaches and schools operating within each subject (e.g. see Katharine Adeney's and Sean Carey approach in politics in Chapter 6). It is the framework of ideas and the focus of research on specific problems which determine whether this or that technique or topic is suitable. Indeed, not all products of the human mind are best addressed by empirical research, let alone quantitative methods.

It follows that there is little point in claiming that any one approach is self-sufficient, or superior to all the others, when it is obvious we need to have theory and practice, concepts and data, and meanings as well as measurement, available within our analytical framework. In privileging the place of quantitative methods in social science research here, we do so not because we wish to denigrate or restrict other forms of scholarship but because our focus on quantitative methods is the outcome of what we see as a pressing need to achieve a *balanced integration* of research methods at a time when this is lacking in much of British social science, and among our skilled labour force. (Indeed, in some other fields, such as medicine, there is a case for arguing the mirror image case, i.e. that a traditional dependence on quantitative methods needs to be balanced by the introduction of more qualitative and mixed methods (Plano Clark and Creswell, 2008)). The reason that quantitative methods have become seen to be so important at the present time is because of the wider numeracy deficit and the national shortage of appropriately skilled social science researchers. It is now time to try to re-establish a more suitable balance and mixture of social research methods.

A crisis of number?

The reader may still reasonably retain some doubts about why we have produced a book dedicated to the greater and more effective use of one group of methods, rather than others. There are several good reasons for this here that can give reassurance. First, as we have indicated earlier, an informed and active citizenry cannot exist without possessing, inter alia, the skills of rational analysis. This country needs fewer MMR scares, less alternative 'medicine', more responsible journalism, and a new generation of more honest politicians. Only if we – meaning both academics and the graduates from their programmes – can reason with numbers, and we *demand* the same of the chattering classes, can we hope to see a decent society.

Second, it will already be apparent that, as editors, we have adopted a methodological pluralist perspective which argues for toleration in alternative approaches to research, and seeks to select the most suitable and rigorous method for the particular research problem that is to hand. Given that undergraduate curricula across the social sciences require students to achieve competence in a range of research and analytical methods, that pluralism must include *quantitative* methods. Despite this simple logic, there is ample evidence that many students do not currently engage effectively with the quantitative components of their studies, and that learning to reason with number is not as effectively taught as it could be – even if as Williams et al. (2004) show, the crisis of number may not be quite as deep as often feared. We want to help to remedy this educational shortfall. Improving teaching and learning processes is central to extending the range of skills that can be deployed, and therefore to enhancing the quality of our social sciences.

There is also a third reason for urging the importance of quantitative methods, and one of arguably more pressing weight. Despite the need for caution and scepticism about political opinions and professional self-interest in policy statements (see below), it is true that contemporary Britain is experiencing a *genuine* shortage of graduates with the number skills and interests that the national economy requires. Anxiety about weak numerical skills among social scientists can be seen as a subset of a wider UK governmental concern about the current supply of 'home grown' scientifically qualified personnel and a shortage of school pupils wanting to go forward to study mathematics, engineering and the physical sciences (HM Treasury, 2002; Department for Education and Skills (DfES), 2004, 2005). 'There has been a rapid increase in the need for quantitatively trained social scientists across all level of government' (ESRC, 2008: 2), but far from finding solutions, the supply of such graduates shows little sign of improving:

There are persistent concerns that UK [*sic*] lacks the critical mass to satisfy such demand ... As the Smith Inquiry [DfES 2004] on Post 14 mathematics highlighted there are fewer and fewer students now seeking qualifications in maths related studies than ever before. The Royal Society's [2006] study – *Degrees of Concern* – revealed how this had led to a 20% decline in 'A' level entries in maths between 1999 and 2005 ... recent evidence points to only a minority of social science students choosing to deploy quantitative tools and techniques in their doctoral work. (ESRC, 2008: 2)

The review of *Strategically Important and Vulnerable Subjects* by the Higher Education Funding Council for England (Roberts, 2005) and parallel studies by the ESRC in conjunction with the Higher Education Funding Council for Wales (Lynch et al., 2007) and the Scottish Funding Council (McVie et al., 2008) have all found undergraduate output inadequate for maintaining national quantitatively skilled labour force levels. The recruitment of appropriately trained graduates to be government social scientists has not been possible (Policy and Innovation Unit (PIU), 2000). To make things worse, the ESRC's *Demographic Review of the UK Social Sciences* (Mills et al., 2006) identifies an ageing and shrinking academic population in England and Wales, raising doubts about the adequate replenishment of such quantitative skills as the older generation does possess. While we may not wish to prioritise labour market outcomes in determining the higher education curriculum, it would be equally short-sighted and indeed irresponsible for the social sciences to ignore these problems.

However, it is important at this point to stress the distinction between the solid evidence of a crisis of number and other less reliable expressions of self-interest or opinion. What we are dealing with here is not just the special pleading of social statisticians or econometricians, as might arguably be alleged against statements emanating from the 2001 Research Assessment Exercise (RAE) Statistics and Operations Research panel, the Committee of Professors of Social Statistics (see ESRC, 2008: 2) or the Oswald Report (1999). Nor are we merely repeating here the short-sighted complaints of British industry and employers (notorious for their under-investment in employee training and career development) as illustrated by Lord Leitch's *Review of Skills Final Report* (2006). On the contrary, 'there is much circumstantial and some direct evidence ... that there is a deficit of quantitative skills in the UK social sciences' (Commission on the Social Sciences, 2003: 57). This evaluation has since been supported by a variety of research and evidence-based documentation. For example, the survey by Lynch et al. (2007) sees this as a problem existing for more than a decade, while in documenting the more recent situation in Scotland, McVie et al. (2008) suggest its origins lie as far back as the 1960s. Similarly, research by Wiles et al. (2005) shows the extent of the UK's need for further training in quantitative, and indeed other kinds of, methods.

Although we believe that the problem is a real one, we acknowledge that not everybody will share our interpretation or concern about it. There are alternative perspectives, which minimise the situation we are highlighting: some colleagues show no wish to embrace our remedies. It would be naïve to believe any 'problem' leaps ready-made into the public arena in a consensual form, without going through an evolving process of recognition, definition and re-evaluation. For example, the Leitch Review not only presents information about a lack of skills training in the UK, but in itself is both an indicator of growing public concern about numeracy skills across all levels of the labour force, as well as being a contribution to the re-definition of the problem it seeks to remedy.

The setting up of the Leitch Review should be seen part of a wider re-constitution of the 'problem', in which we have seen both government and opposition politicians extensively criticise the education system for failing to produce young workers who are literate and numerate. This criticism has frequently been thinly disguised as moral anxiety about the emergence of an underclass deprived of educational opportunity and motivation, in an ever-more rigidly stratified society. For example, several years of laments from ministers and shadow spokesmen (*sic*) about allegedly falling rates of mobility culminated in Prime Minister Gordon Brown's announcement of a White Paper on social mobility in 2008. Ironically, this Whitehall consensus about the handicaps for later life-chances due to a lack of numeracy was based on a highly dubious reading – or should we say, counting – of the numerical research data on rates of social mobility (see Lambert et al., 2007; Payne, 2008)! In a similar vein, the over-estimate of illiteracy and innumeracy in the UK workforce, to the tune of *five million people* (Payne, 2006), provides another case study of how even research involving highly numerate social scientists can produce seriously incorrect estimates.

One might be tempted to dismiss political polemics about low numeracy levels as an over-reaction. After all, such anxieties about the education system are nothing new. In the UK (and other Western countries) there have been previous periods of worry about the numerical abilities and inclinations of students. Today's interest in skills variously echoes British fears about the military rise of the Prussians with their new technical universities, and the challenge of the growing American economy, in the last quarter of the nineteenth century; the justification developed for systematic government funding of higher education during reconstruction after the First World War; Cold War calls for an investment in training as part of the 'white-hot heat of technology' of the 1960s; or the 'shortage of engineers' scam which so disastrously distorted the allocation of higher education funding in the 1980s. Like all researchers, we should retain a degree of healthy scepticism towards panaceas, rhetoric, and political intrigue. Nonetheless, we can distinguish between earlier moral panics and the specific situation in contemporary society. Simply put, the numeracy skills needs of today's citizens and employees have never been greater, and – in our particular concern here – they are not being adequately met in the undergraduate social science curriculum.

Government concerns about qualified personnel have been manifested in the social sciences by ESRC policies aimed at meeting qualified workforce deficits, especially in the fields of economics, demography and social policy (e.g. ESRC, 2000). However, until recently these issues have not always found a ready response among the social science community, except at the level of conversation and anecdote. Indeed, in Britain the debate among academics about quantification has been largely isolated from these national concerns, apart from occasional negative initial responses to earlier ESRC consultations (such as those concerning recognition of Master's courses and the introduction of the '1+3' pattern for doctorates) by those who wished to maintain what they saw as their intellectual independence, including their own less quantitative styles of research.

As shown by Martin Bulmer's reflections in Chapter 4 on past difficulties in teaching quantitative methods in social policy and sociology, there has certainly been no uniformity of support for strengthening the quantitative skills within the social sciences. Such resistance is not restricted to these two subjects. In the words of a recent ESRC document:

> enhancing undergraduate teaching in quantitative methods ... will be a formidable challenge as the current appetite for both the teaching and learning of quantitative methods across the UK social science community is, in many disciplines limited. (2008: 1)

Even when offered additional concrete assistance to find and describe quantitative examples for introduction into their modules, some lecturers actively refuse to modify their teaching (as Jane Falkingham and Teresa McGowan report in Chapter 7).

The interim report of the ESRC Initiative on Undergraduate Teaching of Quantitative Methods indirectly offers two explanations for this. On the one hand there is a

> perception of QM as always positivist and empiricist and usually conservative or uncritical in character or even incompatible with many more mainstream methodologies or epistemologies (e.g. feminist and interpretivist approaches, ethnography, grounded theory) *when anyone with a basic knowledge of QM would know this not to be the case.* (MacInnes, 2009: 3; emphasis added)

Quantitative methods are labelled by many social scientists as 'positivist' and therefore only marginally relevant, a view that is

> rarely rooted in any profound epistemological critique of QM, nor does it lead (as it might very usefully do) to any emphasis on learning about the social construction of data, or the ways quantitative evidence can be used or misused to make arguments not just within academic but in wider civic and political debate. (MacInnes, 2009: 3–4)

MacInnes also offers a rebuke to social scientists for their narrow conception of their own professional competence:

although we as yet have no documented evidence of this, it is almost certainly the case that the majority of teaching staff in social science departments (excluding Psychology and Economics) do not have the basic QM skills that many departments (including their own) expect their students to have. (2009: 8)

The result is at best indifference, or often hostility, towards quantitative methods, and a pervasive culture in which they are deemed irrelevant and inaccessible. Not only do staff lack basic number skills, but they also display little motivation to remedy the situation, and indeed could be accused of complacency (although we shall see below, innovating staff skills is no easy matter in today's universities):

unlike other research and analysis skills which all staff are assumed to possess by virtue of being competent members of their profession, quantitative skills, no matter how basic, have come to be seen as the exclusive responsibility of those with much more advanced quantitative skills, as if reading a simple contingency table had more in common with the skills needed to undertake advanced multivariate analysis, than, say, the ability to distinguish interpretative and positivist approaches in the philosophy of social science, or approach the analysis of an interview transcript. (MacInnes, 2009: 8–9)

Despite this record of opposition, since the turn of this century there have been signs appearing of a shift away from such fundamentalist resistance. A *modus vivendi* of mutual non-communication emerged from earlier states of methodological warfare, slowly followed by a new awareness of governmental priorities as they gently cascaded down from the academic hierarchy. ESRC policies have played a central role in this. Programmes such as a long-term investment in providing enhanced access to archived datasets, better initial research training for graduate students via '1+3' routes to the PhD, the introduction in 2006 of Advanced Quantitative Methods Enhanced Stipends for postgraduates acquiring and using quantitative methods, the creation of later career opportunities (not least through the ESRC National Centre for Research Methods since 2004), and research into the nature of the 'crisis of number' (including the post of Strategic Advisor for the Undergraduate Teaching of Quantitative Methods in 2008) have begun to bear fruit. The idea of a predominantly non-quantitative social science has been problematised, as Chapters 5 and 6 demonstrate for sociology and politics. Although there is still some way to go, it is no longer only the specialists who recognise the importance of quantitative methods in social research.

Learners as victims

It is still true, nonetheless, that those who have been most vocal about the crisis of number and the need to enhance quantitative methods have also

been the more numerate social scientists in each discipline, together with many who teach methods of social research. Let us first consider this view from those who are most involved and expert. Without basic number skills, we can see that it is hard for students to learn how to reason with numbers. It is all too easy for lecturers who are at ease with number to slip into common-room 'academic moan-ins'.

We lament our students' limited prior learning in maths, the bad teaching they experience in secondary education, their consequent reluctance to acquire quantitative skills, their lack of interest in such techniques, their failure to engage actively with quantitative datasets during their other studies, and their fear of coping with rigorous argument. In our more generous moments, we also acknowledge the genuine anxiety and even fear that many undergraduates experience when confronted with numbers and statistical argumentation. No one likes to come up with the wrong answer, especially in front of their peers. We know that most first year students have neither practised calculation since the earlier stages of their school education nor been systematically introduced to applied formal logic and numerical reasoning. The great majority have entered higher education through the more relaxed, 'appreciation' curriculum of 'A' level humanities (except of course those who have come through the more progressive Scottish school system where a breadth of subject content has been maintained). Mature students, often with worse school experiences and longer gaps since their use of number, frequently have greater problems.

Even before they gave up on number, our new undergraduates may well have received a less than adequate grounding. It is one thing to possess a certificate as evidence of a pass in GCSE Maths at a minimum of Grade C (or equivalent) – as university entrants to the social sciences in England and Wales are normally required to demonstrate – and quite another for our recruits to have enjoyed good teaching in maths at school. Sadly, the stories that our new students tell, and their limited confidence with number, attest to the basic fact that maths and science teaching in UK schools is at a low ebb. Worse, there is little sign that those responsible for teaching these subjects understand the true nature of the crisis. It is always easier to blame the victims.

So every summer when GCSE and 'A' level exam results are announced, we hear from the proponents of those school subjects who have most resolutely complained of a fall in real achievement, grade inflation and shrinking recruitment, with a regularity and originality akin to the arrival of the first cuckoo in spring. Just as certainly as the media will carry annual 'news stories' featuring young women excitedly opening their exam results envelopes, these messengers of scholastic doom will queue up each August to claim that their own disciplines are the most difficult, most intellectually challenging and rigorous, and therefore morally superior. They will point with inverted pride to low pass rates as proof that a resistance to educational reform and contemporary learning theory has once again 'protected standards'. For many of those charged with teaching maths and sciences the under-achievement is simple to explain: these days the kids are thick, they lack aspiration and 'A' levels are not worth the paper on which they are printed, unlike 'in our day'. The return of the grammar schools would soon sort everything out (whisper it not that for each grammar school there were four secondary moderns where students were *prevented* from studying for a school-leaving qualification in maths!). The blogs and wikis have only made such ill-informed commentary more prevalent.

These doom-mongers show little awareness of the evidence from educational research that school exam pass rates are actually associated inter alia with poor school facilities, teachers whose students find them hard to relate to, syllabi that have little connection with the life-worlds of many of those who study them, and bad teaching practices (lessons that may also apply to other levels of educational provision!). School maths teaching has continued to be structured around the narrow academic needs of the very few pupils who will progress to higher education mathematics, rather than the general needs of the great majority for life skills as citizens who can reason with number in understanding contemporary issues. Even the new 'use of maths' GSCE and A level syllabi promised for 2010, and supposedly designed to promote 'functional mathematical skills' and the application of maths to concrete problems, reads all too familiarly like a conventional programme, despite its expanded coverage of simple statistical and probability calculation (e.g. Edexcel, 2009).

In annual concert, we also hear employers (and opposition politicians, regardless of which party is in power) complaining about a shortage of school leavers possessing the levels of numeracy needed to perform work tasks on their entry to employment. (The previous sentence was originally drafted in the first week of August 2008: on Monday, 11 August 2008, one of BBC Radio 4's morning news headlines was a CBI press release calling for more school pupils to study science, because of problems in finding skilled young workers. This was repeated in August 2009 during the final stages of completion of this book and 2010). They may have a point, but as in all areas of labour force shortage, the employers' own apparently superior numerical abilities do not extend to understanding the numbers behind the working of market forces. Those loudest in promoting the virtues of the free market economy seem incapable of grasping that an upward adjustment of key pay rates for suitable young workers, or providing substantial bursaries for school pupils gaining relevant skills, might well go a long way to attract those who do have the requisite capabilities. Nor do employers seem able to understand that recruitment practices which discriminate against young women, ethnic minorities or the disabled, reduce the field of numerically competent individuals from which companies can recruit.

Similarly the great entrepreneurs and innovators of the British economy have been remarkably slow in adapting their induction, training and career development programmes for new entrants to their workforce so that their organisations could gain a competitive advantage. One of the most common complaints among recent science and engineering graduates is that employers do not allow them to use the expertise that was so hard won in their degrees. It is easier to blame 'the government', the schools, or young people themselves, than to innovate in management, let alone to adopt a more socially responsible form of capitalism that might see some merit in contributing – or more likely avoiding – fair corporation tax to the rest of the society on which every so-called 'wealth producing' business actually depends.

This is not to deny that an educational problem exists. The shortage of teachers who are competent to teach maths effectively in primary schools sets the process off on the wrong foot. This is compounded by the widespread poor quality of maths and science classes at secondary level. England's archaic system of narrow subject specialisation after (and sometimes prior to) GCSEs, so deeply entrenched in our elitist culture dominated by Oxbridge and Civil Service traditions since way before the current mode of exams, offers an escape route from the monotony and confusion of number, into the sunlit uplands of the humanities – and many bright kids are only too eager to take their chances.

The humanities offer less rote-learning, fewer rigid conventions of work process and written presentation, greater sophistication over what constitutes 'right' and 'wrong' answers, much less dependence on the systematic accumulation of mutually interdependent skills, and an escape from the constraints of reasoned and evidenced argument. This is not so much a 'flight from number' as a 'flight *towards* the greater flexibility of arts subjects': the loss of number is only consequential. Even if the experience of GCSE Maths has been less dispiriting than the admittedly somewhat pessimistic vision presented here, there are few opportunities for most 'non-science' students at A-level to use and practise the number skills they had previously gained. The old adage 'use it or lose it' was never more apposite than in numeracy, and nowhere more relevant than during the two years spent studying arts 'A' levels. University lecturers are left to pick up the pieces, but few of us have the necessary pedagogic skills, or the motivation in these RAE/REF (Research Excellence Framework)-dominated days, to do so.

We academics have also been slow to stop blaming the victims and to do something to tackle the problem. In the foreseeable future, we will continue to be faced with intakes of students who are markedly less numerate than we would like. It is therefore up to us to adapt our own educational service to provide solutions. Nor should we confuse low levels of numeracy competence with resistance by students or a 'flight from number'. A recent report notes:

> the widely held belief (consistently refuted by surveys of students themselves) that students choose social science subjects to 'avoid' numbers. This appears to be a 'myth' in the true sociological sense of the term, that has grown up to legitimate almost universally low expectations of student attainment in QM, and correspondingly low levels of teaching provision (MacInnes, 2009: 3).

Effective solutions depend on understanding the proper nature of what it is that we want to solve. The contributors to this book offer a spread of perspectives which starts with understanding why students struggle with number, what proportion struggle with which elements, and the features of our system that contribute to their difficulties. The later chapters move on to explore strategies for coping with this and the resources available to lecturers who wish to develop their own solutions. The focus is less on the detail of classroom practice and lesson design and more on identifying a basic approach within which not only each discipline, but also each lecturer, can select items and construct teaching sequences which will meet the needs of their own students' learning. Unless we are willing to take this on board, there is little point in railing against the inadequacies of others.

Targets and tactics

With the above discussion in mind, where in the system is the best place to seek to intervene: schools; undergraduate education; postgraduate training; or mid-career development? Action is needed on all four levels (ESRC, 2008; Wiles et al., 2005), but as we have already signalled, in this collection, our target is the undergraduate curriculum (although this includes any repercussions for subsequent MRes degrees). When we say 'the undergraduate curriculum', we do indeed mean exactly that, rather than the *research methods syllabus*. As several of our contributors argue (for example, in Chapters 5 and 6), if quantitative methods are shut off in their own isolated module(s) there is little prospect of substantial improvement. Not only does this isolation send the message that quantitative methods are irrelevant to the rest of a degree's content, it actively deprives students of opportunities to practise and develop the skills of numerical analysis and argumentation, so that what they may have learned in a previous specialist module is soon forgotten. The solution must be to enable lecturers in 'substantive' modules not only to use, but also to draw attention to, quantitative examples in their own classes.

Despite the difficulties inherent in this, the capacities of modern electronic communications now offer a genuine prospect of successful innovation. Just as half a century ago, the then new generation of large IBM machines facilitated the development of modern techniques of modelling and statistical analysis (e.g. work coming out of Chicago (not least SPSS), Ann Arbor, Berkeley and Harvard in the 1960s), so the internet now allows e-access to stores of *resources for teaching*. These open up promising possibilities for further change at a more basic level. Provided these resources contain exercises and examples in a flexible and adaptable format, with user-friendly 'front-ends', individual lecturers can select the elements – and only those elements – which they wish to graft on to their own bespoke classes (see Chapters 8–10). The more these elements and examples held in the electronic resource centres are based on real-life situations to which students can relate, the better they will work within the research methods' syllabus, and the stronger will be their message in the other modules which make up the undergraduate programme. Lecturers no longer have to re-invent the wheel. There is nothing dishonourable about borrowing successful practices and case studies from elsewhere. Although still involving the lecturer in time inputs to implement, the pick-'n'-mix model saves time, is relatively cheap to use, and so is cost-effective. It is, however, a style of academic working that is challenging because of its novelty.

Using relevant, tried-and-tested resource elements will help to overcome what McVie et al. (2008: 29–30), in their scoping study of Scotland's capacity building in quantitative methods, identify as *antipathy*: the reluctance of students to engage with quantitative methods, which is a key obstacle to progress. Our contention is that the right methods, at the right point in the programme, presented in the right way (i.e. with lots of examples relevant to the core discipline being studied) can overcome much if not all of this resistance. McVie et al. identify two further blockages: *accessibility* to further staff training (training not being readily available at present), and *enabling resources* to provide time off, to fund access to such training and to facilitate collaboration. As editors, we can do little about the second and third of these blockages, beyond adding our voice to the supporting lobby, and indicating how e-social science can provide one route forward (see Chapters 9 and 10).

However, if for tactical reasons than for no other, we see the next step as being somewhat different from those identified in the McVie report. Perhaps not surprisingly considering the authors and their remit, the McVie team lays an emphasis not on basic education for undergraduates, but on the more advanced techniques which depend on that prior learning, and on the need to enhance the infrastructure by means of which these more advanced techniques can be acquired by professional researchers. Two issues arise from this orientation.

While there is a strong case to be made for improving the infrastructure of funding and provision of training – and we are in no way opposed to that – *on its own* it may well not be the solution intended. It is essentially a top-down approach, in more than one sense (even allowing for the McVie respondents who indicated the original need). Central provision of facilities, and intervention directed and controlled from an external body, however well meaning, run the risk of being seen as a further imposition on a work-force that already perceives itself as over-burdened. In the first place, even 'hub and node' models of provision remain too distant from the daily life of many local departments. Enhancing the infrastructure is not meant to be for the benefit of those who are already relatively expert in, and convinced of the need for, quantitative methods. It is more important to support and involve those who not only lack the skills, but also may first need convincing that their lack of skills is problematic. Even if there are academics who would recognise their need to up-skill, they often feel insecure and threatened by their lack of quantitative expertise. Successful innovation has to involve a sense of ownership, involvement and local support. If quantitative methods are seen as an externally driven imposition, or as an attempt by quantitative specialists to enforce their own methodological approach on other, less numerate colleagues (often in work situations of inadequate resourcing), the prospects for success are slim. An old saying comes to mind about equine relocation and the failure of central directives to enforce liquid ingurgitation.

Increased provision is no guarantee of uptake. The mechanics of cascading information to promote awareness, generating grass roots enthusiasm, freeing up time, and ensuring that resources are allocated to the right point in every university, represent formidable obstacles. Tackling McVie's blockage of 'accessibility' involves ensuring that the enabling resources are both sufficient and also directly and easily available to those members of staff who most need to take advantage of the increased access. The valiant efforts of the ESRC's great and good carry the same limitation: academics may pay lip service to government labour force planning, or even to the goal of enhanced teaching and learning, but anecdotal observations of one's colleagues suggest that we are as yet a long way from achieving a systematic commitment and motivation to change. Aiming to 'integrate training across each level to create a multi layered national training infrastructure' may be incompatible with discipline self-identities and the creation of 'a framework which is flexible enough to meet the particular skill requirements of individual researchers' (ESRC, 2008: 3). Although recent collaborations with the funding councils are welcome (e.g. ESRC, 2006a, b), as is the acknowledgement of other bodies such as Quality Assurance Agency and Higher Education Academy as stakeholders (ESRC, 2008: 6), the structural separation of the ESRC as dealing with research and postgraduate training continues to be a stumbling block. This separation is highlighted in an underlying uncertainty about ultimate goals and the means of achieving them, which characterises the literature and current policy debates that in turn revolve around three possible targets. Is it the intention to produce:

- a small elite band of highly expert quantitative social scientists with even greater technical skills than those of contemporary specialists;
- a larger supply of statistically competent professional employees to service the needs of government, commerce and academic research projects;
- or a higher level of quantitative understanding among all social science undergraduates?

The three options listed above are not mutually exclusive, although a shortage of resources means that priorities have to be set. It will already be apparent that as editors we favour the last of these options, not only for its own importance in the intrinsic development of our social sciences, but also because a stronger base will in turn provide the larger supply of statistically competent professional employees who will be needed as well. We are less comfortable with the case for a new elite of the kind that more specialist quantitative researchers and statisticians have recently advocated, because although it may be cheaper and easier to deliver, it will not solve the difficulties we have identified with the undergraduate learning experience, and this option is less likely to add appreciably to the supply of graduates wanting to enter this field. In many ways this uncertainty over goals eerily echoes an earlier Social Science Research Council debate over who should be carrying out social survey research; market research companies outside academia, or university-based social scientists trained in the skills of questionnaire design, sampling and survey operations (e.g. Payne, 1979, 1981; Abrams, 1980; Harrop, 1980)?

In turn, the means for attaining one's target will largely depend on which target is selected. We have already expressed doubts about top-down solutions that do not take sufficient account of how universities are actually run, and the conditions under which social scientists work. However urgent the shortage of skilled researchers is, a quick-fix approach is unlikely to provide a long-term answer. Trying to rectify current shortcomings in research capacity, regardless of how urgently this is needed, runs the risk of treating the symptoms of a malaise which has its deeper root causes in the education system.

Future researchers and lecturers do not arrive ready-made in this world. They are a product of their prior experiences. Their quantitative skills, and their attitudes towards quantification, have been inculcated through a long process of learning. Poor numeracy may start in schools but it is all too often reinforced during higher education. It is from the body of methodologically disenfranchised and disenchanted undergraduates that postgraduates are chosen, postgraduates who, lacking a proper grounding in quantitative methods, quite reasonably tend to select doctoral topics and methods that move them further away from a quantitative perspective. If this is true for those who go on to become social scientists in higher education, it is even more true for those who go on to become teachers of A level social science subjects: recruited from the same body of methodologically disenfranchised and disenchanted undergraduates, they are trapped into training up the next generation of A level students to become our next round of non-numerate undergraduates. The key to preventing this is to stop trying to convert people *after* they have entered the social science profession and to do this earlier in their careers. We are unable to change their schooling, but it is certainly within our remit to change their undergraduate experience. This does not mean changes to research methods teaching on its own (important though this is): rather it means enhancing the visibility and use of quantitative methods *across the curriculum*.

It follows that this book, although presumably sometimes preaching to the converted, is aimed not only at convincing fellow lecturers of the need for change, but also at showing the economical and effective ways in which these changes can be made. Each of our contributors is an enthusiast, but they are neither quantitative nor educational geeks. They are realistic about the task to be faced. Indeed, most of the chapters claim at best only a partial success for the particular innovations that they report. This modesty of achievement is all the more significant because it applies to the easier task of promoting *simple* quantitative methods, not the more advanced techniques. We would not dispute that the latter skills are necessary for tackling many research questions, and even for a basic competence in some of the more numerate disciplines, but they are unrealistic goals for many social science students at this point in educational history. The first steps to take must be the introduction of our reluctant undergraduates to levels of quantitative technique that may seem laughably straightforward and elementary to more numerate colleagues. Those of us who teach introductory modules in research methods find a proportion of our students struggling with percentages, averages and basic maths notation. As Malcolm Williams and Carole Sutton show in Chapter 5, the current situation is that in some disciplines students find anything beyond a visualisation of bivariate data 'hard' to accomplish. For instance, many do not take the notion of correlation any further than inspecting scatterplots, and typically give up at what they see as the Byzantine complexity of chi-square and similar tests of association. Until we can improve achievement at this basic level, the more sophisticated techniques will have to wait.

Working around the blockages: a practical way forward

The rather gloomy assessment presented above is grounded in research findings (Williams et al., 2008). However, the current state of affairs does not mean that nothing can be done: indeed we would optimistically argue that it demonstrates both the scale of the challenge, and the potential scope for intervention. Most of the chapters that follow suggest ways forward, but to illustrate how fresh thinking can contribute, it is worth briefly considering what can happen if we set aside the traditional order and content of knowledge accumulation that comes from mathematical statistics, and ask, in any discipline and any degree programme: *What do students really need to know and master at any point in their studies?* It may be that there are different sequences of learning that fit better with the curriculum as a whole, even if they do not quite follow the conventional logic and sequence of teaching statistics. In this approach (which does assume that quantitative methods modules are being taught not by a specialist statistician but by a member of staff in the core discipline), it is possible to keep other dimensions of the research process running alongside the number work. Each quantitative technique has to earn its place in the module by virtue of the needs of other modules and research methods frameworks, not by mathematical rationale and rigour alone. 'Mathematical proofs' and examples drawn from outside social science fields have little place here. The key point about this approach is that it sets the students' learning needs at the centre of the process, enabling them to understand the purpose and relevance of what they are studying.

As an illustration, Table 2.1 sets out one way of organising the presentation of quantitative material for a degree in sociology. Of course, other disciplines would work within their own frames of reference, and indeed by no means all sociology departments would be enthusiastic about what is outlined here. Table 2.1 is intended to be illustrative and heuristic, not

Table 2.1 Developing and integrating basic quantitative methods: an example from sociology

Core numerical activity	Purpose	Practical skills	Critical pragmatics	Social science models
Simple counts: Uni-variate frequencies; basic tools (revision of basic maths such as percentages). Charts and graphs: levels of measurement	**Context:** Local/national comparisons, outside the immediate study, to give a sense of the topic's importance, scale or a framework to the study	**Accessing** numerical data: sources of hard copy national statistics; online datasets and 'Teaching Datasets'; hunting down data	**Limitations:** Of national statistics, and other secondary analysis sources; primary versus secondary data; problems of access/format	**Epistemology:** Philosophy of social science: how do we 'know'? What do we want to know? What is a sociological question? Methodological pluralism
Bi-variate counts and interactions: *Simple cross-tabulation*	**Literature review:** What do earlier studies *claim* to have found?	**'Reading' data:** Charts and graphs; selecting and reporting numerical data	**Numerical reasoning:** Media misrepresentation; lying with statistics; 'risk'	**Explanation:** Realism; logic; causes; prediction; falsification; analysis level
Handling numbers: *Using* tables, charts etc. to investigate, describe and illuminate	**Description:** Core features of own data; sample size and basic picture of face-sheet variables	**Sampling:** *Introduction* to probability, sample size; basic types of sample design	**Generalisations:** Resource limits to sample design/ fieldwork; gatekeepers; evidence and conclusions	**Ethics:** What are the limits of research; the public intellectual's responsibility; neutrality, stance and bias?
Reasoning and writing about numbers: Connecting numbers to interesting problems; communicating findings	**Exploration:** Very basic features of the data; any *obvious* patterns (e.g. class/gender/ethnicity differences?)	**Statistical package:** *Introduction* to, e.g. SPSS variables/values/ labels/ very simple cross-tabs; reading the output	**Operationalisation:** What do measurements show; What is a 'variable'? Levels of measurement; range/ outliers	**The research process:** Rigorous research design to produce a proper answer to the research question posed
Data manipulation: Merging; new variables	**Clarification:** Working *on* the data	**Statistical package:** New variables, merging	**Sources of bias:** Problems in data collection	**Elaboration:** Beyond primary and sense data
Complex associations: N-way cross-tabs; measurements of association	**Testing propositions:** Looking for more complex patterns and how variables are associated	**Pattern testing:** Scattergrams; correlation; chi-square, etc.; propositions; significance tests	**Thinking with numbers:** Prediction and falsification; conventions of interpretation	**What is a sociological theory?** The limitations of non-quantitative methods

prescriptive. Its purpose is to demonstrate the logical development of working from disciplinary-relevant starting points: in this case, that most sociological variables are nominal or ordinal, and that the most useful tools of analysis for first- and second-year sociology students are visual representations and the contingency table.

The structure of the grid has a vertical dimension reflecting a progressive development from simple to more complex skills and knowledge, and a horizontal dimension connecting and integrating the core numeracy elements within their context: what do we need these techniques for, what do we actually do with them, what are the limitations to their use, and how do the specifics of numbers connect to wider methodological issues? Thus, reading down the left-hand column takes us from the simplest ideas of measurement, proportions and charts, through simple cross-tabulations and the use of number to illuminate, to adapting and manipulating data, the logic of comparative analysis using several variables and *using* this kind of information as evidence in reasoned argument, to the standardised analysis of cross-tabulation. The second column leaves open the choice of a concrete topic(s) which can used to exemplify *what each technique is used for*, in each stage of the research process (following the steps of the research process is generally regarded as the most effective means of learning research methods). Thus the methods element is immediately and continuously grounded in the substantive content of the degree programme. The 'practical skills' column lists the hands-on activities (for example using very basic sub-routines in SPSS) that will allow students to *apply* their new conceptual knowledge in a concrete way (again a tried-and-tested teaching model), while the fourth and fifth columns follow through a critical awareness of the *limitations* of what is being offered by quantitative methods, and how this needs to be seen as part of the *philosophy* and *professional practice* of doing sociology. Each column is intended to follow a cumulative and progressive pedagogic path.

An alternative way of using the grid is to read across the rows from left to right, as well as up and down each separate column. Each of the columns' 'phases' of learning consists of sequentially related elements but also directly connects with what was learned at the same or previous stages in other columns. For example, manipulating data formats (column six: phase five) is best tackled once students have started working with SPSS so that they can create 'new variables' etc (column three, phases four and five) while at the same time being encouraged to think about what measurements really mean (column four) and the need for good initial research design (column five). However, there is plenty of scope for varying the sequencing as required. The size of the cells reflects the number of words they have to contain, not their importance or the amount of tuition associated with them. For example, the grid contains a potentially too extensive content in column six for the final phase. To repeat, the purpose of the grid is not to be prescriptive. Its point is that quantitative skills involve a grounding in hands-on activity, illustration from 'real' cases, and a context of the discipline-related issues that impinge on its research activity. How we set this up should depend as far as possible on the needs of each discipline, not on mathematical theory.

If there is any hidden agenda in Table 2.1, and indeed in this collection of essays as a whole, it is that the teaching of research methods not only has yet to deliver graduates with quantitative skills, but that it also offers tremendous scope for innovation and improvement. It is never easy to escape from traditional frames of reference, and all the more so if research methods are isolated in a discrete module, ignored by other colleagues, and often allocated as teaching duties to junior colleagues in their early careers. The chapters in this collection are designed to challenge conventional practice by offering research-based insights into the underlying causes of underachievement, and to indicate alternative approaches with the potential to deliver substantial, if not seismic, shifts in the way quantitative methods are taught and learned in the UK's social sciences.

References

Abrams, M. (1980) 'Social research and market research', *Sociology*, 14 (1): 113–15.

Brewer, J. and Hunter A. (2006) *Foundations of Multimethod Research.* Thousand Oaks, CA: Sage.

Brown, G. (2008) '*Education and social mobility*', Speech to the Specialist Schools and Academies Trust, London. Available at: http://www.number-10.gov.uk/output/Page15837.asp (accessed 2 July 2008).

Commission on the Social Sciences (2003) *Great Expectations: the Social Sciences in Britain.* London: Academy of Learned Societies for the Social Sciences. Available at: http://www.acss.org.uk/docs/GtExpectations.pdf (accessed 20 August 2008).

Department for Education and Skills (2004) *Making Mathematics Count.* Report from Professor Adrian Smith's Inquiry into Post-14 Mathematics Education, February 2004. Available at: http://www.tda.gov.uk/upload/resources/pdf/m/mathsinquiry_finalreport.pdf (accessed 20 August 2008).

Department for Education and Skills (2005) *14–19 Education and Skills.* Government White Paper, February 2005. Available at: http://www.dfes.gov.uk/publications/14-19educationandskills/ (accessed 20 August 2008).

Economic and Social Research Council (2000) *Strategy for Underpinning Social Science Research.* Swindon: ESRC.

Economic and Social Research Council (2006a) *Demographic Review of the UK Social Sciences.* Swindon: ESRC.

Economic and Social Research Council (2006b) *Development of Undergraduate Curricula in Quantitative Methods* (call for proposals). Swindon: ESRC.

Economic and Social Research Council (2008) *Strategic Advisor for the Undergraduate Teaching of Quantitative Methods* (tender document). Swindon: ESRC.

Edexcel (2009) *GCSE from 2010: Mathematics.* Available at: http://www.edexcel.com/quals/gcse/gcse10/maths/Pages/default.aspx (accessed 4 August 2009).

Harrop, M. (1980) 'Social research and market research: a critique of a critique', *Sociology*, 14 (2): 277–81.

HM Treasury (2002) *SET for Success: the Supply of People with Science, Technology, Engineering and Mathematics Skills*. The Report of Sir Gareth Roberts review, April 2002. Available at: http://www.vitae.ac.uk/policy-practice/1685/Roberts-recommendation.html#set (accessed 19 December 2010).

Jary, D. (ed.) (2002) *Benchmarking and Quality Management: The Debate in UK Higher Education*. Birmingham: C-SAP Monograph No 1, LTSN Centre for Sociology, Anthropology, and Politics, University of Birmingham.

Lambert, P., Prandy, K. and Bottero, W. (2007) 'By slow degrees: two centuries of social reproduction and mobility in Britain', *Sociological Research Online*, 12 (1). Available at: http://www.socresonline.org.uk/12/1/prandy.html (accessed 1 June 2009).

Leitch, Lord S. (2006) *Review of Skills Final Report*. Norwich: HMSO for HM Treasury.

Lynch, R., Maio, G., Moore, G., Moore, L., Orford, S., Robinson, A., Taylor C., and Whitefield, K. (2007) *ESRC/ HEFCW Scoping Study in Quantitative Methods Capacity Building in Wales: Final Report*. Swindon: ESRC/HEFCW. Available at: http://www.esrcsocietytoday.ac.uk/ESRCInfoCentre/Images/Scoping%20Study%20to%20Identify%20Quantitative%20Methods%20Capacity%20Building%20Needs%20in%20Wales%20-%20Final%20Report_tcm6-15717.pdf (accessed 20 August 2008).

MacInnes, J. (2009) *ESRC Initiative on Undergraduate Teaching of Quantitative Methods. Interim Report of the Strategic Advisor*. Swindon: ESRC.

McVie, S., Coxon, A., Hawkins, P., Palmer, J. and Rice, R. (2008) *Scoping Study in Quantitative Methods Capacity Building in Scotland: Final Report*. Swindon: ESRC/SFC. Available at: http://www.sccjr.ac.uk/library.php?catID=5&type=doc&id=56 (accessed 20 August 2008).

Mills, D., Jepson, A., Coxon, A., Easterby-Smith, M., Hawkins, P. and Spencer, J. (2006) *Demographic Review of the UK Social Sciences*. Swindon: ESCR.

Oswald, A. and Machin, S. (1999) *Signs of Disintegration: A Report on UK Economics PhDs and ESRC Studentship Demand: Final report*. Swindon: ESRC. Available at: http://www2.warwick.ac.uk/fac/soc/economics/staff/faculty/oswald/esrcrep.pdf (accessed 20 August 2008).

Payne, G. (1979) 'Social research and market research', *Sociology*, 13 (2): 307–13.

Payne, G. (1981) 'Social research and market research', in D. De Vaus (ed.), *Social Surveys*. London: Sage, 2002.

Payne, G. (2006) 'Re-counting "illiteracy"', *British Journal of Sociology*, 57 (2): 219–40.

Payne, G. (2008) '*What do They Mean, "More Social Mobility"?*', Cambridge: Paper presented at the Social Stratification Seminar, Clare College, September.

Payne, G., Lyon, S. and Anderson, R. (1988) 'The Teaching of social research methods', in Eggins, H. (ed.), *Review of Sociology Courses and Teaching*. London: CNAA.

Payne, G., Williams, M. and Chamberlain, S. (2004) 'Methodological pluralism in British sociology', *Sociology*, 38 (1): 153–63.

Payne, G., Williams, M. and Chamberlain, S. (2005) 'Methodological pluralism, British sociology and the evidence-based state: a reply to May', *Sociology*, 39 (3): 529–33.

Plano Clark, V. and Creswell, J. (2008) *The Mixed Methods Reader.* Thousand Oaks, CA: Sage.

Policy and Innovation Unit, Cabinet Office (2000) *Adding It Up.* London: HMSO. Available at: http://www.nationalschool.gov.uk/policyhub/docs/addingitup.pdf (accessed 20 August 2008).

Roberts, G. (2005) *Strategically Important and Vulnerable Subjects: Final Report.* Bristol: HEFCE 2005/24. Available at: http://www.hefce.ac.uk/pubs/hefce/2005/05_24/ (accessed 20 August 2008).

Royal Society (2006) *A Degree of Concern? UK First Degrees in Science, Technology and Mathematics.* London: The Royal Society. Available at: http://royalsociety.org/displaypagedoc.asp?id=23118 (accessed 20 August 2008).

Tashakkori, A. and Teddlie, C. (eds) (2003) *Handbook of Mixed Methods in Social and Behavioural Research.* Thousand Oaks, CA: Sage.

Wiles, R., Durrant, G., De Broa, S. and Powell, J. (2005) *Assessment of Needs for Training in Research Methods in the UK Social Science Community.* Swindon: ESRC. Available at: http://www.ncrm.ac.uk/research/outputs/publications/documents/Assessment%20of%20training%20needs%20Final%20Report%202005.pdf (accessed 20 August 2008).

Williams, M., Hodgkinson, L. and Payne, G. (2004) 'A crisis of number? Some recent research from British sociology', *Radical Statistics*. 85: 40–54. Available at: www.radstats.org.uk/no085/Williams85.pdf (accessed July 2008).

Williams, M., Payne, G., Hodgkinson, L. and Poade, D. (2008) 'Does British sociology count? Sociology students' attitudes toward quantitative methods', *Sociology*, 42 (5): 1003–21.

Best Practices in Quantitative Methods Teaching: Comparing Social Science Curricula Across Countries

Jonathan Parker

Teaching in higher education tends to be seen and experienced as a solitary activity. Academics like the freedom and independence to teach their classes as they see fit and often begrudge interference, criticism or judgements from peers and others. Much of the scholarship of learning and teaching tacitly accepts this individualistic model of teaching by examining, categorising and analysing classroom practices or interventions within single modules. Though team-taught modules and other cooperative approaches can be incorporated, most studies of learning and teaching focus on the level of the individual module in isolation, and the literature on teaching quantitative research methods follows a similar pattern.

This body of literature most commonly analyses the relative effectiveness of one technique or intervention compared with another (see Garfield and Ben-Zvi, 2007, for an overview). There is a host of studies examining the content of introductory statistics modules, the obstacles to teaching introductory statistics, the most important topics to be included, and which teaching models or techniques are most effective. This book, as a case in point, contains many excellent examples of such research. There are very good reasons to carry out research at modular and classroom levels since it is the main organising structure of teaching in higher education across most countries. However, viewing and researching teaching exclusively from the perspective of the module and classroom obscures the importance of learning at programme or degree level, which is the normal level of analysis used for auditing purposes.

The expansion of scholarship on the teaching of quantitative methods and statistics has provided welcome and needed resources to support what is a difficult subject to teach. However, if one takes a wider perspective on how to prepare and train social science undergraduates, it is the accumulation of learning outcomes over an entire degree that matters. Quality assurance systems in higher education, particularly in European countries, focus on degree outcomes rather than individual modules. If you are interested in the accumulation of learning over an entire programme, this attention must expand beyond examining how well quantitative methods is taught within any one class or module. No matter how finely designed and implemented, one particular class in research methods or statistics is only a small proportion of a degree. The relationship of quantitative methods to the degree as a whole has a huge impact on students' motivations for taking quantitative methods, the use to which they put their skills, and, ultimately, what they retain from such training. It is therefore essential to examine the place of methods in the overall curriculum when discussing best practices in teaching.

Quantitative methods cannot be viewed in isolation, which can be a particular weakness of the scholarship in this area. They are a key part of a wider effort to develop an understanding of the scientific method, the way in which research is designed and implemented, and the various techniques that can be wielded in this effort. An understanding of quantitative data and their analysis is a crucial skill in doing scientific research, but it is only a part of the broader concept of what it means to be a scientist. Students should understand why their discipline is part of the social sciences and how this conception frames the process of doing research. Quantitative methods should neither be seen as separate from general research methods, including qualitative methods, nor be seen as separate from the practice of doing research. These three types of teaching – quantitative methods, research methods and research practice – reinforce one another and should all be found on a degree programme. To consider overall degree outcomes, we have to examine training in general research methods, quantitative methods training and how students will apply these skills throughout their degree.

Quantitative methods within the degree programme

Many studies document how quantitative methods can put students off because they are not about a particular subject content and are also difficult and complex (Garfield and Ben-Zvi, 2007). These classes develop research skills that are the tools with which students may study different content areas. This makes the relevance of quantitative methods dependent on the requirements, content and structure of the overall degree programme. For example, not all degrees require students to take quantitative methods early in their undergraduate programme. Students' fear of these classes in the social sciences is well documented. In countries that allow undergraduates more latitude over the sequencing of their programme of study, particularly in the USA, students will often wait until the end of their degree to take any required methods. Methods classes taken as a final part of a degree, by definition, cannot be of much use to students in the study of that subject. The sequencing of methods classes can definitely pose an obstacle to teaching the subject, but that is not the only problem.

Many degree programmes require quantitative methods to be studied early, so that students may develop research skills before taking upper level content. However, these later modules do not always require methods as a *prerequisite*, and other classes can frequently fail to link their content and practice to prior methods training or will not apply these methods in their coursework. The impact of quantitative methods depends on the extent to which subsequent coursework follows up on this training and gets students to apply their skills. Many programmes see quantitative methods as a 'Good Thing' that should be required of all students, but then place all the training and statistical content for the degree into one (very unpopular) module and nowhere else. Students do not see the point of learning difficult skills that will never again be employed in a degree subject. The seeming irrelevance of such learning, combined with its difficulty, then undermines the efforts of methods instructors before anyone even sets foot in the classroom. It leads to heavy workloads, poor student ratings and difficult teaching assignments for (often junior) staff: a heavy disincentive even for those who are interested in and committed to teaching quantitative methods.

The curriculum of a degree programme determines when students will develop their skills in statistics and research methods, the depth to which students will develop these skills and, finally, the ways in which these tools will be used by students, not just within the methods module itself, but also in all subsequent teaching in the degree subject. These factors go beyond what, when and how quantitative methods are taught and emphasise the issue of *why* they are taught. Will these methods be required for and applied in subsequent modules in the degree? Will students have to conduct research projects in which these skills are applied? This reinforcement is crucial to hone these skills and keep them from disappearing after the final exam in introductory statistics. The purpose, place and application of methods in the whole degree will influence student skills in quantitative methods as much as what happens within the statistics classroom. The relationship of research methods to the rest of the degree should be the first principle discussed when planning such modules.

To put this issue in perspective, consider a hypothetical programme from any social science subject. The most common model for teaching research methods in the social science disciplines is to require one module of introductory statistics and one module of general research methods. This typical sequence would account for between 5 per cent and 9 per cent of a degree, depending on the credit weighting and number of years of study. The burden of developing student skills in designing, carrying out, analysing and presenting research cannot rest on such a small proportion of undergraduate class time. Two modules worth will not turn undergraduates into social scientists. Students cannot possibly gain sufficient data handling and hands-on research experience if it is confined to methods classes, although that is often what degree programmes will suggest for how they approach the teaching of social science.

Training students to be social scientists is the collective responsibility of an entire programme rather than a burden on methods teachers alone. Methods modules of all types are only sufficient preparation and training for students when the rest of the curriculum shoulders its share of the responsibility for continuing to develop scientific research skills. Basic skills learned in methods modules must be repeated, reinforced and applied in subsequent classes. When a curriculum segregates methods teaching it sends a clear message that these methods are not necessary for doing that subject. Students pick up on these signals and perceive methods as largely irrelevant because they will have little or no bearing on the rest of the curriculum. The value of methods teaching in a programme is more than just the sum of its parts. The way in which all elements of research training and their application fit together, and are reinforced through the curriculum, matters deeply. It is the whole degree and the way in which its elements fit together that will determine the overall effectiveness of quantitative and research methods teaching.

Making international comparisons

An examination of social science programmes in different countries reveals a diverse set of approaches to teaching methods in the social science curriculum. The following section is based on the Economics and Social Research Council (ESRC) report *International Bench-marking Review of Best Practice in the Provision of Undergraduate Teaching in Quantitative Methods in the Social Sciences* (Parker et al., 2008), which examines quantitative methods training at the undergraduate level in the USA, Sweden, Norway, Finland, Spain, the Netherlands, Canada and Australia. These eight countries were selected because of their long-standing track record in producing social scientists, particularly those with quantitative methods skills (ESRC, 2006). Selection relied on a ranking based on the number of social science PhDs produced (National Science Foundation, 2006). The state of undergraduate methods teaching across a range of social science disciplines was surveyed to gain an indication of current practices. Degree requirements for each discipline were analysed across universities in each country. The study included the subjects of economics, business studies, human geography, political science, psychology and sociology; however, the results presented in this chapter exclude human geography because it was not always taught as a separate subject and could not be compared reliably across countries. Importantly, this study examined quantitative methods training by placing it in the wider context of the undergraduate degree by measuring the extent to which all types of research methods are taught and practised in these subjects.

A sample of universities was surveyed in each country, focusing primarily on leading research universities because these institutions produce most postgraduate students (National Science Foundation, 2006). Each subject's degree components were analysed to determine the requirements for:

- quantitative methods;
- general research methods;
- undergraduate research, such as a thesis or a dissertation.

Quantitative methods are research methods concerned with numbers and anything that is quantifiable. Such methods modules would include a graphical, mathematical and econometric representation of ideas and analyses; the manipulation, treatment and interpretation of statistical data; statistics, numeracy and quantitative skills, including data analysis, interpretation and extrapolation; survey design and analysis; psychometrics; experimental design; and mathematics.

Any methods modules not classified as quantitative methods in the study were classified as 'general research methods'. This definition encompasses a broad range of topics, but generally describes modules covering epistemology and methods. These modules define the scientific method and what research is, categorising the different types of research and various ways it can be carried out, and explaining the various methodologies used to conduct it. The aim of all of these courses is to introduce students to the scientific method and improve their research skills, which could be either qualitative or quantitative in character. This definition could incorporate many different types of content for different disciplines. Typically in the study, these modules included were simply named 'research methods', 'scope and methods', or 'research design'. There is some risk of this category becoming a label that refers to *qualitative* research methods. However, that is not a problem because *few programmes explicitly require qualitative methods.*

The category of 'theses, dissertations and research projects' consisted of modules where students designed and engaged in their own research. It was often defined as a thesis, dissertation, capstone course or senior seminar. Such modules are usually dedicated to the practice of research, the research process, and should involve designing and conducting research or participating in a research project.

The survey retrieved mandatory course requirements for undergraduate degrees or majors in each subject from university catalogues, reports and websites. Modules in quantitative methodology, general research methods and student research projects were coded using the course titles and descriptions from the websites. This approach differs from many surveys of quantitative methods teaching that examine classroom practices and module level content. This review did not seek to find out the best way to teach quantitative methods in the classroom. It sought to examine the place of methods in the curriculum and examine best practice for the type, timing and extent of methods teaching and undergraduate research. Consequently, it evaluated the content of the whole programme or degree rather than a single module.

Comparing modules across universities in just one country presents a daunting challenge due to the multitude of credit systems and student workloads that exist across different institutions. Extending the comparison across countries greatly multiplies this problem. One possible solution is to calculate the number of credits needed for an undergraduate degree and classify each module as a set percentage of that degree. For example, in the USA a typical three-credit module in a BA of 120 credits would constitute 2.5 per cent of an undergraduate degree, whereas a lab-related module of four credits would be 3.3 per cent. Countries also differ on how many years of study are needed for the completion of an undergraduate degree. Many countries will require three years instead of four, and others will demand an additional fourth year to attain an honours degree. Programmes can also require four modules per semester rather than five. These large variations across countries inhibit any attempt to quantify the exact value of a training module in methods. Identical modules in terms of curriculum content and hours of work required could have different weightings depending on the length of the degree. For example, the typical three-credit module found in the USA is 2.5 per cent of a degree, but the same module in a three-year programme would be 4.2 per cent.

Deciding on whether to weight the percentage of a degree or the amount and level of coursework is a difficult trade-off. Standardising module weighting to the percentage of a degree would prove far too cumbersome, time consuming and difficult, while the results would be misleading in terms of how much training a student actually receives. This study adopted a simple rule of thumb that modules are all generally equivalent. Most universities operate on an eight to 10 module workload per year. Credit weightings were collected in order to classify modules as a half, single or double, according to their relative weight in the particular system being used. This system gives a relatively accurate way of comparing how much course time is allocated to teaching and applying research methods.

National patterns

Comparing mean numbers of required quantitative methods modules across all eight countries (Table 3.1) gives a good overview of different approaches to training in undergraduate social science degrees. Consistent similarities and variations across disciplines and countries suggest some international trends.

There are distinct differences between disciplines that appear across countries. Business and economics are the most quantitative subjects in all countries, as one would expect, although the level of training can vary strongly by country. The most common model, particularly for economics, is two quantitative methods modules. Psychology and sociology also consistently require

Table 3.1 International comparison of mean number of required quantitative methods modules

	Australia	Canada	Finland	Netherlands	Norway	Spain	Sweden	USA
Business	0.7	2.0	1.6	2.0	1.3	1.5	0.1	1.4
Economics	0.7	2.0	1.9	2.8	2.2	2.0	1.2	2.0
Political science	0.0	0.2	0.3	1.1	0.3	1.0	0.1	0.2
Psychology	0.2	1.2	1.5	3.4	0.8	0.6	0.6	1.1
Sociology	0.0	0.7	1.0	3.2	0.6	1.6	0.4	0.9

quantitative methods, though at lower levels. Quantitative methods training in psychology and sociology varies more widely within countries than for business and economics, but is fairly evenly distributed around the standard of one module, which is the most common requirement. Finally, political science provides the least training with only two of the eight countries requiring a full module and most requiring well under half a module on average.

The effectiveness of the quantitative methods training that does occur also relies on the extent to which the skills are required, reinforced and practised in classes outside of methods training. Advanced statistical training is of little use if students are never asked to practise or apply it as part of other modules in their subject. The extent to which such skills are embedded in a curriculum will strongly indicate to students how important it is to that discipline. Economics, for example, is considered the most quantitative subject, not just because of its training requirements, but also because its students are most likely to need and use these skills in their coursework throughout the subject (Ballard and Johnson, 2004; Siegfried et al., 1991).

Quantitative methods should not be viewed in isolation from other training in scientific research methods, and a more complete view of the students' experience should include all methods training and its application in undergraduate research activities. General research methods requirements are usually found alongside quantitative methods, and the two are often taught in the same module. Given this strong linkage, the extent to which general research methods acts as a complementary partner to quantitative methods across subjects and countries is an important issue to examine (see Table 3.2).

General research methods requirements vary more than those for quantitative methods but show similarly consistent trends across disciplines and countries. Economics and business show an inverse relationship between levels of quantitative methods and research methods. Countries with high quantitative methods requirements often have low general research methods requirements. Similarly, countries with lower quantitative methods requirements in those subjects, such as Australia and Sweden, have correspondingly stronger requirements in general research methods. This inverse relationship could occur if some quantitative methods were included in general methods modules, but none of the module descriptions indicate any such content. In

Table 3.2 International comparison of mean number of general research methods modules required

	Australia	Canada	Finland	Netherlands	Norway	Spain	Sweden	USA
Business	1.2	0.1	0.4	4.4	0.3	0.3	0.6	0.2
Economics	1.6	0.1	0.1	1.7	0	0.7	0	0
Political science	0.5	0.3	1.1	3.3	0.5	1.9	1.1	0.3
Psychology	1.8	0.9	1.8	2.8	1.0	3.3	1.5	1.0
Sociology	1.4	1.2	2.0	2.7	1.0	4.8	1.3	1.0

general, economics and business demand little training in general research methods across most countries, aside from Australia and the Netherlands.

All other subjects show a positive correlation between quantitative methods and general research methods. Psychology and sociology show the strongest and most consistent general research methods requirements, with each discipline requiring a mean of at least one module in all but one country. Political science, again, has the lowest requirements of the social sciences. While its standards are much higher than for quantitative methods, it fails to require a mean of one module in half the countries surveyed.

Levels of general research methods training rarely exceed a mean of two modules for a degree. As with quantitative methods, there are few instances of particularly advanced and sustained levels of training. However, just as quantitative methods cannot be separated from general research methods, the overall levels of methods training should not be separated from actual undergraduate research, which offers students the chance to apply their skills.

Undergraduate research requirements vary widely across countries (see Table 3.3), but unlike the results for quantitative and general research methods do not vary much across disciplines. Clearly, some countries' systems of higher education promote or require the inclusion of a research project, thesis or dissertation as part of their undergraduate curricula. Those countries adopt such requirements consistently across the social sciences, though the levels still vary by subject. The Scandinavian countries of Finland, Norway and Sweden, along with the Netherlands, all have consistent requirements for a student thesis or research project across all subjects while the four other countries do not. In addition, about 12 per cent of students in Australia take an extra year to complete an honours degree, which includes a similar requirement. Again, these figures only refer to required modules. The data do not indicate the extent to which elective elements contain student research projects.

Undergraduate research is a popular and growing trend in many countries, the USA and Canada for example, and is often linked to work or placements in local communities. However, these courses are electives and reserved for a few select students (Jenkins, 2007). The ESRC report demonstrated that half the countries surveyed had explicit requirements for all students to design and conduct their own research. Despite the lack of formal requirements in many

Table 3.3 International comparison of mean thesis/dissertation module requirements

	Australia	Canada	Finland	Netherlands	Norway	Spain	Sweden	USA
Business	0	0	0.7	1.9	0.7	0.1	0.8	0
Economics	0	0	0.4	1.0	0.4	0.1	0.9	0
Political science	0	0	0.6	2.1	0.3	0.1	1.6	0
Psychology	0	0	0.3	1.7	1.0	0	1.3	0.1
Sociology	0	0	0.7	2.3	0.6	0.1	1.5	0.1

countries this arrangement is held up as 'good practice' and is more common among the best students, as well as in institutions with excellent reputations for teaching, such as liberal arts colleges in the USA.

Identifying best practice in teaching quantitative methods

The results of the survey give a good indication of how universities approach methods teaching in different countries. Combining the details of this practice with the literature on learning and teaching reveals a good deal of consensus over best practice. The overall results, across most countries and disciplines, show that the requirements for quantitative methods teaching, when viewed in isolation, seldom involve the advanced training of undergraduates. However, there are strong trends across both subjects and countries in how research methods are integrated into an overall discipline or degree. Quantitative methods are often taught as one particular way of conducting scientific research. This approach is usually combined with a more general scope and methods course, which teaches students about the scientific method as well as how to design and conduct research. In some cases the more general research methods course may include quantitative and/or qualitative methods. While either quantitative methods or general research methods coursework may not seem extensive on its own, when combined they can constitute a substantial proportion of a degree. These requirements should be viewed together as a package of research training and practice because quantitative methods, qualitative methods, and scope and methods/research design all complement and reinforce each other, helping to create a more coherent curriculum.

The way in which these different types of training are put to use also matters, with many subjects and countries showing strong trends in requiring students to carry out hands-on research. The combination of these trends, alongside a body of theoretical and empirical literature, suggests substantial cross-subject, international consensus over best practice in research methods training in the curriculum. This consensus can be simplified into the two key approaches:

- an integration of quantitative skills and data analysis throughout the programme;
- rigorous methods training as part of a wider programme of scientific research in the social sciences.

Requiring students to take a single course in maths or statistics does not ensure that they will develop the level of skills required. More recent literature on quantitative literacy recommends the integration of quantitative skills throughout a curriculum. Such skills cannot be learned or retained without continuing practice to reinforce them, so they must be embedded within many different modules or classes throughout a programme (Levine et al., 2002; Schneider, 2004; Howery and Rodriguez, 2006). The American Mathematics Association has played a leading role in developing quantitative literacy and actively supports the adoption of minimal quantitative training standards for all students, as well as the use of data and quantitative skills in modules throughout a student's programme (Gillman, 2006). The National Science Foundation, the social science funding council in the USA, endorses this integrated approach to quantitative skills and student research (Levine et al., 2004).

A 1994 initiative involving a group of sociology departments in the USA, the Minority Opportunities through School Transformation (MOST) programme, sought to raise the achievement of students with a minority background. The project took the approach that *all* students need to be addressed, not just minority groups, in order to raise achievement across the board. The project departments agreed to integrate quantitative data throughout the curriculum, enhance research-based practice and discussion in all courses, and provide mentors for all students. Several institutions also added capstone courses to their major requirements, which emphasised hands-on research, often connected to the neighbouring community (Levine et al., 2002). The programme was a success for the entire student body but was particularly successful in boosting the achievement of minority students.

The success of the MOST programme led to the Integrating Data Analysis (IDA) project. IDA was funded by the National Science Foundation and undertaken by the American Sociological Association. The IDA project builds on the assumption that drove the MOST programme: that curricular change demands departmental change and cannot be left to individual faculty members or limited to isolated modules (Howery and Rodriguez, 2006). The objective of the IDA project is to introduce students to data analysis early, frequently and sequentially throughout the curriculum. The project created datasets and lessons that could be easily adapted for classroom use, and it also provided training for departments on how to use these resources.

Evaluations suggest that long-term projects such as MOST and IDA can make lasting changes in the culture of a department. An assessment of the IDA project shows that students' reactions were generally positive and initial data on learning outcomes demonstrated gains in research knowledge. The assessors suggested that the IDA project will result in cohorts of undergraduate students with a better understanding of sociology, of what sociologists do and of the applicability and importance of the discipline. IDA staff interviews with students in participating institutions showed students to be more positive about learning maths or quantitative skills when they served a purpose or were relevant to the students' life experience. Students were able to connect to what was taught in the classroom with actual hands-on types of data analyses and research experiences (Howery and Rodriguez, 2006). The National Science Foundation endorses the MOST and IDA projects' approaches to teaching, particularly their emphasis on adopting curriculum changes across whole departments rather than in individual modules (Levine et al., 2004).

Undergraduate research

The USA has long promoted undergraduate research as a valuable part of higher education. In 1998, the Boyer Commission of the Carnegie Commission on Higher Education recommended that universities provide research-based learning, undergraduate research and internships. In its recommendations of best practice for teaching social science, the National Science Foundation reaffirmed this commitment, alongside an endorsement of the integration of data analysis and hands-on research throughout an entire programme (Levine et al., 2004). Discipline reports on recommended practices in the undergraduate curriculum for both psychology and sociology promoted undergraduate research (Halonen et al., 2002, 2007; McKinney et al., 2004). Practising social science is seen as the best way to develop higher level skills and learning outcomes while engaging students' interest and enthusiasm (see Healey, 2008, and Jenkins et al., 2003 for reviews of the literature). The different countries which advocate this approach to teaching share a concern about increasing student understanding of the scientific method and developing the skills to apply it by carrying out research. This approach clearly emphasises teaching the scientific method and engaging students in research rather than developing quantitative skills *per se*, even where there are explicit concerns over the need for such skills. The *type* of method is not seen as being as important as the *experience of doing* scientific research. The most common example of this approach involves a large final year research project, thesis or dissertation.

However, viewing the final year project as the be-all and end-all of undergraduate research seriously underestimates the aims of the integrated approach that is adopted by many countries and recommended in the literature. The final project should simply be the culmination of a sequence of research methods training and practice. It is the whole programme of study which is supposed to develop a student's ability to carry out research. Just as the teaching of methods should not be confined to a single module, students' hands-on experience of doing research should not be limited to a final dissertation module.

Modules throughout the programme should not only cover how to do research but should also engage students in large or small hands-on projects. Research councils in the USA and Canada have funded efforts to make data, particularly from large datasets, easily available for use in the classroom as part of the effort to encourage students to work with such data (Levine et al. 2002; Social Sciences and Humanities Research Council of Canada (SSHRC), 2002, 2005; Howery and Rodriguez, 2006). The provision of undergraduate research skills such as data-handling and data analysis throughout the curriculum demonstrates their importance to students, allowing them to practise these in order to develop their skills. The USA and Canada promote an integrated package of research methods and under-graduate research as best practice for the social sciences as an aspiration for their universities, many of which do not yet follow such an approach. However, universities in European countries such as the Netherlands, Finland, Norway and Sweden do follow this approach in the social sciences as an explicitly identified requirement of an undergraduate degree. All of these countries have relatively centralised, state-controlled systems of higher education. This stronger top-down control combines with a greater consensus over the proper way to teach the social science to create a very structured and research-based approach to teaching undergraduates.

The Netherlands demonstrates the most rigorous use of this integrated approach to undergraduate research, but the pattern is similar in the Scandinavian countries. Students take classes on research methods early on in their programmes of study, and they continue to take methods modules throughout their degree. This high level of training in research methods is also put to use throughout the degree. The integrated approach is clear in this pattern: methods training and hands-on research, sometimes referred to as theory and practice, are carried out repeatedly by students throughout their programme rather than only in a few modules near its end. Social science degrees train students to understand and apply the scientific method as researchers. The strong system of quality assurance in the Netherlands strictly enforces this ethos, and external auditors inspect programmes down to the number, content and timing of modules in a student's programme (Quality Assurance Netherlands Universities (QANU), 1999, 2001, 2002, 2003, 2004). Finland, Norway and Sweden provide similar social science curricula and systems of quality assurance, although with fewer required modules. All of these countries require an integrated package of methods training and undergraduate research that is not restricted to just a final year dissertation.

There is an international consensus among countries in the ESRC survey that the best practice for the teaching of quantitative methods consists of the integration of methods training and hands-on research across as much of the programme as possible. Applying research skills is the most effective way of showing the relevance of this training and reinforcing those skills. Six of the eight countries either advocate or practise this approach to social science degrees.

The importance of providing a coherent and consistent approach to research training throughout a programme is critical. Where this approach is adopted, it promotes active student engagement with scientific research. When quantitative methods are included frequently and as part of the research process, rather than isolated in a single module that does not connect to any other coursework in the programme, students will engage with these key skills. More importantly, it is *doing* research that gets students enthusiastic about methods. Even better, this approach shows particular success in engaging students from a minority or disadvantaged background (Levine et al., 2002).

Learning the lessons

The international experience of teaching social science methods, alongside the scholarship of learning and teaching, has led to the following recommendations about undergraduate degrees:

- Developing good methods skills requires engaging students in the process of scientific research throughout their degree. Undergraduates should learn about research methods but, most importantly, they should also apply them in order to better understand the scientific method, reinforce the skills they have learnt, and experience the benefits of using them rather than seeing methods as a purely theoretical exercise. A major research project should be a required part of an honours degree in the social sciences, but the student experience of research should not be confined to that one project.
- Methods training, particularly quantitative methods, and hands-on research should be integrated throughout the modules of a social science degree. For too long, quantitative methods teachers have carried out, in isolation, the difficult job of teaching a topic both feared and disliked by many students. All students should become used to collecting, reading, manipulating and analysing numerical data in modules throughout a degree. Numerical data inspire less fear and hostility from students if they occur frequently across many different subject topics rather than only in a single module of 'quantitative methods' or 'introductory statistics'.

These recommendations build on the existing strengths of undergraduate methods teaching and research in UK universities. There is a long tradition of undergraduate research, with a strong emphasis on the dissertation in most disciplines. There is also a widespread culture of hostility towards mathematics throughout many subjects. The lack of sustained and widespread mathematics training among secondary school students, and their fear and suspicion of taking up maths or statistics once they have entered university, create a substantial impediment to quantitative methods training, particularly in the increasing competition for student numbers that will occur over the next decade.

Quantitative methods can be integrated into ordinary subject modules rather than entirely isolated within 'methods' or 'statistics' modules. This will present the use of such skills as a normal part of the process of doing social science research. Some practical issues for the reader to consider include:

- Does your programme offer a dissertation? If not, then why not? There is not much point in teaching methods if they are not going to be used.
- Is the dissertation optional? If so, then why? If everyone should be taught methods then should not everyone apply what they have learned?
- What kind of quantitative methods or data analysis is used in the other modules in your programme? Ask colleagues which methods are used in the articles and books they assign to their students. Many people are surprised at the extent to which descriptive statistics are used in introductory textbooks or subjects that are not seen as quantitative.
- Tailor your teaching to the skills students will need and actually use in their degree.
- Ask your colleagues to get students to practise the skills they have learned by doing small, hands-on data analysis projects in their modules. It can be as simple a project as reviewing an opinion poll or analysing a chart or graph, but it will reinforce the idea that quantitative skills are important and are used everywhere.
- Even those colleagues who seem hostile to quantitative methods will usually expect their students to be able to find and use descriptive statistics, so incorporating these skills into small assignments or projects is not too much to ask.
- Use lots of small assignments to build up student skills in doing more complicated work. For example, if everyone uses a particular large dataset, students will become more familiar with the data and software. They can then gain the skills and confidence that are necessary to use such a resource in a larger project such as a dissertation.
- If you want to achieve more ambitious outcomes with your students, particularly multivariate techniques, then these skills should be referred to, reinforced and practised in other modules. Students should be asked to read, review, and use these techniques in many different modules if they are to be retained.

Resources

The sociology department at Southwestern University in Georgetown, Texas, USA, has integrated research training throughout its curriculum. You can read a journal article about it as a case study (Kain, 1999) and look at their *Handbook for Sociology Majors*, which provides a description of the skills that are developed in each different level of modules offered. The handbook is available at: http://www.southwestern.edu/academic/depts/socanthro/HandbookSoc.html.

The political scientist Gary Klass (2008) has written a book on skills and expertise that are not often covered in qualitative or quantitative research methods and statistics texts and courses, but are still directly applicable to students' subsequent coursework. The book and its accompanying webpage at http://lilt.ilstu.edu/jpda/ provide some excellent examples and techniques for doing practical exercises in social science classes.

Concluding advice

Teachers tend to be most comfortable in the privacy of their own classroom teaching their own materials to their own students. Shifting this approach to a more collective responsibility can be challenging, but it is particularly critical for research methods and practice. You are providing students with a framework on how to view the world and how to go about becoming a scientist. It is too extensive, complex and important a goal to accomplish by yourself or even in a handful of modules. It takes practice and reinforcement to fully achieve these outcomes beyond the last final exam. Spreading these skills throughout a curriculum may encounter some resistance. However, the *International Bench-marking Review of Best Practice in the Provision of Undergraduate Teaching in Quantitative Methods in the Social Sciences* study (Parker et al., 2008) provides an evidence base on which an argument can be built as well as many practical examples of techniques to try out. The workload implications for one's colleagues are not heavy, and the legitimacy of the case for change is now well established.

References

Ballard, C. and Johnson, M. (2004) 'Basic math skills and performance in an introductory economics class', *Journal of Economic Education*, 35 (Winter): 3–23.

Economic and Social Research Council (2006) *Invitations for Expressions of Interest: International Bench-marking Review of Best Practice in the Provision of Undergraduate Teaching in Quantitative Methods in the Social Sciences*. Swindon: ESRC.

Garfield, J. and Ben-Zvi, D. (2007) 'How students learn statistics revisited: a current review of research on teaching and learning statistics', *International Statistical Review,* 75(3): 372–96.

Gillman, R. (2006) *Current Practices in Quantitative Literacy.* Washington, DC: Mathematics Association of America.

Halonen, J., Appleby, D., Brewer, C., Buskist, W., Gillem, A., Halpern, Hill, W., Lloyd, M., Rudmann, J. and Whitlow, V. (2002) *Undergraduate Psychology Major Learning Goals and Outcomes: A Report.* Washington, DC: American Psychological Association.

Halonen, J., Appleby, D., Brewer, C., Buskist, W., Gillem, A., Halpern, Hill, W., Lloyd, M., Rudmann, J. and Whitlow, V. (2007) *APA Guidelines for the Undergraduate Psychology Major.* Washington, DC: American Psychological Association.

Healey, M. (2008) *Linking Research and Teaching: A Selected Bibliography.* Cheltenham: University of Gloucestershire. Available at: http://www.glos.ac.uk/shareddata/dms/5B8F006BBCD42A039BA6832547DBAC47.pdf (accessed 16 July 2008).

Howery, C. and Rodriguez, H. (2006) 'Integrating Data Analysis (IDA): working with sociology departments to address the quantitative literacy gap', *Teaching Sociology,* 16: 23–38.

Jenkins, A. (2007) *The Effective Adaptation and Mainstreaming of USA Undergraduate Research to the U.K. and Other National Contexts.* Warwick: Reinvention Centre for Undergraduate Research.

Jenkins, A., Breen, R. and Lindsay, R. (2003) *Re-Shaping Teaching in Higher Education: Linking Teaching and Research.* London: Kogan Page.

Kain, E. (1999) 'Building the sociological imagination through a cumulative curriculum: professional socialization in sociology', *Teaching Sociology,* 34: 5–22.

Klass, G. (2008) *Just Plain Data Analysis: Finding, Presenting, and Interpreting Social Science Data.* New York: Rowman and Littlefield.

Levine, F., Rodriguez, H., Howery, C. and Latoni-Rodriguez, A. (2002) *Promoting Diversity and Excellence in Higher Education through Department Change.* Washington, DC: American Sociological Association.

Levine, F., Abler, R. and Rosich, K. (2004) *Education and Training in the Social, Behavioral, and Economic Sciences: A Plan of Action.* Washington, DC: National Science Foundation.

McKinney, K., Howery, C., Strand, K., Kain, E. and Berheide, C. (2004) 'Liberal learning and the sociology major updated: meeting the challenge of teaching sociology in the twenty-first century', in *A Report of the ASA Task Force on the Undergraduate Major.* Washington, DC: American Sociological Association.

National Science Foundation (2006) *Science and Engineering Indicators 2006.* Arlington, VA: National Science Foundation.

Parker, J., Dobson, A., Scott, S., Wyman, M. and Sjöstedt Landén, A. (2008) *International Bench-marking Review of Best Practice in the Provision of Undergraduate Teaching in Quantitative Methods in the Social Sciences.* Swindon: ESRC.

Quality Assurance Netherlands Universities (1999) *Sociologie.* QANU: Utrecht.

Quality Assurance Netherlands Universities (2001) *Psychologie*. QANU: Utrecht.

Quality Assurance Netherlands Universities (2002) *Sociale Geografie*. QANU: Utrecht.

Quality Assurance Netherlands Universities (2003) *Economie*. QANU: Utrecht.

Quality Assurance Netherlands Universities (2004) *Politicologie*. QANU: Utrecht.

Schneider, C. (2004) 'Setting greater expectations for quantitative learning', *Peer Review*, 1(6): 26–7.

Siegfried, J., Bartlett, R., Kelley, A., McCloskey, D. and Tietenberg, H. (1991) 'The status and prospects of the economics major', *Journal of Economic Education*, 22 (Summer): 197–224.

Social Sciences and Humanities Research Council of Canada (2005) *From Granting Council to Knowledge Council: Renewing the Social Sciences and Humanities in Canada*. Ottawa, ON: SSHRC.

Social Sciences and Humanities Research Council of Canada and Statistics Canada (2002) *Final Report: Joint Working Group on the Advancement of Research using Social Statistics*. Ottawa, ON: SSHRC.

The Place of Quantification in the Professional Training of Sociologists: Some Career Reflections

Martin Bulmer

The brief for this chapter was to offer some personal reflections on the place of quantitative methods in a British sociological education over a period of close to half a century. During the period 1960–2010 much has changed, not least the establishment and expansion of sociology as a serious academic and professional practice by 2010 which scarcely existed half a century before. In 1960, Halsey observed that there were about as many professional sociologists teaching in all UK universities as there were academic historians at the University of Oxford – one hundred in each case. The expansion which began in the 1960s has altered the situation out of all recognition so that today there are several thousand teachers and researchers of sociology in higher education, cadres of graduate students in sociology being educated, and a substantial number of persons employed as social researchers, most in non-academic locations, a considerable number of whom would claim some connection with sociology. Whether comparable strides have taken place within sociology in regard to quantitative methods will be one aim of this chapter to explore. Some trends remain constant. It is a broader issue, but the dominant anti-quantitative ethos of UK metropolitan life and particularly of its leading newspapers and journals remains as strong today as it was half a century ago.

Early years

My own encounter with sociology began in the early 1960s when I briefly studied history at Cambridge University and was exposed to a range of speakers in the student Sociology Society. There was considerable interest in sociological approaches to historical subjects and to the history of political thought on the part of historians such as Peter Laslett, Moses Finley, Philip Abrams and James Cornford. Ferocious arguments took place with the History Faculty about the reform of the tripos, and more traditionally minded figures such as Maurice Cowling (1963), Geoffrey Elton (1967) and Charles Wilson (1964) did not hesitate to denounce sociological tendencies and the lure of generalising concepts, which they saw as insidious and a threat to traditional historiography. Three works that influenced me disproportionately at this time were E.H. Carr's *What is History?*, published in 1961, Gunnar Myrdal's *An American Dilemma* (1944), which I encountered while taking a course in American history, and Garry Runciman's *Social Science and Political Theory* (1963), an elegant overview of the relationship between empirical and normative statements in the social sciences. All suggested that a sociological perspective had much to recommend it and significant advantages over an historical one, and I resolved to study sociology.

At this stage, I was not exposed to anything concerning sociological research methods. Although I can recall Donald Stokes speaking at the student society on the British election study in which he was engaged with David Butler (1969), exposure to considerations of methods was minimal. A couple of papers in sociology were offered in Part 2 of the Economics tripos, taught by recent appointments David Lockwood and John Goldthorpe, and Michael Young fleetingly held some kind of lectureship appointment. But what was offered as a way of studying sociology around 1964 in Cambridge was insubstantial – the establishment of the Chair of Sociology and of the Social and Political Sciences Faculty was still five years in the future – so I resolved to move in 1964 to the London School of Economics and Political Science (LSE) to begin a full undergraduate sociology degree there. This was a move that I have never regretted, and it brought me into closer acquaintance with many aspects of the subject. This chapter is about quantitative sociology, so I shall confine myself to what was taught to undergraduates at the LSE during this period.

Sociology after the Second World War had cast off the yoke of Hobhouse and Ginsberg and had broadened its reach, partly under the influence of other LSE teachers such as David Glass, T.H. Marshall, Edward Shils and Jean Floud, and also through closer involvement with the department of statistics. The details of courses may be consulted in the annual LSE *Calendar*, but the main research methods course at this period was entitled 'Survey methods in social investigation' and was taught by Claus Moser (now Lord Moser), who was professor of social statistics. His textbook of that name, later revised with Graham Kalton (Moser and Kalton, 1967), stemmed from this course, and gives a fair idea of its content. This was what I studied. It was backed up in the sociology department by teachers of a quantitative bent such as John Westergaard, assisted by the young Wyn Lewis in statistics (who later moved to the sociology department at Warwick). There was also a stimulating class in sociology taught by Asher Tropp, Westergaard and Alan Little on the sociology of modern Britain, which incorporated much quantitative material into the course, and helped to reinforce the relevance of the survey methods course within the sociology degree. Their approach to methods was, however, broader than survey methods and encompassed ethnographic and case study research. At this period, the LSE degree probably offered the leading single honours sociology degree in the country, and the methods component thus had a markedly quantitative content, so much so that 'research methods' was more or less equated to 'survey methods', although the existence of other methods was recognised.

Taking stock: 1979–1981

The main focus of this chapter is not a chronological history of sociological research methods in the UK since the 1960s, but rather to provide a personal view. However, it seemed to the writer that he could most usefully focus on a series of reflections and assessments which appeared 30 years ago, in the period 1979–81. These various contributions in turn reflected on the first 30 years of British sociology as a professional academic activity, from approximately 1950 to 1980.

Writing in 1981, I attempted to characterise the teaching of research methods in the UK more generally:

> Much discussion of the current state of methodology teaching is characterised by what may be called 'the myth of the positivist past' (Platt 1981). British sociology has never been as strongly quantitative and statistical as is nowadays widely thought. Despite the statistical and survey emphasis apparent in Peel (1968) few sociology departments taught their undergraduates more than a basic course in social statistics (Rosenbaum 1971: paras 31–45). It was difficult at that time to find sociologists sufficiently strong in quantitative methods to work on topics demanding advanced statistical competence. In 1972 a conference on the teaching of statistics in the social sciences heard that 'for a majority of sociology students, research methods courses – with or without a statistics component – represent the only significant contact they have with quantitative and formal modes of thinking and analysis'. Such courses were also often uninspiring, ill thought-out and marginal to sociological concerns (Coxon 1973: 43), frequently taught by statisticians or economists for students in the social sciences generally, leaving sociology students to make their own substantive applications. (Bulmer, 1981: 540)

A sense of the period can be gained from the following long extract from John Wakeford's 1981 critique:

> Examination questions probed for evidence of a firm grasp of these specific procedures, and of the students' ability to manipulate quantitative data. 'Methods' utilised a static model of social science in which the research enterprise was conceived, presented and assessed as a set of scientific techniques, detached from the substantive and theoretical concerns of contemporary sociological work. Data, it was implied – in tests,

syllabuses and examination questions – could be gathered independent of their source or meaning.

Most of the texts used were not written specifically for sociology but rather for the social sciences as a whole – notably those by Selltiz, Moser, Madge, Oppenheim, Festinger and Katz and Goode and Hatt – replete with implicit epistemological and methodological assumptions. For instance, in the most quoted text, *Survey Methods in Social Investigation*, Moser makes his methodological position explicit:

> I have at many points in the previous three chapters referred to errors that may occur in the collection of survey data.... What is meant by response errors? Let us assume that for each individual covered by a survey there is an individual true value (ITV). This value is quite independent of the survey, of the way the question is asked, and by whom. If we ask the respondent how old he is, there is one correct answer; if we ask him how much he spent on chocolate last week, there is again a unique correct answer. It is true that many questions are not so simple and – for instance, with opinion questions – I would often be difficult to define the ITV. However, the difficulty is beside the point here. (Moser 1958: 246)

Such a perspective may not have been shared by all teachers, but how often were the contradictions between methods text and sociological models explicitly discussed in class? (1981: 506)

In 1979, Wakeford had compiled a collection of undergraduate research methods syllabuses from UK departments, which now provides a useful snapshot of the state of research methods teaching at the time. In his 1981 commentary, Wakeford observed that the LSE offering at the time:

> is composed of only two sections – one being 'entirely a course in elementary statistics taught under the auspices of the Department of Statistics', the other covering the 'basic issues and methods of social research', by almost exclusive attention to the execution and analysis of material from social surveys. (1981: 508)

This was basically the course that I had taken 15 years earlier, though as Wakeford noted, with the advent of a new interdepartmental lecture course and the appointment of new staff (Dr Christopher Husbands and myself), courses had been modified to place less emphasis on survey methods and more on theoretical context. Indeed, the edited text (Bulmer, 1977) which I had recently published put much more emphasis on the interconnection of theory and method, and the range of available methods which could be drawn upon.

A remarkable regularity revealed in the Wakeford compendium of courses was that the most cited methods text appeared to be A.V. Cicourel's *Method and Measurement in Sociology* (1964) which, inter alia, provided a critique of interviewing and fixed-choice questionnaires. It was essentially a work of critique, not so much setting out what could be done in the course of research as dwelling on the limitations of the standard procedures. It is a measure of the methodological ferment associated with the expansion of British sociology between the mid 1960s and the late 1970s that such a work should come to occupy a commanding place in the teaching of research methods. Yet perhaps one should not be surprised. Even at the LSE, that bastion of traditionalism in methods teaching for so long, changes in personnel in the sociology department meant that support for quantitative methods tended to be a minority activity within the department. Indeed, in the late 1970s, when the acquisition of the WH Smith warehouse made possible the creation of what is now the British Library of Political and Economic Science (rebuilt again in 2001), considerable movement took place among departments within the school. The internal planning document for this extensive set of moves written by Pro-Director Cyril Grunfeld (1978) included the statement (made, of course, in the days of a reliance on mainframes for all data analysis) that 'the Sociology Department will not need to be near the computer'.

Christopher T. Husbands put the matter succinctly in a paper given to the British Sociological Association conference in 1980: 'As cognoscenti will already know, the discipline of sociology in Britain lacks the sympathy to quantitative approaches that marks the subject in the United States' (Husbands, 1981: 88). His paper presents a variety of empirical evidence, including analysis of the content of British journal articles, to support this proposition.

One of the traits held against survey research in particular, implicit in the quote from John Wakeford above, is that such research was 'positivistic'. Jennifer Platt dissected the meaning of 'positivism' quite extensively during this period, and concluded that perhaps the contrast was not as great as was commonly thought: 'It seems possible that the main *practical* difference between "positivist" and other methodologies is in the degree of explicitness with which they state in principle, and describe in individual instances, the intellectual procedures that they employ at different stages of research rather than in their ontological and epistemological assumptions' (Platt, 1981: 82, emphasis in original).

Catherine Marsh, developing the teaching of sociological research methods at Cambridge University in the social and political sciences tripos, and then moving to the University of Manchester, where she held a joint appointment in sociology and econometrics before her untimely death in 1993, sought to examine whether the problems faced by the survey method were:

> intrinsic philosophical problems which place absolute constraints on the method, or whether they are technical problems which are in principle capable of a solution. It is my contention that, behind the war-cry of positivism, attacks that have been parading as fundamental criticisms of the epistemological basis of survey research have very often been either criticisms of a practical technical nature ... or have raised problems to do with

any kind of data collection in social science, which stem from the problem that the subject matter of our research is conscious, communicates in anguage whose meaning is not capable of unique determination, and is capable of changing very rapidly. This is a problem for any social scientist, from the experimenter to the ethnographer, and is not confined to surveys. (1979: 293, emphasis in original)

As indicated above, one preponderant response to the perceived limitations of surveys was to reject the survey as a tool of sociological investigation, through an over-reaction to the earlier LSE-based model of how to teach research methods. Indeed this view was still surfacing in the first decade of the twenty-first century, in the argument of Savage and Burrows (2007) that face-to-face questioning of the population was passé, and sociologists could rely much more on databanks of administrative data built up by commercial organisations. As Crompton (2008) pointed out in a justifiably trenchant critique, this was resurrecting, perhaps not intentionally, the arguments of 40 years earlier against quantitative methods, and was scarcely more persuasive. Crompton added another dimension to the argument by suggesting that some of the proponents of quantitative methods in the 1980s and 1990s, particularly those associated with Nuffield College, Oxford, had put forward their arguments *for* quantification in an unnecessarily abrasive and contentious manner, which did not lead to a resolution of the arguments but to stalemate. This need not have been the outcome. George W. Brown, at a conference held at the end of 1979 at the University of Warwick to consider graduate training in sociological research methods, argued for a finer-tuned approach to data collection via surveys and face-to-face interviews and a less intransigent position.

The last fifteen years or so has seen some efforts to return to using that most valuable of all resources that we have in the social sciences – the humanity of the investigator. Cicourel's *Method and Measurement in Sociology* published in 1964 made important criticisms of survey research, but by and large this has led to a movement that has rejected the survey as a viable approach. (Others have rejected it for a somewhat different set of reasons, e.g. Yarrow 1963.) This paper deals with alternatives to outright rejection that accept the critical importance of survey-type research and have worked to improve existing methods of approach. It should not be overlooked that the traditional questionnaire has important achievements particularly with more census-type inquiries and its emphasis upon the importance of standardisation does reflect a significant insight. Its error has been to be far too inflexible in the interpretation of this principle. It is now clear that error and bias need to be combated by a range of approaches, and that the notions surrounding the idea of standardization are only one of these. Indeed, I would go further to suggest that methodological and technical advances can probably never lead to a final solution and that we need also to depend on the theoretical implications of a particular set of results – something along the lines of what psychologists have called 'construct validity' (Cronbach and Meehl 1955). (Brown, 1981: 556)

Marsh, in discussing assessment procedures at the end of the 1970s suggested that the conventional three-hour examination was particularly unsuited to assessing the skills taught in research methods courses. Such examinations were good at testing 'verbal fluency and conceptual acumen' (Marsh, 1981: 521) but other skills were not adequately grasped by the traditional examination. Marsh suggested a range of research skills that research methods courses were trying to impart, but which were not assessable in the traditional way. These included:

- research creativity;
- numeracy;
- data analytic flair (this she observed was scarcely assessed at all);
- social sensitivity;
- intellectual craftsmanship;
- computing;
- knowledge of data sources;
- knowledge of library sources.

Written 30 years ago, these considerations are still highly relevant to the themes of this book. Discussing numeracy, Marsh considers the issue of standards in not very demanding numerical sections of a course, and the importance of using the full range of marks even if this does not accord with the conventions used on other papers in a sociology examination.

At the battlefront: personal experiences

My own perspectives on the place of research methods in the teaching of sociology underwent a considerable change in the mid 1970s as a result of which my acquaintance with the world of quantitative methods increased. After six years of teaching research methods at Durham University, I made a career change and entered the Government Statistical Service as a statistician in 1974. Assigned to the newly created Office of Population Censuses and Surveys (OPCS), formed from the merger of the General Register Office (founded 1837; Nissel, 1987) with the Government Social Survey (founded 1940; Moss, 1991), I found myself working with statisticians, demographers and social survey officers in a very different environment from that of an academic sociology department. My own duties in the Population Statistics Division concerned 'immigrant statistics', statistics of the population termed of 'New Commonwealth and Pakistan ethnic origin', both in answering parliamentary questions on the subject and taking part in the preparatory work towards a possible ethnic question in the 1981 Census of Population. This experience underlined the differences in perspective which it was possible to hold, albeit in an environment with a strong professional ethos and many colleagues who had been academics before entering government, notably the head of the Government Statistical Service at the time, Claus Moser, who had been appointed to this position from the LSE by Premier Harold Wilson.

In fact, as a social scientist in government, I found myself a bit of a square peg in a round hole, since although the role of statistician (like that of economist) was well established, that of sociologist was not. There existed a class of 'research officers' engaged in diverse kinds of work, but in the days before the establishment of Government Social Research (GSR), and the cadre of some 1,000 GSR officers which exists today, these researchers occupied a backroom and rather marginal role, and there was little opportunity to provide policy advice except in a few specialised locations such as the Home Office Research Unit. Quite rapidly I decided that the opportunities were more varied in academia, and after a year moved to a lectureship in social policy at the LSE, next door to the OPCS offices at the bottom of Kingsway, where I taught research methods to social policy, sociology and other students for 17 years. I never regretted that move, but found the short time that I spent in the OPCS an eye-opening and valuable experience, and one which considerably influenced my appreciation of the range of methods open to the sociologist.

This move also widened my view of the social survey. The sceptical reader may at this point pose a question: why should there be a particular affinity between the discipline of sociology and the practical activity going under the name of social survey research? Part of the warrant for considering that there is some connection between the two lies in the history of empirical social investigation. The social survey has been a major tool of social investigation for more than 100 years, and although not synonymous with the development of academic sociology, it has been an important part of that tradition (see Bulmer et al., 1991). The UK poverty studies of Charles Booth and Seebohm Rowntree in the late nineteenth and early twentieth centuries were important both as steps in the establishment of the systematic study of society on a scientific basis and in making the institutionalisation of empirical social inquiry possible. In Europe, sociology developed somewhat later as a growing subject in universities, but the existence of the social survey was an important signal of its distinctive subject matter. In the early development of sociology in the UK, the subject often had particularly close links with the study of social policy and administration, where the social survey tradition held a powerful sway.

The early history of the social survey prior to 1940 was the history of studies of social conditions usually conducted in particular localities without benefit of ideas of probability sampling or representativeness. There were a few exceptions to this – the Norwegian statistician Kiaer and the English statistician A.L. Bowley – but the first major application of probability sampling in surveys was in the US market research industry in the 1930s by pioneers such as George Gallup. The triumph of Gallup's 1936 presidential election prediction over the flawed *Literary Digest* poll was an early marker. Social survey research began to become established in the federal government, and studies such as *The American Soldier* run by a team of academic survey specialists helped to establish the reputation of surveys based on probability sampling methods. The US Current Population Survey began as a government survey based on probability methods in 1940 within the Works Progress Administration, devoted initially to surveying economic activity and providing a measure of unemployment in the national economy (Bregger, 1983). Parallel developments began to take place in European governments after the end of the Second World War in 1945, for example the initiation of the Family Expenditure Survey in the UK from 1953. In 1951, P.C. Mahalanobis inaugurated the Indian National Sample Survey, the first national household sample survey in the world.

Parallel with the development of survey research in government and the private sector, academic survey research flourished in the immediate postwar period. In the USA, scholars such as Paul Lazarsfeld, Samuel Stouffer, Louis Guttman, Hannan Selvin and Peter Rossi established the social survey as an instrument of sociological research, and institutions such as the National Opinion Research Center in Chicago, the Columbia Bureau of Applied Social Research and the Michigan Institute of Social Research became the leading centres for the dissemination of survey research into academic social science. In the UK the developments were somewhat slower, and there was a failure to institutionalise social survey methods, but individual sociologists such as David Glass, W.G. Runciman, A.H. Halsey and John Goldthorpe undertook major social survey projects and emphasised the centrality of social survey research for sociology.

The OPCS was centrally concerned with survey methods and this experience was complemented by interacting with colleagues from other disciplines in the UK, and by encounters with overseas specialists in research methods, in UK associations such as the Social Research Association and the Royal Statistical Society, and in international and overseas associations such as the Research Committee on Logic and Methodology (RC33) of the International Sociological Association, and the American Sociological Association. This served as a useful reminder that a purely sociological perspective on research methods is a limiting one, and one which confines itself just to the research undertaken by sociologists is too narrow. One form which this involvement took was an engagement from the LSE in activities linked to government social research, allied to a developing interest in the usefulness of social science applied to policy (for one example of the results of this interest, see Bulmer, 1987). The Social Scientists in Government network, which Stuart Blume coordinated for a time, provided one informal route to such connections, as did an informal dining club of which I was a member that was run by Bill Daniel of the Policy Studies Institute (PSI), Chris Caswill of the Economic and Social Research Council (ESRC), Peter Brannen of the Department of Employment and later the International Labour Organisation (ILO), and Peter Healey of the Science Policy Support Group. I maintained my interest in survey research via an informal group in which some LSE staff as well as staff from the Social and Community Planning Research

(SCPR; now NatCen) and City University attempted to collaborate in teaching survey methods, with modest success at first. All of these activities, however, opened up perspectives on research methods from outside the discipline of sociology. Moreover, being a member of the interdisciplinary LSE Department of Social Science and Administration, which brought together sociologists, social historians, economists, political scientists and social philosophers, helped to maintain a broader perspective on the methodological issues being debated. (For another take, see Bulmer et al., 1989).

The international angle was also a useful reminder of some of the short-comings of research methods among the 'softer' social sciences in the UK. Exposure to North American sociologists taking numerous graduate courses in research methods, regardless of their own inclination or ultimate PhD research topic, was a reminder that gaining a thorough grounding in research methods was a significant component in a professional education in sociology. A consideration of developments in survey research in the USA compared with the UK also reinforced the value of these international comparisons (cf. McKennell et al., 1987). Britain lagged not only in terms of developments within the academy, but also in terms of building bridges between the academic and non-academic branches of social research. Creating the institutional conditions in the UK for a fruitful collaboration along the lines of the National Opinion Research Center at Chicago or the Institute of Social Research at the University of Michigan had proved a greater challenge. Consider for example the fate of the Survey Research Centre at the LSE, founded by Maurice Kendall and led latterly by William Belson, which effectively closed down in the 1970s, and the short-lived SSRC (Social Science Research Council) Survey Methods Unit under Mark Abrams between 1971 and 1975, which then fell victim to expenditure cuts (cf. Hall, 2009). Until recently, SCPR/NatCen failed to develop an academic link, whereas the Institute for Social and Economic Research (ISER) at Essex did not develop a survey capacity analogous to the large American centres of survey research.

It is my impression that until the mid 1980s, there was comparatively less pressure from the research councils to bolster postgraduate training in research methods. There was interest in the issues, as the 1979 conference on Teaching Research Methodology to Postgraduates at Warwick (Burgers, 1979; Burgess and Bulmer, 1981) showed, but it was not immediately translated into research council policy. There has been a good deal of change in the kinds of topics tackled in sociology PhDs over the years; in the 1970s studies in areas such as stratification, industrial sociology and organisation, and voting behaviour were more common and have since somewhat fallen from fashion (for a useful discussion, see Payne, 2007). The first form taken by intervention was to seek to improve the lamentable completion rates of those who held awards from the SSRC/ESRC. Under three chief executives of the ESRC who were strongly committed to both improving completion rates and bolstering quantitative training, Howard Newby (sociologist), Gordon Marshall (sociologist) and Ian Diamond (demographer), great improvements were made in completion rates, and from the *Horizons and Opportunities* report of 1987, through the various versions of the ESRC training guidelines, pressure to improve the postgraduate training of ESRC award holders, including sociologists, became much more insistent.

At the LSE, as one of the teachers of research methods to postgraduate students, I became involved with interdisciplinary attempts to foster research methodology at the school between the late 1980s and 1993. This was part of an attempt to shape the LSE's response to the first promulgation of the ESRC training guidelines and to lay down a framework of more formal training for PhD students alongside improvements in the completion rates of ESRC-supported research students. I was a member and secretary of an interdepartmental working party, chaired by Pro-Director Derek Diamond, which led eventually to the establishment of the LSE Methodology Institute as a cross-cutting centre within the school. This was not all plain sailing. Disciplines differed in the importance attached to research methods, as well as the extent to which they wished to participate in interdisciplinary teaching. Economists and social anthropologists seemed particularly reluctant to so engage, seemingly considering that their own provision was quite adequate for meeting their needs. The government department even at one stage opined that the teaching of 'such techniques' had no place in an undergraduate education, though it later relaxed this view and made appointments of lecturers who were able to contribute to the school-wide programme.

The interdisciplinary challenges posed by creating postgraduate training programmes in research methods are very considerable, and although the ESRC has brought about and is still bringing about a changing landscape in this respect, the UK is still a long way, in disciplines such as sociology and political science, from establishing the kind of rigorous postgraduate training which is a *sine qua non* of the world leadership of the USA in empirically oriented research in those two disciplines. I did not remain at the LSE to take part in the development of the Methodology Institute, preferring to devote my efforts at Southampton University, and then for the last 13 years of my career at the University of Surrey, to programmes which provided a thorough training in empirical social research, particularly at Master's level. I remain convinced that these are essential, although other sociologists (for example see Abrams, 1981) have expressed scepticism about their value.

Face to face with promoting quantitative methods in the social sciences

The focus of my activities then shifted from research training as such to developing research resources. For the last 12 years or so prior to retirement, I was involved in two research council-funded enterprises, the ESRC Survey Link Scheme and the ESRC Question Bank, intended to promote certain aspects of social survey research, which led to some firsthand acquaintance with the difficulties that British social science faces.

The Survey Link Scheme (Bulmer, 2008), founded by Aubrey McKennell in the 1980s, which I ran from 2002 to 2007, was the lesser of the two activities. This was a very modest attempt to build a bridge between the academic world and professional survey research by providing participants with a two-day experience, which began with them attending a seminar in a university laboratory centred on a particular large-scale government survey such as the General Household Survey or the Family Resources Survey. In the morning participants were given an introduction to web resources about surveys and to Computer Assisted Personal Interviewing (CAPI), which is not widely covered in UK social science methods courses (see Couper et al., 1998). The morning ended with a 30-minute video about interviewing produced by the National Centre for Social Research, the UK independent professional survey organisation, in which four of its interviewers talked about aspects of the interview process in considerable detail. In the afternoon, professional staff of the organisation which conducted the survey, such as the Office for National Statistics (ONS), NatCen or the British Market Research Bureau, would focus on one survey, go through the CAPI version of the questionnaire, and discuss aspects of the design of the fieldwork of the survey. The focus was heavily on the data collection side of the survey, and not on data analysis.

The second day provided participants in the scheme with the opportunity to go out for the day with a professional interviewer to experience survey research at first hand. This was arranged between the participant and the survey organisation under the auspices of the Survey Link Scheme, and could take place in different parts of the UK according to where participants lived. It did not involve such extensive travel as participating in the first day, and had an even more practical emphasis. Feedback from those who took part in the scheme indicated a high degree of positive evaluation, and that the experience had been an eye-opening one, even for those who were involved in the analysis of data from a particular survey. One aim of the scheme, of course, was to do something to counterbalance the very strong emphasis in quantitative methods courses in sociology on data analysis and suitable software (e.g. SPSS, STATA) for handling data. Aspects of data collection (e.g. questionnaire design) are relatively neglected topics in survey pedagogy, and one aim of the scheme was to remedy this lack of information.

The scheme was tasked with increasing the number of participants, and successfully did this over three years. My overriding impression, however, was that much of this interest came from disciplines other than sociology, and that those directing social science postgraduate training programmes in disciplines such as sociology, anthropology, political science and psychology had little interest in sending their students on short courses such as those provided by the Survey Link Scheme. Since the time demand was modest and the costs of the participants were met, I concluded that many of these postgraduate directors did not consider that a detailed firsthand knowledge of survey research was a necessity for their students.

My experience of survey research was more extensive and intensive through my association with the ESRC Question Bank (Qb). The 'Qb' was started in 1995 and went public on the internet in 1996, as part of the Centre for Applied Social Surveys (CASS) under the direction of Roger Thomas at NatCen and Chris Skinner at the University of Southampton. The Qb had a five-year life at the National Centre for Social Research, with myself as Academic Director, and for eight years at the University of Surrey, from 2000 to 2008, again under my direction. The Qb is now part of the Survey Resources Network (http://surveynet.ac.uk/), since January 2009 located at the University of Essex as part of the UK Data Archive. I think that the Qb in its first decade did a good job in identifying and making available the questionnaires of major UK probability sample surveys, presenting these in the form of PDF files, and making them searchable using a fairly sophisticated search engine that could highlight words in the resulting files that were discovered. By the end of the project at Surrey we had some 70,000 pages accessible on the Qb website.

What proved a much greater challenge was to write material about the conceptualisation and measurement of key variables appearing in many of the surveys presented by the Qb. Very good work has been done in the UK over the past decade focusing on the standardisation and measurement of social class (see Rose and Pevalin, 2006), but this topic has tended to be the exception. For many other social variables, there was much less material available, although the Qb was committed to trying to commission commentaries on key social variables and improvements in their measurement. This proved very challenging, one reason being that the professional researchers in survey agencies such as the ONS and NatCen had no time to write material for academic consumption, since this was a diversion from the tasks which occupied them in their paid employment. The number of academics in the UK with the capacity and time to write such material was very limited, providing further evidence of the narrow base of survey specialists within disciplines such as sociology. One volume of material is, however, forthcoming from this set of activities (Bulmer et al., 2010) and for an earlier collection, see Burgess (1987).

The situation is even more serious in relation to methodological research on social survey data, where the number of sociologists in the UK carrying out such work can be counted on the fingers of both hands. The problem is not simply one of sufficient personnel engaged in survey research. There are inherent problems in standardising the measurement of many social and political variables which, with the exception of social class, are not being tackled (see Heath and Martin, 1997). The Survey Resources Network is also coordinating a set of research projects on the methodology of survey research, which may do something to advance research capacity (http://surveynet.ac.uk/sdmi/introduction.asp).

Where do we go from here?

What will UK sociology look like in 2020, and will it have got to grips with the problems inherent in providing adequate training in quantitative methods? The tension between humanistic and scientific elements, or to put the matter in extreme form, between sociology and social research, is likely to remain, and also to remain unresolved, though pluralism is much to be preferred to dogmatism (Halsey, 2002; Halsey and Runciman, 2005). The tension exists and is likely to persist. The past 40 years have not provided a solution, and to some extent each generation seems to reinvent the wheel.

Aspects of school education in the UK carry through into higher education. Mathematics education could be stronger, and the early specialisation and lack of a thorough education in maths right the way through secondary education is one contributory factor to the problems faced in undergraduate and postgraduate sociology. A further awkward question relates to the knowledge and skills of those teaching sociology to the large numbers of students taking the subject at A level. How many of these teachers have a sound grounding in all aspects of research methods? Does the humanistic critique of the scientific pretensions of sociology predominate, making the acquisition of quantitative skills in higher education more difficult? Do quantitative methods in higher education in sociology need embedding much more firmly into substantive courses in the subject, and being treated much less as an (optional) 'add on' which is kept in a separate course? This is a feature of disciplines such as psychology and economics, where quantitative methods are much more firmly established. If so, how is this to be achieved, given the non-centralisation that is characteristic of a lot of UK higher education?

The strongest pressure for change seems likely to come from the ESRC so far as sociology is concerned. At the time of writing, the shape of its proposed doctoral training centres (DTCs) and doctoral training units (DTUs) is not yet clear, since the outcome of the competition is not yet known, but the commitment to bolstering quantitative methods is clear.

> [T]he skills deficit in quantitative research methods – at both a basic and advanced level ... will remain priorities for funding through the new DTC and DTU network and the ESRC will welcome applications that seek to address the imbalance in these areas through new and innovative postgraduate training provision as well as through the supply of undergraduates able to make full use of postgraduate training in these areas. (ESRC, 2009: 2)

The ESRC provides the major component of full-time postgraduate research student support, so its voice is likely to be influential.

Pressures from the job market may also make themselves felt if there are major cuts in expenditure on higher education and fewer academic jobs as a result. Empirical social research in all its aspects is a major employer in government, the private sector, the third sector and elsewhere (see Bulmer et al., 2001). Some estimates suggest that as many as 20,000 people work in this sector, far more than the number of jobs in academic sociology. Economic necessity may point to some reorientation of priorities to make the skills of sociology graduates more marketable in tougher times. Sociology has no monopoly over quantitative methods, and another possibility is that the opportunities created for those who are well trained in quantitative methods may accrue disproportionately to those coming from other disciplines where quantitative methods is more firmly embedded in the core subject matter of advanced education and training. The future is difficult to foresee, and it may be that the best we can do is to dissect and seek to learn from past experience and failings.

References

Abrams, P. (1981) 'Visionaries and virtuosi: competence and purpose in the education of sociologists', *Sociology*, 15(4): 530–8.

Bregger, J./Bureau of Labor Statistics (1983) *The Current Population Survey: A Historical Perspective and the BLS's role*. Washington, DC: Bureau of Labor Statistics. Available at: http://www.bls.gov/opub/mlr/1984/06/art2full.pdf (accessed 15 February 2009).

Brown, G. (1981) 'Teaching data collection in social survey research', *Sociology*, 15(4): 550–7.

Bulmer, M. (ed.) (1977) *Sociological Research Methods: An Introduction* (2nd edn, 1983). London: Macmillan.

Bulmer, M. (1981) 'Approaches to methodology course content', *Sociology*, 15(4): 539–44.

Bulmer, M. (1987) *The Social Basis of Community Care*. London: Allen and Unwin.

Bulmer, M. (2008) *A Description of the ESRC Survey Link Scheme 2005–2008 for Bidders (Based Upon Its Final Report)*. Guildford, Surrey: Department of Sociology, University of Surrey. Available at: http://surveynet.ac.uk/SQB/QB/slsdocs/docs/Description%20of%20SLS%20for%20bidders%20(web).pdf (accessed 5 November 2009).

Bulmer, M. and Burgess, R. (1981) 'Which way forward for methodology teaching?', *Sociology*, 15(4): 586–9.

Bulmer, M., Bales, K. and Sklar, K. (eds) (1991) *The Social Survey in Historical Perspective, 1880–1940*. Cambridge: Cambridge University Press.

Bulmer, M., Lewis, J. and Piachaud, D. (eds) (1989) *The Goals of Social Policy*. London: Unwin Hyman.

Bulmer, M., Gibbs, J. and Hyman, L. (eds) (2010) *Survey Measurement Through Social Surveys: An Applied Approach*. Aldershot: Ashgate.

Bulmer, M., Sykes, W. and Moorhouse, J. (2001) *The Directory of Social Research Organisations in the UK* (revised edition). London: Continuum.

Burgess, R. (ed.) (1979) *Teaching Research Methodology to Postgraduates: A Survey of Courses in the UK*. Coventry: Department of Sociology, University of Warwick (mimeo).

Burgess, R. (ed.) (1987) *Key Variables in Social Investigation*. London: Routledge.

Burgess, R. and Bulmer, M. (1981) 'Research methodology teaching: trends and developments', *Sociology*, 15(4): 477–89.

Butler, D. and Stokes, D. (1969) *Political Change in Britain: Forces Shaping Electoral Choice*. London: Macmillan.

Carr, E.H. (1961) *What is History?* London: Macmillan.

Cicourel, A. (1964) *Method and Measurement in Sociology*. New York: Free Press.

Couper, M., Baker, R., Bethlehem, J, Clark, C., Martin, J., Nicholls, W. II and O'Reilly, J. (eds) (1998) *Computer Assisted Survey Information Collection*. New York: Wiley-Interscience.

Cowling, M. (1963) *The Nature and Limits of Political Science*. Cambridge: Cambridge University Press.

Coxon, A. (1973) 'Formal foundations for research methods: the matching of methodological needs', *International Journal of Mathematical Education in Science and Technology*, 4(1): 43–9.

Crompton, R. (2008) 'Forty years of sociology: some comments', *Sociology*, 42(6): 1218–27.

Cronbach, J. and Meehl, P. (1955) 'Construct validity in psychological tests', *Psychological Bulletin*, 52: 281–302.

Elton, G. (1967) *The Practice of History*. London: Methuen.

Economic and Social Research Council (2009) *ESRC Postgraduate Training and Development Guidelines 2009*. Swindon: ESRC.

Hall, J. (2009) *Journeys in Survey Research: the website of John F Hall*. Available at: http://surveyresearch.weebly.com (accessed 5 November 2009).

Halsey, A.H. (1986) 'Provincials and professionals: the British post-war sociologists', in M. Bulmer (ed.), *Essays on the History of British Sociological Research*. Cambridge: Cambridge University Press.

Halsey, A.H. (2002) *A History of Sociology in Britain: Science, Literature, and Society*. Oxford: Oxford University Press.

Halsey A.H. and Runciman, G. (eds) (2005) *British Sociology Seen from Without and Within*. Oxford: Oxford University Press for the British Academy.

Heath, A. and Martin, J. (1997) 'Why are there so few formal measuring instruments in social and political research?', in Lyberg, L., Biemer, P., Collins, M., de Leeuw, E., Dippo, C., Schwarz, N. and Trewin, D. (eds), *Survey Measurement and Process Quality*. New York: Wiley-Interscience.

Husbands, C.J. (1981) 'The anti-quantitative bias in Postwar British sociology', in

Marsh, C. (1979) 'Problems with surveys: method or epistemology?', *Sociology*, 13: 293–305.

Marsh, C. (1981) 'The assessment of skills in research methods', *Sociology*, 15(4): 519–25.

McKennell, A., Bynner, J. and Bulmer, M. (1987) 'The links between policy, survey research and academic social science: America and Britain compared', in M. Bulmer (ed.), *Social Science Research and Government: Comparative Essays on Britain and the United States*. Cambridge: Cambridge University Press.

Moser, C. (1958) *Survey Methods in Social Investigation*. London: Heinemann.

Moser, C. and Kalton, G. (1967) *Survey Methods in Social Investigation* (2nd edn). London: Heinemann.

Moss, L. (1991) *The Government Social Survey: A History*. London: HMSO.

Myrdal, G. (1944) *An American Dilemma: the Negro Problem and Modern Democracy*. New York: Harper and Row.

Nissel, M. (1987) *People Count: A History of the General Register Office*. London: HMSO.

Payne, G. (2007) 'Social divisions, social mobilities and social research: methodological issues after 40 years', *Sociology*, 41(5): 901–15.

Peel, J.D.Y. (1968) *Courses Mainly Concerned with Sociological Theory and Methods in 29 Universities*. 15th Conference of Sociology Teachers Section of the BSA. London: British Sociological Association (mimeo).

Platt, J. (1981) 'The social construction of "Positivism" and its significance in British sociology, 1950–1980', in Abrams, P., Deem, R., Finch, J. and Rocke, P. (eds) (1981), *Practice and Progress: British Sociology 1950–1980*. London: Allen & Unwin. pp. 73–87.

Rose, D. and Pevalin, D. (2006) *A Researcher's Guide to the National Statistics Socio-economic Classification*. London: Sage.

Rosenbaum, S. (1971) 'A Report on the use of statistics in social science research', *Journal of the Royal Statistical Society A*, 134: 534–610.

Runciman, G. (1963) *Social Science and Political Theory*. Cambridge: Cambridge University Press.

Savage, M. and Burrows, R. (2007) 'The coming crisis of empirical sociology', *Sociology*, 41(4): 885–99.

Wakeford, J. (ed.) (1979) *Research Methods Syllabuses in Sociology Departments in the United Kingdom (Undergraduate Courses)*. Lancaster: Department of Sociology, University of Lancaster (mimeo).

Wakeford, J. (1981) 'From methods to practice: a critical note on the teaching of research practice to undergraduates', *Sociology*, 15(4): 505–12.

Wilson, C. (1964) *History in Special and in General: An Inaugural Lecture*. Cambridge: Cambridge University Press

Yarrow, M. (1963) 'Problems of methods in parent-child research', *Child Development*, 34: 215–16.

Challenges and Opportunities for Developing Teaching in Quantitative Methods

Malcolm Williams and Carole Sutton

As with governments, we get the academic disciplines we deserve. The collection of work in this volume is predicated on a belief that even though this may be currently true in respect of quantitative methods in social science disciplines, we need better, if they are to continue to be relevant. The disciplines we refer to in this chapter are those sharing epistemological roots with sociology and might include political science, social and public policy, criminology and human geography. In the UK, each of these disciplines is suffering a crisis of quantification: that is, practitioners and students opposed or indifferent to the use of quantitative methods within their disciplines.

Just as the kind of teaching and learning practised will shape the future of the discipline, so too will the kind of discipline(s) we have in turn shape current teaching and learning. For this reason, the first part of the chapter will consider what is wrong in a disciplinary sense, before moving on to describe the challenges in teaching and learning. But this chapter is not pessimistic! It is not pessimistic for several reasons: that there are plenty of examples (in the UK alone) of excellent and successful practices in the teaching of quantitative methods and several of these are presented in this volume. There is evidence that at least a minority of students like and do well in quantitative methods and even some of those who do not like 'quants' still do well. In the second part of the chapter we discuss one teaching and learning initiative that aimed to build such enthusiasm through an experiential learning approach.

As disciplines we face several challenges. There is a 'quantitative deficit' within social science disciplines as practised. That is, while the problems and questions presented in the UK are somewhat similar to those of other countries, here there is a much greater reliance on the use of qualitative methods in mainstream social research. The 'science wars' or the *methodenstreit* dispute of the 1960s to 1980s has left its mark, perhaps less in an outright hostility towards scientific method in social science and more in an indifference to its use. There exists a residual relativism that gives an epistemological equivalence, whereby one's choice of method is perhaps more aesthetic than problem-driven (Denzin and Lincoln, 2003: 6).

Alongside this there is a wider numeracy problem in the UK of the inability or unwillingness of young people to enter disciplines or careers that require well-developed numeracy skills (Department for Education and Skills (DfES), 2004, 2005). Universities and employers have difficulty recruiting for science and technology subjects. Because the social sciences are not usually seen as 'numeric' disciplines and because what numerically inclined people there gravitate towards are science and technology, social science subject intakes in universities are primarily non-numerically inclined students. In England and Wales virtually all undergraduate students possess a minimum qualification in mathematics (usually GCSE grade C or better/equivalent), yet a majority of them shun quantitative methods, many of them are fearful and a significant number do not achieve well.

In addition to the above primary challenges, there are secondary ones relating to employment and recruitment. It is far from easy to establish practical schemes to support the 're-skilling' of the current social science workforce in academia and beyond. There is a shortage of 'home grown' graduates who might join PhD programmes. Meanwhile, there has been the growth of a 'social research' industry outside social science disciplines, with its reliance on a non-social science trained labour force (Williams, 2000a). While *some* UK social scientists do produce 'cutting edge' quantitatively orientated work, there is a danger that they will become 'ghettoised' outside of 'mainstream' social science.

Despite these challenges there are a number of grounds for optimism. Particularly in recent years, there is some evidence of a cultural change among professional social scientists in attitudes and outputs, often in the context of opportunities created by institutional support for employability, and therefore numeracy, skills more generally as UK universities embrace the post-Leitch Report agenda. Nor should we lose sight of the well-researched evidence that quantitative methods are not only taught but are also usually core to the curriculum in our universities. Studies also show that there is a substantial minority of students who have a positive view of quantitative methods and do well in them. And as this book and other recent publications are beginning to demonstrate, better, more imaginative, and interactive teaching materials are being developed.

The disciplinary challenge

Much of the evidence in this chapter for the challenges presented to social science comes from a series of projects conducted by the editors of this book and their colleagues, over a five-year period, mainly in sociology. The reason for focusing on this discipline, apart from it being the 'home' discipline of the investigators, was that sociology can be seen as the epistemological 'root' discipline of social research, not only in the development of methods and techniques, but also in the practical task of the day-to-day teaching of methods in most universities. Indeed, where there is evidence from cognate disciplines, it is that the problems and challenges in sociology do exist elsewhere and are often writ large.

The roots of the 'quantitative problem' go deep, both historically and within contemporary disciplines. In the UK, at least, there never has been a 'golden age' of 'scientific' social science, yet alone sociology. That is not to denigrate the social administration tradition, which provided many examples of statistical descriptions of communities, famously those of Seebohm Rowntree in York, nor some fine examples of large-scale surveys and the use of quantification in sociological analysis in the second half of the twentieth century (see, for example, Goldthorpe et al., 1969; Westergaard and Resler 1975; Wellings et al., 1994). Similarly, the UK has a tradition of 'political arithmetic' in government censuses and surveys, comparable with or better than most industrialised countries. Yet despite this, within sociology and its cognate disciplines there has not been a strong academic, or community, tradition of the social survey such as that found in the USA (Platt, 1998) since the 1920s. Moreover, outside epidemiology and to a lesser extent criminology, experimental method (again unlike the USA) is rare (Oakley, 2000). How it came to be that the UK – and indeed to a great extent other Anglophone countries – developed differently from the USA is beyond the scope of this chapter, though it is itself an object worthy of study if we wish to promote a more scientifically grounded social science.

Sociology in more recent years has not been quantitative, at least in terms of its output. A content analysis of two years' output of articles in the four main UK sociology journals and papers presented at the British Sociological Association (BSA) annual conference showed quantitative output, generously defined as using at least univariate analysis, *as* a very small proportion not only of all papers published, but also of papers reporting on empirical findings (Payne et al., 2004) (Table 5.1). Univariate analysis was far more common than bivariate analysis, let alone multivariate analysis. The BSA conference papers yielded no multivariate contributions at all, which is somewhat worrying given that this is a forum traditionally favoured by many postgraduates and early career researchers. Analyses on this last point were informative. Compared with publications from more senior staff, authors who were 'junior' staff were more likely to use qualitative than quantitative methods, perhaps indicating a greater ambivalence/dislike of quantitative methods among younger cohorts of sociologists.

This is not to suggest that there is any great animus towards the use of quantitative methods in research, or the teaching of them. A survey of BSA

Table 5.1 Level of quantitative analysis (per cent)

Dataset	Theoretical	Qualitative	Univariate	Bivariate	Multivariate	Total
Mainstream*	37.7	40.2	10.7	5.3	6.1	244
Conference	35.3	47.1	15.7	2.0		102
WES	4.3	40.3	14.9	8.5	31.9	49

*Journals in sample: *Sociology, Sociological Review, British Journal of Sociology* and *Sociological Research Online* (and presented separately, *Work, Employment and Society*).

conference delegates in 2003 (Williams et al., 2004: 17–18) indicated a 100 per cent agreement with the statement 'Quantitative methods are necessary in many research contexts'; two-thirds thought quantitative and qualitative methods were equally used in British sociology; but only half of the sample thought that more quantitative methods should be used! Thus there is evidence of tolerance and even of 'methodological pluralism' in principle, but much less of an inclination towards using quantitative methods in practice. Some of this disinclination probably lies in a skills deficit and possibly in an unwillingness to change what one does methodologically. One-third of the BSA sample had not enjoyed learning and quantitative methods and 54 per cent found them 'difficult'. However, one still finds the seismic aftershocks of the *methodenstreit* dispute in occasional outright hostility to quantification, particularly in political science and international relations (see the 'Perestroika' debate in Laitin, 2003); although more usually it is found in the rather tired, but relatively ubiquitous rhetoric of equating 'positivism' with quantification/ explanation/prediction and 'anti-positivism' with more 'progressive' qualitative methods (Williams, 2000b: Chapter 5, p. 87). This latter is more than a rhetorical point, in that it becomes an issue in teaching and learning, as we will go on to describe below. However, in summary, the 'quantitative problem' and its challenges and solutions must be seen within the context of a social science (at least evidenced from sociology) that is mostly pluralist or tolerant, but does not practise that pluralism in research.

The teaching and learning challenge

Until fairly recently we knew very little about what our students thought about quantitative methods, or indeed what they were taught and what their teachers thought about what they were taught! We still have a lot more to learn about these areas, but two studies in the past five years have provided a fair amount of mutually confirmatory findings around practices and attitudes. The first of these studies, supported by the BSA and the Higher Education Academy Subject Network for Sociology, Anthropology, Politics

(C-SAP), was an 'inventory' of the type and amount of quantitative methods taught in UK universities, along with consultations with teachers of methods (Williams et al., 2004). The second study, funded by the Economic and Social Research Council (ESRC), was of undergraduate student attitudes towards quantitative methods. This study was a sample survey of sociology and politics students in English and Welsh universities, along with student focus groups in a subset of these (Williams et al., 2008).

Both studies confirmed that most students are taught at least basic quantitative methods. In the first of these it was found that only two out of the 82 responding departments taught no quantitative methods. This was confirmed by the students themselves in the second study, when by stage three of their degrees all of the students in the sample had studied some quantitative methods and over 80 per cent had studied statistics. At two dissemination events following the first study, lecturers in research methods reported a range of negative student views (see Box 5. 1), and although the validity and reliability of these would usually be considered weaker than the survey findings they should be given some credence, because they arise from the direct experience of teaching methods. These teachers also complained of experiencing ambivalence and some hostility from *colleagues* toward quantitative methods, though such hostility was not apparent in the BSA survey. (There would, perhaps inevitably, be a selection bias in favour of quantitative methods at these events and those opposed to quantitative methods may have been the non-responders in the BSA conference survey.)

Box 5.1   Student views described by teaching staff at consultation days

- 'quantitative research is unfashionable'
- 'quantitative researchers are number crunchers'
- 'quantitative research produces lies, damn lies and statistics'
- 'it is not possible to pursue sociological theory through quantitative research'
- 'quantitative methods are not perceived as "cool"'
- 'people who do quants are just techies in the lab'
- 'quantitative research is less valid than qualitative research'
- 'it's not important to be numerate in social science'
- 'qualitative research is an easier option as you do not have to learn all the procedures associated with, for example, different types of reliability and validity'

Despite the almost universal presence of quantitative methods in the curriculum, the students surveyed in the second study expressed both negative views about learning quantitative methods, as well as ambivalence about quantitative and more 'scientific' approaches to social science. Presented with a series of attitude statements about quantitative methods, in a Likert scale, over 40 per cent of respondents said they did not enjoy learning about surveys and 64 per cent would rather write an essay than analyse data. Yet there was little evidence to indicate that large numbers of students were studying sociology or politics to avoid number. Sixty-six per cent disagreed with the statement 'I don't think sociology students should have to study stats' and 75 per cent disagreed with the statement 'One of the reasons I chose this degree is because I don't like maths'. This evidence of anxiety and ambivalence over statistics and mathematics was echoed in the focus groups.

Table 5.2 also shows how the students performed in their methods modules by their attitude toward them. Those who said they enjoyed learning about surveys fell into two categories, those who got better marks, and those who were more likely to fail methods modules. A bad school experience of maths, or a negative attitude towards maths/stats/quantitative methods, was associated with lower marks. This is an interesting finding, but it needs interpreting with care. We cannot know the causal direction here. Do those who have a 'positive' attitude do better, or do those who do 'better' develop a positive attitude? Indeed there may well be complex patterns of reinforcement or discouragement between results and attitudes.

Although all of the sample had been taught quantitative methods, the evidence showed that for many this has been fairly rudimentary and that this has been particularly so with statistics. Only around half had studied chi-square, a third had studied simple regression, and only a quarter Cramer's V, Z tests or Spearman's rho. Moreover, in all of these around half of the students had found them 'difficult'. Only relatively simple (and mainly visual) techniques, such as bar charts, pie charts, and also mean, median and mode, were considered easy by students.

It would perhaps be a mistake to see these results and indeed the wider issue of the 'numerical/quantitative crisis' as just being about number. There was some evidence, in the study of student attitudes, that they did not think of social science as 'scientific', or at least if they did, they did not see themselves as doing 'science'. They were asked to indicate, on a five-point semantic differential scale, whether they saw sociology as closer to science or the arts/humanities. Overall 71 per cent scored towards the arts/humanities end of the scale, 14.5 per cent towards the science end of the scale, and 15.5 per cent chose the middle category. To some extent this finding (in the sample as a whole) could be explained by the predominance of humanities subjects studied at A level. After sociology, English was the second most popular choice (54 per cent). Nevertheless, 30 per cent took psychology and 5 per cent mathematics. The majority of students taking these subjects (67 and 68 per cent, respectively) still thought sociology closer to the humanities than the sciences. The students with the most 'scientific' attitude were those studying information technology/information and communication technology. Twenty per cent of them saw sociology as closer to science and 23 per cent (the largest number) in the 'neutral' category. Of those who had studied sociology at A level, 70 per cent saw the subject as closer to the humanities.

Table 5.2 **Student views of quantitative methods and achievement in research methods**

	Student view	N	Per cent fails or 3rds (0–49 per cent) in research methods assessments taken	Per cent 1sts or 2.1s in research methods assessments taken
Had a bad experience of maths at school				
Agree	42.9	279	16.1	45.6
Disagree	50.1	328	9.8	58.5
Not sure	6.6	43	14.0	48.9
On the whole not good at maths				
Agree	41.9	274	15.7	46.3
Disagree	44.1	288	8.3	60.8
Not sure	13.9	91	17.6	44.0
One of the reasons I chose this degree is because I don't like maths				
Agree	19.2	126	23.0	38.8
Disagree	75.0	491	9.2	56.2
Not sure	5.6	37	24.3	45.9
I didn't expect to have to do so much number work				
Agree	44.0	288	17.0	45.5
Disagree	46.6	305	8.9	60.7
Not sure	9.3	61	11.5	42.7
I don't think sociology students should have to study stats				
Agree	23.7	155	24.4	34.8
Disagree	69.7	455	8.8	58.2
Not Sure	12.7	83	18.0	43.4
Learning statistics makes me feel anxious				
Agree	52.4	342	17.8	46.5
Disagree	38.8	253	7.2	60.4
Not Sure	8.7	57	7.0	52.6
I enjoyed learning about surveys				
Agree	42.5	277	7.6	58.5
Disagree	41.0	267	18.7	43.1
Not sure	5.1	107	11.2	58.9
I'd rather write an essay than analyse data				
Agree	64.0	418	15.7	47.6
Disagree	19.1	125	11.2	60.0
Not Sure	16.8	110	2.7	60.9
Using stats detaches you from your research topic				
Agree	21.7	142	21.2	40.1
Disagree	59.5	389	8.5	58.9
Not Sure	18.8	123	16.8	54.5
On the whole you can't trust statistics				
Agree	44.1	288	8.3	60.8
Disagree	41.9	274	15.7	46.3
Not sure	13.9	91	17.6	44.0

$P = <0.05$

Statements were presented as a five-point Likert scale, but have been aggregated into a three-point scale in order to achieve the same significance level in each question.

Notwithstanding their A level experience, that students at university continue to see sociology and politics as humanities subjects is perhaps unsurprising given that the 'professional' sociologists who teach in universities themselves overwhelmingly favour the use of qualitative methods in their own work. Moreover, the sociology/politics/criminology curriculum 'ghettoises' research methods into separate classes and the vast majority of the substantive teaching is not grounded in empirical research. Some of the most 'popular' sociologists in the UK (e.g. Anthony Giddens and Zigmunt Bauman) will not undertake empirical work and will often not base their sociological conclusions on empirical work, yet books produced by such authors are influential bestsellers among undergraduates. When students are exposed to empirical work it is more likely to be qualitative and this results in a mindset that sees the disciplines in a particular way. For example, some of the quotes from the focus groups acknowledged the existence of a more 'scientific' sociology, but saw it as not for them, as 'other', perhaps echoing the methodological relativism among their teachers.

> [it depends on] whether you want to define it as science and whether you want it to fit into a category of science ... it's whatever you want it to be.

> There are sociology courses you can do that I didn't think were part of sociology, they take a very different consideration of sociology [numeric, scientific]...

> There's two different kinds of academia. There's like the numeric one which is more like the chemistry and physics and maths and stuff ... And then there's the 'words' one, which is English and history and stuff [in which sociology was included].

The teaching and learning challenge is complex. It is not simply about making number simple and attractive, it is about developing quite a different view of social science subjects as 'scientific', or at least analytic. This probably means persuading students to become 'detectives', as Cathie Marsh (1982) once put it, and to become excited about answering 'real' questions about the social world, rather than regurgitating existing sociological/political science perspectives, many of which do not base their reasoning on empirical research. In other words, the social sciences need to become 'doing' rather than ruminative disciplines.

The professional challenge

None of these things can come to pass unless professional social scientists can be persuaded to take the quantitative crisis seriously. At present we seem to have a vicious circle within which academics (in disciplines such as sociology or political science) are overwhelmingly inclined towards humanistic approaches and/or lack quantitative skills themselves, but are responsible for the training of a new cadre of social scientists, who then reproduce the methodological culture of their trainers. Although quantitative teachers can be trained and others 're-skilled' to have at least a minimum competence, if there is in principle a disinclination or ambivalence toward quantitative methods more generally, the circle cannot be broken. This does not necessarily mean the disciplines themselves will disappear, it is simply that they could become less universally relevant.

The social sciences, as well as contributing to 'pure research' about the nature of society and how it can be known, have significantly and perhaps increasingly traded on their relevance as policy disciplines. Most major funding bodies, for example the ESRC and the Rowntree Foundation, wish to fund research that can bring social and economic benefits either directly or indirectly. Disciplines that do not 'count' can still do such research, but they are much more limited. Moreover, an inability to do work that enumerates, explains or predicts means that social policy and solutions for social problems are hampered. An excellent example of the latter is that of 'homelessness' research. The overwhelming body of research literature (and it is a very large literature) is concerned with the *experiences* of, or policy towards, the homeless in general, or subgroups of homeless people. Virtually all of the research is qualitative, yet governments and non-governmental organisations (NGOs) who wish to tackle the homelessness crisis need statistical data on the size and composition of the homeless population. With very few exceptions, this in unavailable, not because it cannot be obtained, but because those people who research homelessness do not usually have the skills or inclination to conduct this kind of research (Williams and Cheal, 2001). Furthermore their 'clients' in government or NGOs are themselves often not methodologically literate enough to discern the possibilities beyond those on offer from the qualitative scholars who currently research in this area. A similar example is the retreat by sociologists from studying social inequality in general, and social mobility in particular (Payne, 2010).

This is not to suggest that quantitative social research is not happening in Britain. Far from it: the quality and quantity of large-scale survey research is possibly greater in Britain than any other country with the exception of the USA. In recent years the ESRC has funded a number of academic and quasi-academic initiatives to develop cutting edge excellence in quantitative methods, in particular those within the rubric of the National Centre for Research Methods, or its predecessor the ESRC Research Methods Programme. Similarly, the market research sector has pioneered quantitative applications in survey research (e.g. CAPI, CATI) and more recently transactional data and data mining (Savage and Burrows, 2007). This, then, begs the question of who is doing all of this work?

In truth we do not really know, though there is some anecdotal evidence that recruitment to generic non-discipline-based 'social research' is not from the traditional social sciences, such as sociology, social policy or political science, but from a broader spectrum of academic backgrounds (Williams, 2000a). If this is the case then the 'traditional social science disciplines' will eventually cease to be relevant to policy-makers.

Engaging students with quantification: opportunities and developments

We have so far focused on the challenges that face the social science disciplines in terms of engaging students with quantitative approaches to understanding the social world. What we now want to offer is an approach that attempts to address some of the issues raised that seek to more actively engage every student in the research process. Most academics will be aware of deep, surface and strategic approaches to learning. In an ideal world we would hope that students engage with research with enthusiasm, that they would be inquiring and have a curiosity that a deep learning approach brings. The reality is that students will use a mixture of learning processes according to their perceptions of the study tasks set. The findings from the projects discussed above are that, at best, students employ a strategic 'What do I have to do to pass?' approach, and at worst a surface approach with the individual memorising set examples from the research field with no application to new research areas. This 'play it safe' and 'avoidance of potential failure' style of responding to learning has become entrenched across higher education, but it seems particularly marked in the field of quantitative methods.

Faced with this tendency, we need to consider alternative ways of engaging students ambitions. For example, can students be given opportunities both to achieve and to demonstrate the 'distance travelled' beyond assessment, including professional development planning and employability? Students learn many valuable things during their time in higher education which are not necessarily captured in formal assessments – many aspects of employability fall into this category. In other words, 'measurements' may only cover part of the 'distance travelled' by a student (Burgess, 2004: 26).

The challenge for academic staff involved in the teaching of quantitative research methods and analysis is to encourage a deep approach to learning where students are active and enthusiastic learners, engaging not just with the research approach but also with the wider sociological imagination required to interpret and make sense of research outcomes. As Ritchey (2008) emphasises in his key statistical text, linking the *statistical* imagination to the *sociological* imagination is what makes a good social scientist. A competent researcher is one who can engage with the context, bring statistical data alive and be able to produce a narrative that is supported by scientific empirical evidence.

Engaging students in research-based learning can involve a number of different teaching strategies. Students can learn *about* discipline-based research, and they can also learn about *how* to do research and how to be *active participants* in the research process (University of Plymouth, 2008:12–14). To get beyond the initial learning about a discipline, there are a number of pedagogic approaches available: use of problem-based learning techniques; work-based learning involving placements in a suitable research environment; and fieldwork. These techniques in turn need to be matched to what can realistically be expected of the learner at each stage. Learning 'to do' and 'active participation' can involve various practical tasks that may stand alone or may be joined with a common theme that links the various stages in the research process. Problem-based learning strategies are of particular value, when they combine both learning tasks, in the case of applying research methods, and are also set within a wider framework of development through linking to an understanding of project management. For example, from a research brief students are asked to write a project proposal and eventually to design the project. Each phase of the research process involves the students managing their learning at research team meetings, which also involve minute taking and assigning a rotating chair. The research topic may be hypothetical or topical for the locality that the university resides in. Depending on teaching time, course requirements and student numbers, the research may be executed in the field, with collected data analysed and research findings discussed and conclusions drawn.

However, whether as small tasks or as a linked assessment process these projects are often detached from the real world of research and will influence students' perceptions of what academic research entails. There is often a disjuncture in students' understanding of the theoretically ideal research project and real-world research. This is hardly surprising given that most learning takes place in the constructed world of higher education where learning is clearly stipulated and structured (Fry et al., 2003: 135). In this context learning (even problem-based learning) can be seen as an idealised form that does not reflect the messiness and decision-making processes of real-life research. Similarly, there may be a failure to understand how a small research project may relate to larger, established research projects and processes, both qualitative and quantitative. The learning experience, not least in dissertations, often turns out to be a series of over-simplified exercises using tiny amounts of data, at a level that is not even equivalent to what would be a pilot study in 'proper' research.

An alternative strategy is to include a work-based learning element in the curriculum, one that places students in a research environment with a public or private sector research unit. Such a strategy utilises the Kolb learning cycle model of experiential learning that 'is based on the notion that understanding is not a fixed or unchangeable event of thought but is formed and re-formed through "experience"' (Fry et al., 2003: 14). Work-based learning provides the stimulus for experiential learning where students transfer knowledge and ideas to and from the placement context. There are of course practical constraints with larger student numbers and the availability of suitable work-based learning opportunities. Modules with lower student numbers offer greater opportunities for innovative teaching.

The social sciences can learn from the natural sciences where fieldwork forms part of the staple diet of learning experiences (Kent et al., 1997). Fieldwork experiences (in British universities) may vary from one- or two-day visits to areas close to the institution, week-long trips to European destinations to longer trips to more exotic places. Shorter field trips may be compulsory with costs absorbed by the institution and longer trips optional with students covering the costs. However there are multiple challenges for staff who wish to engage their students in fieldwork activities. The financial costs associated with increasing numbers of students are often cited as the initial difficulty (Boyle et al., 2007). Successful fieldwork does not just happen. It has to be properly planned and embedded into the student learning process: 'Effective learning cannot be expected just because we take students into the field' (Lonergan and Andreson, 1988: 70). Students have to be fully prepared before the fieldwork commences, they need to be familiar with the environment and understand how the classroom work relates to the fieldwork, and staff need to be sensitive to the possibility of student anxieties about the field trip itself (Fry et al., 2003; Fletcher and Dodds, 2004). These issues are arguably of particular complexity for the social sciences where field trips focus on the intricacies of the social world.

Case study: fieldwork trip to Belfast, Northern Ireland

The following case study details how small changes in the established curriculum supported the inclusion of a stage two pilot fieldwork trip on a BSc (Hons) Social Research Programme. The 'minor pathway' in social research at the University of Plymouth involves students studying 40 credits of social research-specific modules at each degree stage. Students can combine the minor pathway with the major subjects of international relations, sociology, criminal justice studies or criminology, but as a specialist programme, student numbers tend to be relatively small. The modules are arranged hierarchically to build on previously acquired knowledge and skills. They sit alongside a generic social research content that is delivered to a wide range of social science subjects. The emphasis in the specialist modules is on the philosophical, methodological and practical skills of social research. Students are eligible to top up their final degree with the Market Research Society (MRS) Advanced Certificate qualification (MRS, 2010).

At stage two (second year) there are two specialist modules. In 'The Research Process' students learn through a combination of lectures and problem-based workshop tasks about all stages of research, both social and market research, from design to presentation. The module uses a problem-based learning approach that emulates the research process in social and market research. The students design a project, including methodological design, sampling, resource allocation, costing and timing. This is conducted by research groups who must present their interim and final work as if they were presenting to the research sponsors.

In the second specialist module, 'Analysing the Social Survey', students build on basic descriptive analyses covered in year one, concentrating on bivariate, parametric and non-parametric analyses, and managing common data analysis problems. Secondary data sources are utilised for the data analysis tasks and assessment processes. It was here that synergies were initially established between the two stage two modules. The intention in adding a field trip for the social research students was to enhance these links between the content of the two existing modules. A successful bid for Research Informed Teaching monies, drawn from the Teaching Quality in Education Fund (TQEF) at the University of Plymouth, was made to develop the fieldwork element of the programme. The aims of the project were to:

1 develop a deeper understanding and appreciation of all stages of the research process;
2 gain an understanding of the various factors that contribute to the running of a successful research project;
3 develop an understanding of applied social research in an organisational setting;
4 gain practical experience of professional social and market research data collection techniques;
5 understand how research is subsequently used in areas such as policy development;
6 organise, conduct and manage a group-based research project;
7 understand how research is organised in a professional research organisation and the employment opportunities available to social research graduates.

There was also one final aim to give our students an opportunity to do something 'a bit different', to 'travel a little further' both geographically and academically, and to add to 'the offer' of a degree in a social sciences. The vision was to place students in a familiar and equally unfamiliar environment to challenge them to really reflect on research processes in a social setting and also to make quantitative methods exciting.

Northern Ireland was chosen for the field trip site because it is historically, socially, politically and economically an interesting place. It also has many web-based resources that enable students, and staff, to familiarise themselves with the environment before 'entering the field' and which could support teaching initiatives in the classroom. These included the freely available Northern Ireland Life and Times Survey (NILT) web-based resources (www.ark.ac.uk/nilt) containing methodology, data collection tools and SPSS-formatted data files, together with the wider social, historical and political information from ARK (Access Research Knowledge, (www.ark.ac.uk) and CAIN (Conflict Internet Access; www.cain.ulst.ac.uk). The Research Process module focused research tasks around Northern Ireland and analysis of relevant NILT datasets, enabling students to build a more complete picture of life in Northern Ireland.

In addition, students were required to work in small research groups to develop a research project on a related topic of their choice. The only stipulation was that the topic should lend itself to the adoption of a quantitative research design. Adopting a problem-based learning approach, students managed their own project, keeping minutes of their research meetings and charting progress for a portfolio assessment. This supported the fieldwork's three main aims: to give added extra experiential knowledge about Northern Ireland; to enhance knowledge of existing academic research and research organisations; and to execute a street survey planned in the university classroom.

The academic team approached the ARK and NILT teams to request if some input from the team would be possible. We were delighted when they offered a training event that met the needs of our students. The key areas covered were additional background on NILT and ARK, hands-on practical experience of using CAPI and CASI techniques, something we were unable to offer at the university, the process of cleaning and checking survey data, and disseminating to different audiences. Box 5.2 details the four-day field trip programme which was the outcome.

Box 5.2   Field trip timetable

Day one	Travel to Belfast	
	Evening: Briefing	
Day two	NILT workshop at Queen's University Belfast.	
	AM:	Welcome. Introduction to ARK
		Introduction to NILT: From concept to design
		Using CAPI/CASI interactive workshop
	PM:	Cleaning and checking survey data
		Dissemination: Research updates; reports; policy outcomes.
Day three	AM:	Historical, social and political tour of Belfast
	AM/PM:	Conduct street survey
	Evening:	Survey reflections over a group meal
Day four	AM:	Conduct street survey
	PM:	Travel to Plymouth
Day five	Back at the University:	One week later, data input and preliminary analyses

Evaluation took place both before and after the field trip. Pre-field trip evaluation used a self-completion survey, so that the academic leader could check that the students were happy with the arrangements and also gauge their expectations. Students expressed a high degree of satisfaction with the travel and workshop arrangements. When asked what aspects they were looking forward to, students highlighted 'learning more about NILT', 'experiencing what a street survey is like', and (for some) the prospect of doing these in an unfamiliar environment. One unanticipated aspect was that this was the first time some students had ventured 'abroad' and travelled by plane. Half the students mentioned that it was welcome 'time out' from the familiar time-table of university life, and for some this included family life. They enjoyed being able to tell their peers on other courses that they were going on a field trip. While learning about research processes was mentioned, it was the novel event of a trip away that appeared to be uppermost in their thoughts.

Post-field trip evaluation consisted of a second self-completion question-naire and a focus group discussion. All the students agreed or strongly agreed that the field trip had enabled them to develop some practical fieldwork skills, improve individual confidence to conduct their own research and that the NILT workshop provided a valuable insight into how professional research units function and the career opportunities available to them. However, when asked if they felt that the field trip had contributed to their professional devel-opment portfolio (PDP), half of the group felt that it had not (which may of course indicate something about the relevance of PDP *per se*).

In the focus group students were asked if attending the NILT workshop had made them think any differently about the research process. In the dis-cussion that followed students expressed surprise at the interdisciplinary nature of the research process:

> We have written about BLAISE in one of our research proposals [for course-work] and to see and use it made it 'real' ... and I found the background detail on NILT really useful when I came back [to the university] to com-plete the module assignment.

> I didn't realise that just one or two people were so involved in it from designing to data input to presenting the results. Actually meeting the Director made you realise how the whole process is steered by just a few people. I thought it was a big department. I didn't know that they worked with field work agencies and experts in the different [research] fields to design the actual questionnaire as well.

The additional information and experience of actually visiting different parts of Belfast, mostly connected to The Troubles, was also highlighted by the students.

> From where we were staying it [Belfast] seemed like any other city but within five mins of the tour starting the guide put what we saw around us into context and set the scene.

> You could sit in a taxi and see it [murals] and not really know. You could sit in a classroom and be taught it and not really see it, but getting them both together really made the difference.

> I expected the murals I saw on the internet site to be outside of Belfast. I never expected them to be so close to the city centre.

When asked if they had reflected on the historical, social and political tour in relation to conducting the street survey, a detailed and energised discussion took place about the social setting of the research and the role of the researcher.

> It made me think ... people have actually lived through it [The Troubles] and gives you as the researcher an extra sensitivity when talking to people. It was really important to know about before conducting the street survey.

> Conducting the street survey was real. Some of the people I interviewed had really strong opinions. I think it helped that I wasn't Irish, although being English may have caused some bias.

The students also raised issues about their question construction. Questions that had been piloted in Plymouth and deemed acceptable were now being re-evaluated in light of actually conducting the survey on the target population.

> I felt a lot more comfortable talking to younger people. When I asked some older people I was more tentative especially over some of the question categories we had, especially religion.

> Yeah, I would think about wording the question a bit differently

> People are quite wary when you have a clipboard [in your hand]

> It was a good lesson in how to handle rejection

This discussion continued back in the classroom when entering coded data and unexpected problems that emerged with question wording and categories, and how this become an important consideration at the data analysis phase. From a pedagogic perspective, students were both interested in the SPSS results and in the interpretation and telling of the narrative. It was not just that they had collected some data, it was also that they had travelled both a geographical and an experiential distance, to an unfamiliar place to collect the data.

Fieldwork trips present a 'novel environment' for learning and serve to not only potentially energise students but may also offer a distraction. The post-field trip evaluation suggests that deeper learning had taken place with students linking together the different aspects of the research process. Students were also keen to convey how they enjoyed visiting somewhere different and that this presented itself as a mini-break from the routine of university life. The interesting question to ask, however, relates to the longevity of the learning experience. How do students reflect on the research experience six or 12 months later? How does it relate to conducting their own individual research future research projects – for example final year dissertations – and to how they critically read existing research articles? Perhaps once they return to their final year studies it will simply be remembered as a trip away as part of last year's module. This later point can be overcome by ensuring that outcomes of the fieldwork continues to be reiterated, and reference made to them, in subsequent modules.

Another set of questions concern the viability of field trips in future years, or at other universities. Issues to be resolved include a staff commitment to fieldwork and the need to have institutional support for staff throughout the entire planning and running of the trip. The above pilot trip was funded by TQEF monies that included a buy-out for staff, whereas future trips will need to be integrated into the curriculum and workload management. The module coursework and fieldwork did make use of online resources, and these and other developing technologies may provide part of the solution to issues of staff time and workloads.

Conclusion

The field trip case study described in this chapter is just one example of how it is possible to turn fairly ambivalent students into active and reflective researchers. The interesting thing to note is that in this context the issue of number becomes somewhat redundant, at least for this self-selected group. Students who previously saw the analysis of quantitative data as an issue of numeracy, a test of their ability, or simply as something to be got through and passed, start using quantitative methods as tools in an enterprise in which they feel they have a stake. To some extent one is speeding up a process that happens to some students when they leave university and enter the workplace. Here, if they are conducting research, they quickly find that their learning curve is shaped by the task in hand and the relevance of techniques become apparent.

Field trips, within integrated research-based teaching environments, do offer a great deal of promise, but they are not a panacea for all our problems of teaching quantitative methods. They are relatively resource intensive and probably only suitable for students taking a more dedicated pathway in social research; nevertheless, the principle of 'research ownership' they embody is a good one. Much of our attention (perhaps inevitably) has been focused on the 'numeracy problem', but perhaps the numeracy problem is only a *symptom* of a deeper and wider malaise in social science?

Student chemists, biologists and artists spend time 'doing' in their laboratories or studios. They learn theory and they learn techniques, but the focus of their training is to turn them into active chemists, biologists and artists. In social science this is rarely the case at undergraduate level. Most teaching is classroom based and much of what is learned is about theorising what the world is like, rather than active investigation. Methods modules are rarely integrated with other teaching and their content is seen as artificial. A cultural shift in the curriculum towards helping students to be *active* sociologists (political scientists etc.) would place numeracy issues in the context of investigation to a purpose the student feels they own.

Such a cultural shift will require the active promotion of social science as investigative *science*. This is at the core of the problem and implicit in the evidence we present here. If, as is so often the case at present, social science is not seen as science and even problematised in the curriculum to the point of a rejection of social science as misguided 'positivism', then number and quantitative methods have no point. They are a non sequitor in a humanities programme. This issue goes far beyond the classroom or the laboratory. If quantitative methods are to have any point at all, they must be within the context of an investigative social science with its roots outside the classroom.

References

Boyle, A., Maguire, S., Martin, A., Milsom, C., Nash, R., Rawlinson, S., Turner, A., Wurthmann, S. and Conchie, S. (2007) 'Fieldwork is good: the student perception and the affectionate domain', *Journal of Geography in Higher Education*, 31(2): 299–317.

Burgess, R. (2004) *Measuring and Recording Student Achievement*. London: Universities UK.

Denzin, N. and Lincoln, Y. (2003) (eds) *The Landscape of Qualitative Research*. Thousand Oaks, CA: Sage.

Department for Education and Skills (2004) *Making Mathematics Count*. Report of Professor Adrian Smith's enquiry into Post-14 Mathematics Education, February. Available at: http://www.tda.gov.uk/upload/resources/pdf/m/mathsinquiry_finalreport.pdf (accessed 24 May 2010).

Department for Education and Skills (2005) *14–19 Education and Skills*, Government White Paper, February. Available at: http://www.dfes.gov.uk/publications/14-19educationandskills/ (accessed 24 May 2010).

Fletcher, S. and Dodds, W. (2004) *Dipping Toes in the Water: An International Survey of Residential Fieldwork Within ICM Degree Course Curricula*. Littoral 2004: 7th International Symposium; Delivering Sustainable Coasts: Connecting Science and Policy, Aberdeen Scotland, UK, Volume 1, pp. 305–309. Cambridge: Cambridge University Press.

Fry, H., Ketteridge, S., and Marshall, S. (2003) *A Handbook for Teaching and Learning in Higher Education: Enhancing Academic Practice*. Routledge: Abingdon.

Goldthorpe, J., Lockwood, D., Bechhofer, F. and Platt, J. (1969) *The Affluent Worker in the Class Structure*. Cambridge: Cambridge University Press.

Kent, M., Gilbertstone, D., and Hunt, C., (1997) 'Fieldwork in geography teaching: a critical view of the literature and approaches', *Journal of Geography in Higher Education*, 21(3): 313–32.

Laitin, D. (2003) 'The "Perestroikan Challenge to Social Science"', *Politics and Society*, 31(1): 163–84.

Lonergan, N. and Andreson, L.W. (1988) 'Field-based education: some theoretical considerations', *Higher Education Research and Development*, 7(1): 63–77.

Marsh, C. (1982) *The Survey Method: The Contribution of Surveys to Sociological Explanation*. London: George, Allen and Unwin.

Market Research Society (2010) *The MRS Advanced Certificate in Market & Social Research Practice*. Available at: http://www.mrs.org.uk/qualifications/cert.htm (accessed 24 May 2010).

Oakley, A. (2000) *Experiments in Knowing: Gender and Method in the Social Sciences:* Cambridge: Polity.

Payne, G. (2010) '*The new social mobility: how politicians took over a sociological idea'*. Paper presented to the BSA Annual Conference, Glasgow.

Payne, G., Williams, M. and Chamberlain, S. (2004) 'Methodological pluralism in British sociology', *Sociology*, 38(1): 153–164.

Platt, J. (1998) *A History of Sociological Research Methods in America (1920–1960)*. Cambridge: Cambridge University Press.

Ritchey, F. (2008) *The Statistical Imagination: Elementary Statistics for the Social Sciences*. New York: McGraw-Hill.

Savage, M. and Burrows, R. (2007) 'The coming crisis in empirical sociology', *Sociology*, 41(5): 885–99.

University of Plymouth (2008) *Draft Learning and Teaching Strategy*. Plymouth: University of Plymouth.

Wellings, K., Field, J., Johnson, A. and Wadsworth, J. (1994) *Sexual Behaviour in Britain: The National Survey of Sexual Attitudes and Lifestyles*. Harmondsworth: Penguin.

Westergaard, J. and Resler, H. (1975) *Class in a Capitalist Society: A Study of Contemporary Britain*. Harmondsworth: Penguin.

Williams, M. (2000a) 'Social research – the emergence of a discipline?', *International Journal of Social Research Methodology'*, 2(2): 157–66.

Williams, M. (2000b) *Science and Social Science: An Introduction*. London: Routledge.

Williams, M. and Cheal, B. (2001) 'Is there any such thing as homelessness? Measurement, explanation and process in "homelessness" research', *European Journal of Social Research* – Innovation, 11(3): 239–54.

Williams, M., Collett, C. and Rice, R. (2004) *Baseline Study of Quantitative Methods in British Sociology*. Birmingham/Durham: C-SAP/BSA. Available at: http://www.britsoc.org.uk (accessed 24 May 2010).

Williams, M., Payne, G., Hodgkinson, L. and Poade, D. (2008) 'Does sociology count: student attitudes to the teaching of quantitative methods', *Sociology*, 42(5): 1003–22.

How to Teach the Reluctant and Terrified to Love Statistics: The Importance of Context in Teaching Quantitative Methods in the Social Sciences

Katharine Adeney and Sean Carey

It was widely reported in the British media in June 2008 that 'a "lost generation" of mathematicians has cost the economy £9 billion' (Woolcock, 2008: 9). This statistic precipitated a debate about standards of education and the impact of a decline in mathematics training in Britain, both of which concern us as social scientists. Perhaps just as worrying was the fact that the methodology for calculating this large number was unclear; and yet the finding was reported uncritically. The lack of debate about the origin of this estimate or its accuracy when the report was first covered in most newspapers was striking (but see Goldacre, 2008). The impact on future earnings was reported with little or no discussion of how such a figure was calculated, for example 'pupils who ditch maths after GCSEs lose £136,000 in lifetime earnings' (Wooding, 2008: 2). The pervasiveness of statistics in the media, especially when they are presented uncritically and used to inform political debate, makes the teaching of tools to evaluate data to undergraduate social science students all the more important. These research skills will enable them to evaluate data not only in 'the real world' but also in research articles.

As emphasised by the Economic and Social Research Council (ESRC), there is a market for quantitative skills in the academic, public and voluntary sectors, and these skills need to be developed during 'the earliest stages of career development' (ESRC, 2006). There should therefore be a strong motivation for students to learn and use quantitative methods as part of their university education. Previous research has found that social science graduates with quantitative skills are not only more marketable and valuable as employees, but that these graduates also report that these skills are subsequently useful and applicable in their chosen occupations as well as other areas of civic life (Andersen and Harsell, 2005). Experience of discussing job applications with final year undergraduates confirms that many stress the skills they have learnt on the second year quantitative methods course on their CVs to demonstrate to potential employers their familiarity with the research process and data analysis. On the other side of the coin, discussing the employability of graduates with representatives from survey organisations who have visited Sheffield has indicated that these organisations are desperate to have applications from undergraduates who already have a familiarity with data analysis and surveys – even at the basic level at which we introduce students to it. The advantages are not only far in the future in terms of career prospects, but also in the present or short-term future.

An understanding of the research process will invariably produce a better understanding of research in other courses taught as part of a student's degree programme. Thus students studying a course on democratisation would be better equipped to evaluate the merits or otherwise of the modernisation theorists of democratisation who rely on comparative data, e.g. Lipset (1971) and Vanhanen (1997). In addition, it will provide a valuable foundation for postgraduate study.

Despite the clear advantages of learning quantitative methods, research has also shown that undergraduate social science students are usually reluctant to learn research methods, and statistics in particular (Williams et al., 2004). This is certainly confirmed in our experience. Reluctance can come in the form of anxiety about maths and statistics, something the vast majority of politics undergraduates thought they had left behind once they had finished their GCSEs, and were relieved to do so. But this reluctance can also come from a denial that quantitative analysis has any place in the study of politics despite the pervasiveness of numerical data in the making of political argument and in supporting theories. Nevertheless, statistical analysis at various levels of sophistication is the most prevalent methodology used in the empirical study of politics (although not in every social science discipline, see Payne et al., 2004), and a familiarity with some of the most commonly used methods is essential for understanding research in our discipline. Therefore our goal is to teach students something that many do not want to learn, but which is essential for them to know. It is this dilemma that drives the choices that we make.

The fact that such courses are frequently compulsory also means that the academic staff member tasked with teaching the course is often not enamoured with doing so. A lecturer's lack of enthusiasm will be quickly conveyed to students, with a predictable disengagement by the vast majority. This is not confined to the teaching of statistics and research methods – enthusiasm on the part of lecturers and seminar leaders is absolutely vital for imparting knowledge at *any* level in the education system. However, it is likely to be more prevalent in the attitude of those teaching compulsory methods courses. The reluctance of students to learn statistics can generate concerns in the academic who is tasked with teaching such a course, resulting in 'stat anxiety' for both student and teacher (Lewis-Beck, 2001: 8), especially in those academics who do not claim specialist expertise in research methods. There is also a perception among colleagues that teaching quantitative methods is difficult, and this can indeed be the case. There is therefore a certain amount of goodwill to be gained from within the department for taking on these courses.

Although the details will vary according to the nature of the course being taught, *the vast majority of research methods and statistics courses at undergraduate level in the social sciences should be able to be taught by non-specialists in this area.* We will lay out in more detail below the types of methods and statistics that we cover in our own modules, but all social science academics should be able to cope with understanding the principles and process of research design, understand and know how to create basic descriptive statistics such as crosstabs, interpret a chi-square statistic and learn the basics of how to work statistical software such as SPSS and Stata (for the sceptical it should be stressed that one of the authors of this article is distinctly non-mathematical). This applies as much to faculty as it does to graduate teaching assistants. What it does require is that the academics and teaching assistants be as open to the subject and its merits as we expect our students to be.

It must also be acknowledged that teaching statistics to students who are mostly reluctant, frequently terrified and sometimes actively resistant requires patience and imagination. Statistics is best taught in a context that will engage those we seek to learn. The strategy that we adopt for teaching quantitative research methods is consistent with recent wider research in good practice for the teaching of undergraduate quantitative research methods in our discipline of political science. We believe that the teaching of research methods cannot and should not be separated from the teaching of theory and substantive topics (Janda, 2001; Quaile Hill, 2002; Thies and Hogan, 2005) and are therefore strong advocates of subject specific training in research methods (Janda, 2001). We see no reason why this principle and our approach would not apply to teaching research methods in other social sciences.

We also believe that it is important to introduce students gradually to the research statistics element of our undergraduate course, and only after familiarising them with the fundamentals of empirical research design and the use of numbers more broadly in the political and social world. This strategy helps overcome the reluctance of students by requiring them to first think about the ubiquitous use of numbers in a social context, not only in the media, but also by politicians, interest groups and many other social actors. This forms a vitally important component of the second year course that we teach at the University of Sheffield. It enables us to make constant use of subject specific examples to illustrate concepts. We are not averse to occasionally widening our pool of examples to popular culture (cartoons, music, television, sport, etc.) to emphasise some points. These often tend to be the examples that students will remember and can work well to elicit understanding of the generalised nature of a concept. However, such examples must be used to reinforce those that can be related to the subject – indeed the use of two examples to make the same point is an important teaching tool.

Experience has also taught us that an emphasis should be placed on application and interpretation rather than on formulae and statistical proofs, as advocated by Adams (2001). This enables students to actively engage with the material and learn how to apply techniques rather than being passive observers. Finally, it is apparent that learning will be enhanced when students conduct their own research using real data and addressing real political problems (Adams, 2001, Lewis-Beck, 2001). By doing so, students not only engage with the material but also feel that they have some 'stake' and interest in the results, especially if (as our course does) they can design a research question in which they are interested in the results.

Mandatory statistics

We teach two quantitative research methods modules in our department. Like many politics departments in the UK we have implemented an undergraduate course in statistics as a requirement for all our students. At the University of Sheffield, this is taught in the second year of study for all students taking politics as a single or dual degree. It involves the teaching of a large cohort (usually over 200) of students using lecture, seminar and workshop formats. We are also involved in teaching an optional quantitative methods track of the undergraduate dissertation, involving the teaching of a far smaller number of students in a combination of workshop and tutorial formats. Thus we attempt to teach basic quantitative methods for all, and advanced quantitative methods for some. Both courses take place over the whole of the academic year and having this length of time available to develop the content of the modules has proved to be important in cultivating the skills we aim to impart.

In this chapter we shall concentrate on the mandatory module, titled 'Political Analysis: Approaches and Methods', which is comprised of four main themes. Quantitative methods comprise the final section of the course and the first three sections directly support the importance of learning and using quantitative methods. It consists of a number of components that place the research and statistical methods in context, and allow them to be introduced gradually. In a bid to overcome the anxiety associated with learning statistics we aim to 'make the learning fun or at least painless' and continually demonstrate that 'statistics increase understanding of how politics works' (Lewis-Beck, 2001: 8). We attempt to do this in a number of ways; by having variation in the type of assessment, much of which is innovative, variation in the teaching format and learning activities, and presenting students with the opportunity to link the learning of quantitative methods with their substantive interests.

The first component of 'Political Analysis: Approaches and Methods' presents students with approaches to conducting research in social science, particularly that of the 'scientific method'. It encourages students to consider the alternatives to the scientific method, e.g. faith, logic or authority, and the problems of using these alternatives to construct political arguments. It also cautions them on the limitations of the scientific method, especially in the social sciences (as compared with the natural sciences). It considers where those approaches students have already been exposed to, such as behaviouralism, rational choice, institutionalism and interpretive theories, fit within the scientific method. This feature of the course is familiar to them as, in a number of respects, it covers material that they will already be aware of.

The second component investigates the use of quantification in politics, such as numerical benchmarks or indicators in political argument and public policy. Notably, this is not the research of political science, but it does concentrate on the political world. This feature of the module is rather unusual, at least for our discipline. In some respects we believe that this may be the most useful aspect of the course for our students. Evidence tends to support the view that a lack of critical engagement with the numbers used in everyday life, particularly in the political, is a potentially serious problem (Best, 2001; Blastland and Dilnot, 2007). This section of the course illustrates how ubiquitous numbers are in almost all aspects of the political world, for example in migration, health and education statistics. We deliberately choose topical areas to focus on, and update these regularly, introducing extremely contemporary examples, e.g. MRSA or C-Difficile statistics in the National Health Service, migration statistics, school or hospital league tables. This enables us to concentrate on the essential elements of quantification in debates that are familiar to the students. More importantly, it also enables us to focus on the potential misuse of numbers by political actors and institutions.

In particular we focus on the ways in which statistics are often used in a misleading fashion, by deliberate or unintentional design or presentation problems. We cover potential problems with design, such as bad sampling strategies. Problems with presentation can include using the graphical presentation of the data in such a manner as to disguise changes over time or to present a snapshot of data out of the wider context; problems with the comparability of data over time; and the cherry picking of selective data to support an argument. We also focus on the importance of understanding the context in which these data were collected. These topics are familiar to all intelligent people, whether studying politics or not, so it is good preparation for students to engage with statistics that they have already been exposed to before introducing them to examples which they have not met before.

The third component of the module introduces students to the main principles of research design in empirical social science research. This is absolutely crucial as it allows them to appreciate where statistics fit into the process of analysis. It aims to dispel the preconception that quantitative methods for studying social sciences are based on barefoot empiricism and demonstrates the importance of theory and appropriate operationalisation.

Students are presented with familiar hypotheses from politics such as democratic peace theory. They are then taught the need for appropriate operationalisation and statistical analysis in order to test whether or not the hypothesis that democracies do not go to war with one another is correct. The methodology is presented within a substantive context in a way in which analysis of numerical data is often the most viable option to evaluate the accuracy of commonly known phenomena. However, the component is not only quantitative, as we also stress the importance of constructing plausible, testable, generalisable and simple hypotheses.

The fourth component finally introduces quantitative research techniques. A variety of quantitative methods are introduced, from descriptive statistical techniques such as crosstabs to inferential statistics such as correlation and linear regression. Students not only learn about some commonly used statistical techniques, they also apply these techniques to analyse real data in order to address the research questions they are interested in. They do so through learning and using basic features of the SPSS statistical analysis software.

Teaching a course that includes such a wide range of material, pedagogical activities and students requires a large and motivated teaching team. We draw our team from both the faculty and postgraduate community within our department. Weekly lectures are given by ourselves, with weekly one-hour seminars or workshops of groups of no more than 15 students led by either a faculty member or a graduate teaching assistant. The teaching team usually comprises five or six people. All of the teaching activities are highly coordinated so that each seminar group is working on the same activity in the same week. While the course deliberately stretches over the academic year, we schedule numerous teaching-free weeks into those two semesters (24 weeks) to enable students to complete assessments. Unlike many other courses the workload on political analysis is reasonably evenly distributed across the length of the course. When students are working on assignments we structure the presentation of ongoing work into seminars in order to monitor their progress, provide formative feedback prior to submission, and prevent students from trying to complete an entire assignment until a day or two before it is due for submission. Students are expected to study six hours a week independent of teaching time.

Assessment

Teaching and assessment for the course are varied. The variation in teaching provision includes didactic lectures, computer-based workshops, student-led seminars, problem-based learning seminars, class discussions and debates. Seminar activities include practical experience in confronting important social science datasets, analysis of (in)numeracy in newspapers, a debate fuelled only by information in data tables, analysing how data are used (well and not so well) in published social science research, presentations and exercises involving the design, sampling and operationalisation of research projects, and presentations based on the use of numerical measurements by political actors. While the preparation of materials for this module is more time-consuming than for regular courses, much of this can be carried over from one year to next, and for those elements which require updating (absolutely essential to ensure the contemporaneous nature of examples) we believe the reward for the students (and instructors) is merited.

Assessing quantitative methods courses tends to differ from that for other courses in the social sciences. In the vast majority of courses there are advantages to be gained from a larger piece of coursework that allows students to develop a number of ideas and produce a substantial essay addressing a single question or topic. Such forms of assessment permit students to demonstrate their ability to synthesise material, construct an argument and demonstrate wider reading around the topic. In statistics, more frequent, smaller assignments with clear marking criteria tend to be more appropriate in both reducing anxiety and making sure that students do not fall behind (Janda, 2001).

We set four assessments, which are related but quite distinct. Assessment includes: the design and piloting of a questionnaire that is placed in the context of an appropriate research question, hypothesis and sampling strategy; an analysis of the role that issues of measurement and quantitative analysis play in an important political or policy issue; and a research paper utilising data analysis using a statistical software program and placed in the context of an appropriate research question, hypothesis and operationalisation. There is also an exam that requires the student to compose a research design to address one of a choice of research questions, and to evaluate how well a number of testable hypotheses are supported by some tables of data.

One theme is present in each of these assignments: we offer students a wide choice of substantive topic in each form of assessment. Our rationale is that students will engage far better with the methods if they can relate to the subject being studied. This extends our belief that the best research methods training is discipline specific, and that an even better understanding of research methods will be achieved when the subject is subdiscipline specific.

The first assignment we set involves the creation of a survey on any topic appropriate for this form of analysis. It is no coincidence that the first assignment is a group effort with students working together in teams of about three or four. Although initially resisted by many students, working in a group has a number of advantages for students in general: it divides the workload, it tends to increase productivity, it encourages communication and cooperation, and it allows for the specialisation of tasks according to ability and experience. We have found that having assessed group projects at the beginning of a course also leads to a relaxed and confident seminar group, whose members subsequently interact well together. This assignment requires students to formulate an appropriate research question in consultation with the wider group and seminar tutor. They are then encouraged to consider what the most appropriate method of conducting the survey would be (e.g. postal, telephone, face to face) and what their sampling strategy would be.

The groups then collectively design (again with input from the wider seminar group and tutor) a series of survey questions to enable them to be able to answer their research questions. Much of the teaching for this assessment requires feedback on the appropriateness of questions, focusing on several different factors including (but not limited to) question type, length, order, and whether the questions are leading, ambiguous or contradictory. We also address the format that these questions can take, for example whether visual aids or alternative scales would be appropriate. We have found that feedback works best when the students from other groups within the seminar group give their feedback – this enables students to apply lessons from other students' work effectively to their own.

Students are then required to complete their survey (with a limit of 20 questions) and 'pilot' it on their 'target population'. Obviously, restricting the choice of questions to those that could be answered by a feasible target population (university students would probably be the only target population available to our groups) would be self-defeating and could also raise ethical problems. Students are therefore instructed to approach friends and classmates and ask them to answer the survey as if they were a member of the target population (which they may or may not be). The point of this exercise is not to yield any useful results (which would be nonsensical) but for students to consider the merits of, and the difficulties with, their survey. A reflection on the limitations of the questionnaire, and a consideration of the changes that would be required, form an important part of the assessment, which is 1,500 words in total. Students have worked on quite varied projects: notable ones include the relationship between gender and recycling, political knowledge and trust in politicians, and the political ideology of university lecturers and the subject taught.

The second assignment involves analysing quantification in the real world. This requires students to analyse the role that quantification plays in the debate surrounding a political issue of their choosing. For this assignment students compare two political organisations, broadly conceived, in order to analyse how they use and interpret statistics on the same political issue to argue for different outcomes (for example the Refugee Council versus Migration Watch or the Labour Party versus the Conservative Party). The types of organisation and the list of potential issues are unlimited, although we do provide some advised areas and most students will choose one of these, for example abortion, crime, migration, ID cards, or government reform. The students' papers engage with the use of quantitative evidence in politics and the manner in which it relates to political behaviour, arguments, interpretations and outcomes.

We ask them to consider a number of questions about the types of statistics organisations use. For example:

- Do they use official government statistics, surveys, indicators, indices or some other types of data?
- Do the organisations collect or commission the collection of data themselves or use externally collated data?
- When and why were the data collected?
- Do they even explain the origin of the data that they use?
- Are the data and the way the statistics are presented consistent with the arguments the organisation is making?
- Is it possible to evaluate the quality of the data used by the organisation?

The students can then contrast the differences and similarities between the two organisations chosen. Drawing on the work of Best (2001), we ask them to be critical of statistics used by organisations and actors with a political agenda, but also to be careful to avoid being either cynical or naïve. Again, this is a short assignment of 1,500 words (although students can add tables of statistics which do not count towards the word limit).

A third assignment involves an analysis of real datasets. This is an important assessment, and one that is introduced near the end of the course so that students can appreciate the different ways in which data are collected and the benefits (and dangers) of using numerical data to construct a political argument before proceeding to conduct their own research project. Delaying the introduction of this assessment also allows them to become familiar with using numerical data and also to become comfortable with their seminar tutors and seminar group. As Clawson et al. warn us, 'locating interesting, informative, and timely applications is one of the most challenging and time-consuming aspects of teaching methods' (2001: 4). While an unlimited choice of topic for this assignment for a cohort of over 200 students would be unmanageable, indeed unfeasible, we do offer considerable choice. This aspect of our course has been extended over time so that we now offer training in the use of four major datasets that students can analyse for their research, including public opinion data from a British Election Study, a Eurobarometer, one of the British Social Attitudes surveys, and international relations data from a number of sources including measures of democracy, human rights violations and economics. The use of real data to analyse research questions has proved to be a key strength of a module taken by large numbers of students with varied interests. From these choices students can, and do, select topics that they are interested in, indeed subjects they are often passionate about, and produce a paper that requires them to test a hypothesis of their own choosing with real data.

The other advantage of using real datasets is that it allows those with more statistical knowledge than the majority of their peers (students studying for a dual economics and politics degree often fall into this category) to utilise more complicated techniques. The students are taught to use the SPSS software through two dedicated computer workshops in computer rooms, run by the faculty and teaching assistants teaching on the course. They are introduced to the basic features of the software, shown how to create crosstabs and calculate a chi-square statistic, and how to present data in a graphical form, e.g. pie and bar charts. They are also taught how to manipulate data, for example recoding variables such as age from raw to grouped categories for ease of use and presentation. As with the other assignments, the word limit for this one is deliberately short at 1,500 words, including at least one table and one graph to illustrate their argument, but not more than five in total. Students have looked at many different issues, including the link between social class and voting patterns, regime type and the protection of human rights, and the change in attitudes towards civil rights before and after a major terrorist incident.

One of the potential drawbacks of using real data for teaching at undergraduate level is the complexity of the major datasets used to address some of the most interesting questions in social sciences. To combat this problem we have condensed these datasets so they are more suitable for study at the undergraduate level. This involved removing some variables and observations from the datasets, producing user-friendly codebooks and recoding some of the variables. While this has proved to be a time-consuming activity it is one that is proving to be less necessary as more and more datasets are increasingly presented in teaching-friendly formats, such as those held at the UK Data Archive as part of its Learning and Teaching Resources scheme.

Our strategy of offering as much substantive choice as is practicable even continues on to our course exam where we require students to write a research design, from theory through to analysis, based on a wide selection of research questions taken from numerous areas of our discipline.

Supporting teaching

One of the major justifications for teaching social science students quantitative research methods is to maximise their employability and teach them transferable skills, which would also be a major benefit for postgraduate research in the social sciences. Although this information is commonly imparted to students at the beginning of such courses, there are ways in which we believe its importance can be better emphasised. One such way is to have representatives from attractive employers talk to the students about the significance of quantitatively trained social scientists. We have brought in external speakers to address the students on our course about the relevance of quantitative methods in their professions. These speakers can also shed light on the challenges and difficult decisions faced when conducting quantitative research. During the most recent academic year we hosted representatives from one of the major political polling companies, the Ministry of Justice and the Prime Minister's Strategy Unit. These external speakers give talks and question and answer sessions in lecture periods dedicated to a key topic.

We support our teaching in a number of ways. Naturally, we provide the usual service of placing lecture and seminar notes and other learning materials on the virtual learning environment (VLE). However, support for students also involves some innovative approaches. Using useful material available at www.intute.ac.uk, and in collaboration with our information literacy staff in the library, we designed an online tutorial for finding data on the internet that was tailored explicitly to the learning objectives of one of our assignments. We do not require students to complete this tutorial (to do so would be no guarantee that they had internalised it) but we do make clear that the marking criteria for the second assessment automatically assume that they are aware of the information and tips contained within this tutorial. This also forms part of the information literacy skills spine promoted by the department at all three levels of teaching in the compulsory core modules.

In addition, we use our VLE in a number of different ways to support students, including producing a page of frequently asked questions for assignments and a module discussion board. We also provide extra time to support struggling students by putting on additional seminars for those seeking more help with assignments. Enthusiastic students also receive extra support: optional workshops are offered for those students who wish to analyse more complicated datasets. This support has proved popular in both alleviating the fears of the most anxious and encouraging the enthusiasm of the keenest. Of course, being accessible within office hours has also proved invaluable – and many students will avail themselves of this opportunity to speak to faculty and teaching assistants if they require further clarification.

By the time the course ends we expect that every student will appreciate the necessity of quantitative research in political science, even if we do not expect that they will all go on to perform statistical analysis in the future. However, we do suppose that some of them will (as evidence from those wishing to take the quantitative dissertation discussed below indicates). We are confident that all students will be better equipped to understand articles that use quantitative techniques, and to question more effectively assumptions found in journal articles and monographs after taking this course. This will aid them when they take their more advanced research-led options in their final year and perhaps in their graduate career, and also help to equip them as educated citizens of the future. In this respect the course is complementary to every other course they will take.

Finally, as well as supporting the students on this course, experience has taught us that support for the team that teaches on this course is vital. The course is constantly adapted to include new examples and also in response to feedback from students. We take into account feedback from our teaching assistants as well, and actively solicit such feedback throughout the year. The nature of the course requires that a high level of coordination is necessary to ensure that teaching assistants are fully aware of the requirements of the assessment, and know about the most appropriate ways to run seminars. This coordination (generally two meetings per semester) has proved invaluable not only in ensuring the continuity of advice given to students in different seminar groups, but also in ensuring that teaching assistants are aware of what is expected of them and are not intimidated by teaching this type of material.

Optional statistics: the quantitative dissertation

Although we believe it is important for all social science graduates to have some understanding of quantitative methods, we also believe it is desirable for some of those students to have sufficient quantitative training to prepare them for either an academic career or employment that predominantly uses those skills. In order to teach the more enthusiastic students more advanced techniques of data collection and data analysis we offer training associated with a substantial research project in a student's final year of study. The undergraduate curriculum in our department includes a compulsory dissertation for all single politics students. Students taking a dual degree including politics also have the option of electing to complete a dissertation. For those electing to take the quantitative track of the dissertation we offer instructional quantitative sessions during the early stages of this project in addition to their regular supervision meetings. In these meetings they are introduced to, and trained in, methods appropriate to the research questions that they are interested in. The format of this training is a hands-on approach with students learning to use and apply quantitative methods on an individual level.

These sessions take place in small groups. We have found that this learning environment is the most appropriate as students benefit from being exposed to the issues and problems of their contemporaries, while the group is small enough for each student to receive sufficient personal attention. The student-led nature of the content of this course works very well in shaping the methods taught to address the research questions of interest to these students. Our experience is that this approach leads to more substance-driven research rather than method-driven research that a set course on certain statistical techniques can lead to, and, for the students and staff involved in this process, it is a very rewarding experience. Indeed, we have found that a significant number within this group of students will continue their studies into postgraduate education, and we feel that this training gives them a distinct advantage at that stage.

Conclusion

There are clearly difficulties to be overcome in teaching undergraduate quantitative methods courses. Frequently there are obstacles to clear in order to teach the course that you see as the most appropriate, whether that may be a different set of priorities in the department, a lack of interest from students or a lack of time available in order to collect the necessary materials. But the teaching of quantitative methods can also be most rewarding. Our students grapple with questions that they are keenly interested in answering, which generates some highly innovative work. We have often found ourselves marking closer to the top end of the marking scale than we would ordinarily do for this level of study. Some students after taking our courses have gone on to produce some highly imaginative quantitative research in the undergraduate dissertations that they produce in their final year of study. Having taught undergraduate quantitative methods courses for a number of years, we have had the pleasure of seeing politics graduates securing funding for postgraduate studies and getting jobs because of what they have learned in our courses (and we are not alone here, see Janda, 2001).

It tends to be the case that undergraduate students in most social science disciplines, and not just in politics, are reticent about taking statistics courses and therefore have relatively low expectations for them. As many other teachers of social science research methods have found, student evaluations of research methods courses tend to generate more negative evaluations than other courses (Carlson and Hyde, 2002; xix). We are no different here, with the aggregate ratings of our compulsory course less positive than the substantive courses that we also teach. However, with this lower mean comes greater variance. A further inspection of student comments suggests that, while expectations were rather low before beginning, many students have found themselves surprisingly enjoying the course. Some of the most pleasing comments we have received on completing evaluations of our courses have referred to a sea change in their attitudes over the duration of the course, from one of dread to one of enjoyment, and even a recognition that the skills learned would be useful both for the remainder of their academic career and even in life after university.

Acknowledgements

The research on which this chapter is based was made possible thanks to an ESRC grant (RES-043-25-004) to develop undergraduate curricula in quantitative methods. More details can be found at http://www.shef.ac.uk/politics/methods. We would also like to thank all of our colleagues, both past and present, who have helped us teach on these modules at Sheffield: Glenn Gottfried, Dominic Holland, John Kingdom, Robert McIlveen, Alistair McMillan, James Meadowcroft, and Louise Strong.

References

Adams, G. (2001) 'Teaching undergraduate methods', *Political Methodologist*, 10(1): 2–4.

Andersen, K. and Harsell, D. (2005) 'Assessing the impact of a quantitative skills course for undergraduates', *Journal of Political Science Education*, 1(1): 7–27.

Best, J. (2001) *Damned Lies and Statistics: Untangling Numbers From the Media, Politicians and Activists*. Los Angeles: University of California Press.

Blastland, M. and Dilnot, A. (2007) *The Tiger That Isn't: Seeing Through a World of Numbers*. London: Profile.

Carlson, J. and Hyde, M. (2002) *Doing Empirical Political Research*. Boston, MA: Houghton Mifflin.

Clawson, R., Hoffman, A. and McCann, J. (2001) 'If we only knew then what we know now: a few reflections on teaching undergraduate quantitative methods courses', *Political Methodologist*, 10(1): 4–5.

Economic and Social Research Council (2006) *Call for Proposals: The Development of Undergraduate Curricula in Quantitative Methods*. Swindon: ESRC.

Goldacre, B. (2008) 'Decline of maths? Just do the arithmetic', *Guardian*, 7 June.

Intute (n.d.) 'Internet for government and politics', *Virtual Training Suite Tutorial*. Available at: http://www.vts.intute.ac.uk/he/tutorial/government (accessed 8 August 2009).

Janda, K. (2001) 'Teaching research methods: the best job in the department', *Political Methodologist*, 10(1): 6–7.

Lewis-Beck, M. (2001) 'Teaching undergraduate methods: overcoming "Stat" anxiety', *Political Methodologist*, 10(1): 7–9.

Lipset, S. (1971) *Political Man*. London: Heinemann.

Payne, G., Williams, M. and Chamberlain, S. (2004) 'Methodological pluralism in British sociology', *Sociology*, 38(1): 153–63.

Quaile Hill, K. (2002) 'The lamentable state of science education in political science', *PS: Political Science and Politics*, 35(1): 113–16.

Thies, C. and Hogan, R. (2005) 'The state of undergraduate research methods training in political science', *PS: Political Science and Politics*, 38(2): 293–7.

Vanhanen, T. (1997) *Prospects of Democracy: A Study of 172 Countries*. London: Routledge.

Williams, M., Collett, T. and Rice, R. (2004) *Baseline Study of Quantitative Methods in British Sociology*. Birmingham/Durham: BSA/C-SAP. Available at: http://www.britsoc.co.uk/publications/BSA++CSAP+Quantitative+Methods+Report.htm (accessed 8 August 2009).

Wooding, D. (2008) '£136K maths losers', *Sun*, 3 June.

Woolcock, N. (2008) 'Can't-do attitude to maths "has cost economy £9bn"', *Times*, 3 June.

Improving the Teaching of Quantitative Methods to Undergraduate Social Scientists: Understanding and Overcoming the Barriers

Jane Falkingham and Teresa McGowan

The problem of a 'deficit' in quantitative UK social scientists has been a policy concern for the government and research councils since the late 1990s (Economic and Social Research Council (ESRC), 2005). In order to overcome this deficit it has been increasingly recognised that the development of quantitative skills needs to take place during the earliest stages of career development (ESRC, 2006). While the problem has been well documented (Higher Education Funding Council for England (HEFCE), 2005; The Royal Society 2008), *how* this 'deficit' can be addressed has been relatively under-researched, with only a select number of studies currently available.

In their survey of delegates at the 2003 British Sociological Association annual conference, Williams et al. found that 'over 70% of the sample believed it was difficult to be a proficient quantitative researcher' and that 'students chose sociology to avoid numbers' (Williams et al., 2004a: 46). In a further consultation with academics about quantitative methods in undergraduate sociology, quantitative research was found to be viewed negatively: 'many students have preconceptions about the numeracy aspect of quantitative research' (Williams et al., 2004b). The authors identified several barriers to the wider use of quantitative methods by students studying sociology, including negative student perceptions often being reinforced by lecturers and tutors, and problems with the level and language of quantitative courses (Williams et al., 2004b).

Drawing on recent ESRC funded research undertaken by the authors at the University of Southampton, this chapter investigates the potential barriers to the use of quantitative methods among undergraduates from a range of social science disciplines, including sociology, social policy, social work, politics, international relations and applied social sciences, and advances some proposals for how these barriers might be overcome. An understanding of how we can address the 'deficit' in quantitative skills will be essential to ensure the UK maintains its international ranking in social scientific research and strengthens its position as global leader in e-social science and research methods.

The study site

Home to the largest group of social statisticians and demographers in the country, rigorous empirical research using cutting edge quantitative methods has long been a hallmark of social sciences at the University of Southampton. The School of Social Sciences has a long-established commitment to the integration of quantitative methods in its undergraduate curricula, with all programmes in the school requiring students to take one or more quantitative methods units in their first year of study, as well as further units in the second or third year. Both the first and second year units are large, with approximately 250 students in each. The content of these modules starts with the absolute basics – descriptive statistics (including tables and graphs) and simple inferential statistics with the use of Excel and SPSS – and very little prior knowledge is assumed. The school has invested a great deal in the teaching of these courses; putting only its most experienced lecturers in charge, introducing new material each year to ensure the lectures reflect contemporary issues and using a variety of teaching methods and resources in an attempt to enthuse and inspire students. Despite this commitment in some disciplines, the number of students applying the skills and knowledge acquired in these units to their substantive work remains disappointingly low. This is particularly noticeable in the preparation of undergraduate dissertations, where, outside economics and population studies, very few projects involve either the collection and analysis of primary survey data or the secondary analysis of datasets held by the Economic and Social Data Service (ESDS) or the Data Archive. Within some disciplines, the inclusion of any numerical data at all within dissertations remains rare, despite the fact that systematic analysis of published administrative data can often provide valuable insights into trends in social, political and economic phenomena. This phenomenon appears to be mirrored in other social science departments across the UK.

Moreover, despite the school's commitment to the provision of quantitative methods training for all students, there remains a tendency

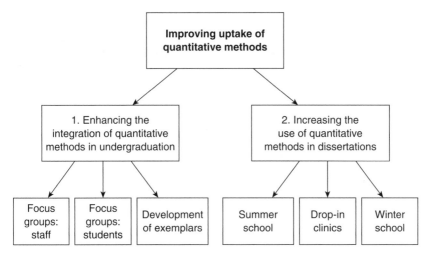

Figure 7.1   Project activities

among both students and (to some extent) staff to regard this training as a 'stand-alone' activity, which is at best imperfectly integrated with the study of substantive subject areas. This is an inherent problem where quantitative methods are taught in separate units/modules, as is the case both here and in many UK higher education establishments. The School of Social Sciences at Southampton, with its extensive in-house expertise in quantitative methods and its multidisciplinary programme structure within a common administrative framework, has therefore provided an appropriate site for exploring the processes of integration and investigating how the barriers to wider use of quantitative methods can be overcome. The work was carried out by one full-time research assistant with some senior staff input.

This chapter reports on some of the findings of two related projects, the first aiming at enhancing the integration of quantitative methods skills in the broader undergraduate curricula, with a focus on first and second year undergraduates and modules, while the second aimed at increasing the use of quantitative methods in third year undergraduate dissertations in disciplines where the use of such methods has been historically low. The project activities are summarised in Figure 7.1.

As a first step, a series of focus groups were held with student and staff in order to explore: the perceptions of the relationship between quantitative methods training and learning in substantive subject areas; the barriers to fuller integration of curricula; and the actions which could be undertaken to overcome such barriers. We shall report generic findings from this qualitative research that may be applicable to institutions elsewhere, before discussing the actions that resulted and an early evaluation of the impact these actions have had.

Understanding the barriers: attitudes to learning and teaching quantitative methods

The sample frame for the six focus groups with students was all first and second year undergraduates studying degree programmes in politics and international relations, sociology and social policy, social work, and applied social sciences during the spring term of 2007 (n = 478). The total number of student participants was 30. In addition, two focus groups were held with staff. Despite our best efforts in recruiting participants, with all staff within the respective disciplines invited to attend (n = 80), nine members of staff attended the first group, whereas only two attended the second. The participants were a self-selected group who were likely to have had a particular interest in quantitative methods, thus the views expressed here are unlikely to be representative of all students and staff. Although the data from the student and staff focus groups were analysed separately, a number of common themes emerged. The most striking finding among both students and staff when asked their views on quantitative methods was a fear of numbers and mathematics.

> Because it's maths people panic about it straight away before we've even started. (Second year student)

> So I know that I've got a bit of a block against it ... But it's not hostility, it's just I don't feel all that wonderfully competent in that area myself. (Staff member)

Students' fear of quantitative methods was exacerbated because they felt they had not known there was going to be a mathematical element to their degree, despite it being advertised in the prospectus. Our consultation with staff revealed that when advertising the course there was often a tendency to 'play it down', as it was assumed the quantitative element would put students off applying. Conversely, on completion of the degree staff said they tended to encourage students to positively highlight this element of their training because it is seen to increase employability. The initial 'surprise' could be viewed as a contributing factor to the overall nervousness among students about quantitative methods:

> It seemed last year that a lot of people didn't realise that we were going to be doing it as part of the degree course. I heard a lot of people saying 'What? Stats!' (Second year student)

Students were also apprehensive about the academic level at which the course would be delivered. As first year students, with little experience of university, many were concerned that the course would be conveyed at a higher level than they had previously experienced. This led to unease that they may not achieve a good result in the examination, thereby heightening their overall anxiety regarding quantitative methods.

> When I realised, when I first came and started doing the course, that we are going to be doing quantitative methods, I was scared really ... it brings to mind, like, people that have ... an A level in, like, maths, and it's 'oh my gosh this is going to be really hard'.

Many students revealed that they did not understand the course title and this in itself was also a cause of anxiety.

> I think a lot of people were just, 'Aghh! I don't understand', you know, and the whole term was just, like, you know, it wasn't really very explained what it actually sort of meant?

The fear of number expressed by staff appeared to be intrinsically linked to their personal confidence in carrying out quantitative methods, verbalising how they considered the use of quantitative techniques unattainable. One participant said:

> With some of the very clever technical stuff about multilevel modelling or regression or whatever, you know I think, even if I were 20 and were, you know, very determined, I would still not be able to do the clever things like that, and even if I spent a lifetime trying to do it, still wouldn't be able to do the clever things that these really clever people can.

A lack of quantitative methods training also contributes to this fear. While the majority of staff had engaged with some quantitative methods during their career, only a couple of staff in our focus groups were currently using it in research. Staff fears of quantitative methods were mainly with respect to teaching. Most said they were comfortable seeking help for the purpose of their own research but felt they were not experienced or current enough to use it in teaching:

> I am also aware that I, myself, would feel very, very uneasy about teaching anything with any quantitative material in it.

The overwhelming consensus among staff attending our focus groups was the opinion that quantitative methods was 'not for them':

> Well if I'm honest, then probably my first reaction is 'Oh that's not for me'.

This view was also expressed by students, who elaborated and rationalised why it was 'not for them', believing that they chose their degree discipline because they had a 'language brain' which lends itself to essay-based subjects (seen as requiring reasoned argument about theory) rather than a 'maths brain' (which they see as having a pre-defined right or wrong answer). Both first and second year students held this belief, although it appeared to strengthen over time with students in the second year believing the two 'types' of thinking were mutually exclusive; one cannot not be good at both essay-based and mathematical subjects.

> I think it's hard, cause some people have, like, analytical brains and some people have, like, mathematical brains, and sociology is so analytical that I think a lot of people just have analytical brains and can't cope with maths so well. (Second year student)

It was clear that students and staff were expressing similar attitudes and concerns regarding quantitative methods. The link between the two was likely to be complex but we could hypothesise that staff attitude will influence or 'trickle down' to students through their teaching and their position as role models. Certainly by their second year, students' views were more entrenched.

Perceptions of the relevance of quantitative methods

In attempting to unpick why students and staff felt 'it's not for me', we explored the extent to which students felt quantitative methods to be relevant, both within everyday life and more specifically within their chosen degree subject. The relationship was complex. One first year student explained how an initial negative attitude to numbers could lead to fears about completing the module, which in turn could lead to individuals questioning the relevance of quantitative methods in the curriculum.

> If you haven't studied maths for a long time and you hated it when you did study it, you're going to come into it thinking 'Oh no'... and a lot of people at the beginning were like 'Why does this kind of matter to social work, how does it like, how can you apply it to social work?'... they maybe found it a lot harder to study, to do, to learn it, because they weren't thinking it was relevant to the subject.

Perceptions of the relevance of quantitative methods varied according to the benchmark to which it was being applied. Most students agreed that the module had been relevant in helping them to appreciate statistics they encountered in everyday life, stating that they were now able to evaluate critically information they encountered in the media. Some students thought the module had been influential in opening up statistics as an option for them in the future, while overall students noted that their computer literacy would be valuable for future employability. Others suggested that the module had helped them achieve a mathematical literacy they had previously not felt capable of reaching and spoke of the self-achievement gained:

> It's a bit of a self-confidence boost as well. Because when you're sat in your room and you cannot do an equation and you think right I'm going to sit there, and you're there for three hours and at the end of it you get it, and it's right, it's a massive self-confidence boost. And you think, 'If I can do this then, you know, I can do it'.

Students discussed how they applied the attitude they had developed through facing their fears towards adopting quantitative methods for other units they were studying. Thus, the quantitative methods module developed an 'I can' attitude that was seen as relevant to other units.

> I think when we say like you know modules overlap theories, what I found with quantitative methods is that I overlapped with my attitude. It's like you know we were saying about how you know when you get an equation and you solve it and you feel really determined. It was that sort of attitude from quantitative methods that you brought into the other aspects of the other modules.

However, while studying quantitative methods was frequently seen as *generally* relevant, many still failed to make a strong connection between what was taught on the quantitative methods course and the *specific content* of their own degree. This was critical because gaining their degree is of foremost importance to students; if they do not feel quantitative methods are relevant, they are not motivated to learn about them. Some students went so far as to say the course was irrelevant to their degree.

> I think it's almost a bit pointless because some statistics obviously are useful, they're particularly descriptive, but once you start doing normal distributions it doesn't seem relevant to any sort of social science ... I think making everyone do something with that level of statistical work, it annoys people.

Overall, students felt it was important to understand quantitative methods rather than be able to manipulate numerical data.

> You need to be able to have a general understanding of it [but] there comes a point where it becomes useless really because you're studying it, you're spending a lot of effort on it, you're probably not going to be using [it].

The historical context of quantitative methods was presented by staff as an important influence on how they viewed its relevance. Discussions highlighted the different traditions of various disciplines in the methods used. For example, staff drew a distinction between 'number crunching' and 'theory' noting that a strong tradition favouring 'thinking theoretically' exists:

> I think in politics, particularly in the UK, you can develop a career without ever having to [use quantitative methods], and it's quite interesting, that quite a few people have developed a kind of position which they can validate as to why they don't ever need to either.

It was also suggested that the technical nature of quantitative methods and the focus on the aggregate rather than the individual have led to a rejection of it in the past. However, staff noted methodological traditions, particularly in sociology and social work, were changing and a move to more quantitative research is now taking place.

> Certainly within social work ... that awe if you like ... in the past has led to a rejection of it, as technical, scientific. Technical and therefore alienating, and alienating from those who use the services of social workers. And so I think there's been that reaction against it, which I think now we're coming back to a rather more considered position about you know what, you know numerical data and it's manipulation can contribute to our understanding of social problems and responses to that, you know without losing the sense of the individual person ... But I think because of this focus on the person, you know the technical expertise is seen as potentially alienating.

Lecturers recognised that this changing nature of methods within the disciplines had altered the character of qualitative methods, giving a greater connection between quantitative and qualitative.

> I think partly the fact that qualitative methodologies have in some sense come to, to mimic quantitative methodology in the sense that the analysis of qualitative data has become much more systematic and so on, so that in some respects it's actually more like the analysis of quantitative data ... I think it brings it closer together.

However, the legacy of a long tradition of qualitative methodologies in these disciplines was still evident, with some staff considering the relevance of quantitative methods limited. Most considered it important for students to understand quantitative methods but that it was not necessary for them to learn to manipulate data/numbers, reflecting precisely the attitude found among the students in our sample.

> I'd certainly say to know about them in the sense of knowing how they're collected and so on. Not necessarily to know how to use those techniques.

Staff also acknowledged that a disincentive for students learning quantitative methods was that staff were not seen using these methods. The modest representation of quantitative methods in published journals also impacted on students' views:

> One [reason students get turned off] is they don't see their staff doing it so why should they do it? Secondly they're being asked to do things when I

Teaching Quantitative Methods

think what they should be asked to be doing is interpret and be able to read. And thirdly is the examples used are not examples that have any interest at all to politics students.

Staff thought it was wrong to think of quantitative methods in isolation. They were aware that students were seeing the quantitative methods modules as separate from the rest of the degree and felt it was important to integrate the modules further into the curriculum, to increase students' sense of inclusion and enhance learning. It would be more coherent to think of a methods package or 'tool kit'.

> When we talk about quantitative methods in isolation that becomes a problem because you're isolating it from the conceptual questions, from the qualitative, from the way that qualitative and quantitative can actually support each other.

They noted that it was important to make the relevance of quantitative methods in the substantive area clearer to students:

> I also think there's something about relevance as well, making it relevant, you know relevant, and I say this particularly for the social work students, so that they can actually, you know I mean, relevant through being able to contextualise it and making the links.

Integration and isolation

One strategy for tackling the problem of perceived relevance is to improve integration. Overall, students did not feel their quantitative methods modules were integrated with the rest of their degree, seeing more integration of subject areas across the social sciences as beneficial.

> I do think people think it's just a little bit of maths on the side.
> (First year student)
>
> I'd say they are separate, all by themselves. They distance, stats, from the others. I'd say they should have been more integrated. (Second year student)

They suggested that more use of quantitative examples during substantive lectures would enable better integration of the quantitative methods modules across the degree programme. Also, running quantitative methods modules in the same semester as substantive modules in which quantitative methods skills were applicable would help strengthen the link.

> I think definitely they need, I think they need more integration personally. I don't think there's enough.

This failure to incorporate quantitative methods into the rest of the curriculum gives students the impression that lecturers on substantive courses do not feel it is important:

> None of my lecturers have really used any quantitative methods at all really. But I think that they could make it a bit more, I think that they could incorporate it a bit more. Even if it's just a few you know, 'Oh this is the statistics that you get for things.' I mean sometimes they do show you statistics and things, but a lot of the time they don't incorporate it whatsoever, but it does kind of lead to the impression that they really don't think it's valid in some ways. And because of that I think then people that are doing the course then tend to have the same view sometimes. I don't think they encourage it as much as they should.

There was speculation that this infrequent reference to quantitative methods was due to some tutors in substantive courses not thinking that they were relevant, believing instead that a 'philosophical' approach should be adopted.

> *First year student:* It seems, they seem, separate. And there's no real reason why it has to be. And obviously the attitude of a lot of the lecturers, the other modules, almost feels that they feel they're doing something slightly higher. And particularly [lecturer X] is quite philosophical and I always get the feeling X doesn't really like quantitative methods creeping in ... I'm not having a go at X, but it's that kind of lecturer and you feel they don't really want maths.
>
> *Moderator:* What is it that makes you feel that way?
>
> *First year student:* Well it's more like abstract, and it's more about thinking certain ways and, well and nothing else, it's that.
>
> *Another first year student:* Yeah, 'cause it's kind of the stuff you're learning in politics is supposed to be like the point of course ... it's not contemporary as such, it's kind of skills that you can apply in any political situation ... learning quantitative methods are kind of not really necessary because you're supposed to be thinking so abstract and so, you know, so you can apply it to any circumstances so it doesn't really matter what numbers you use or what the figures are because it's, that's looking at the present'.

The majority of staff admitted there was little or limited use of, or linkage to, quantitative methods in the substantive lectures they delivered. They critically evaluated their own teaching, agreeing that this omission was sending an indirect message to students about the lack of importance of quantitative methods within the discipline.

> All the examples I choose to produce are really qualitative ones or maybe they inch into sort of mixed methods stuff. But what message am I actually, not explicitly, cause I think I'm probably explicitly saying we're all open minded, all your mixed methods great you know, and all this stuff and quantitative, but here's a [qualitative] example. (Staff member)

You know and it would never occur to me to sort of say you know from your stats, that we know from what you're doing in your stats that you know, 10 percent of the people in Britain are such and such you know, I'd never know to say that. (Staff member)

This is partly due to a lack of communication across the course conveners, leading to staff being unaware which quantitative methods are being taught to students, and when they are being taught them.

They just go off and do their units and they come back and we don't really know quite what they've done .... And also timing wise, you don't know what they're doing at that point in time. If you knew what they were doing at that point in time you might be able to say, 'Well look I know this week you've been studying this in stats, this is a study that has been, that makes use of those kinds of principles,' and sort of play up one that works with it a bit more. So I think that we need to work harder to connect.

The absence of communication was evident to the students, who were quite adamant that more communication between lecturers would improve the overall quality and learning on their degree:

There seems to be a breakdown of communication between the [statistics and substantive course] lecturers. (Second year student)

Just showing, you know, kind of a bit more knowledge both ways .... Between the different first year course leaders about, and it can be an odd sort of casual remark in a lecture about this ties in with ... (First year student)

Staff in our focus groups emphasised that stronger links, connections and dialogue between lecturers teaching quantitative methods and those teaching substantive modules were needed.

Basically a lot more communication really, and maybe some curriculum teams, which go across, across the disciplines. You know it's just, there's a lack of communication I think, about how we can help each other.

There was agreement that this communication should be a two-way process. More examples in the quantitative methods modules should draw on substantive topics and those who were teaching quantitative methods should acknowledge the value of qualitative methodologies.

I think one of the things that is reassuring is that if some of these quantitative experts, you know, acknowledge the value of qualitative work and then that makes the qualitative people feel much more positive.

Many students agreed, suggesting also that hints and tips about where information could be used later in their career would enhance enthusiasm for the module and increase its relevance.

It needs to be more specific, like, with relevant examples to our courses.

I think if they gave examples as well, like saying 'Ah well', when they are explaining whatever, Z-scores, then they say 'Ah well, in a typical job in an office you might use this for this' and then we could see.

A central issue in achieving this enhanced communication and integration is the question of *which disciplines* should be taught together, and *who* should do the teaching. The students were in favour of being taught quantitative methods in separate, single subject groups, by lecturers who were also specialists in each substantive discipline.

It would probably be a good idea for them to have, like, it would probably be a lot of work, but to have tutors who are, like know their stats specific to the course they are teaching.

Staff also discussed the value of teaching quantitative methods separately in each discipline, rather than in a general module taken by students across the social sciences. Some considered it important that students were taught 'in-house', advocating the importance of role models.

If you are first years coming in to do a degree in sociology or social policy or, well social work or whatever, know their lecturers in those disciplines, and then have a quantitative methods course taught by people in another discipline, they may well pick up that, 'Oh well all my role models in my subject are you know not people who are as interested in this'.

It was felt that teaching delivered by social statisticians, rather than from within each substantive discipline, benefited the students through greater expertise. On the other hand, this served to set quantitative methods apart from the rest of the curriculum.

[It has] been both a strength and a weakness I think. It's been the strength obviously in that you have that expertise there. It's been a weakness in the sense that it's, in a sense both students and staff I suspect, it's been a kind of bolt-hole and it's been a kind of added extra rather than something which is integrated ... So in a sense I think that there's always been a kind of structural barrier to integration.

However, while staff tended towards the opinion that teaching 'within house' would overcome the problems of integration, due to the problem of expertise this approach was also seen as problematic:

Because I think one of the problems with embedding it within the politics curriculum is that you can't because we haven't got people in our department who can do, who can actually reinforce.

While recognising their lack of knowledge in quantitative methods, staff pointed out that they could not be experts in everything.

> Don't think we can all be jack-of-all-trades .... Can we? And you know you, obviously at this level we're all trying to sort of develop expertise in, in a niche ... and we can't all be you know thoroughly brilliant at quantitative methods and be great post-structuralists at the same time or whatever can we, so ...?

Much of the restriction upon staff becoming experts in quantitative methods was due to restrictions of time and/or workload. However, some did feel it was out of their reach conceptually, mirroring the student opinion that it was difficult for those with a 'language brain' to also excel in mathematical-based studies.

> One sort of pre-conception of quantitative methods is that, is that a lot of people sort of are a little wary of going there, because they know that however good they become at it, they're not going to be as good as the real sort of experts, because the people who are the real experts in quantitative methods are always going to sort of be beyond, beyond reach, in a way.

It was also reported that the several social science staff with expertise in quantitative methods tended to 'get sent' all the students who needed guidance with it or wanted to use it in their final year dissertations. Because very few students wanted to use quantitative methods extensively, other staff felt it was appropriate that these few staff members should offer their expertise, so to some extent this meant that other staff did not need to learn it.

One member of staff summed up the majority staff belief that it was important for students to have quantitative methods skills and that teaching should reflect the link between discipline and methods:

> I think ... we haven't regarded it as two-way traffic as much as we should have done .... And I think we should be strengthening those kinds of links and looking at how you deal with teaching to strengthen those kinds of links. Partly because I think in my discipline, you should not be turning out a student with a degree in this area who has not demonstrated some basic level of competence in their understanding of those areas.

Language, pace and mode of delivery

A large number of the students found quantitative methods difficult due to the use of technical language and equations. They became confused by technical terms: lectures were difficult to follow because new information was introduced too quickly. There was not enough time to grasp new terms and concepts, causing confusion over which techniques should be applied, what it all meant and how to interpret results. Conversely, a minority of students thought parts of the module were too easy, leading to a lack of attention and boredom.

To overcome this diversity in prior knowledge students suggested streaming, with a separate group for those who had done A level mathematics:

> The people who had had an experience with maths before, and stats, found it too easy and therefore boring and some other people who found maths daunting were put off by that, perhaps because some of it they could click with and some of it was a bit too much perhaps. So again, maybe instead of that module, there was a distinction between perhaps a lower and another group of people who had had experience of it.

Some staff also favoured streaming by A level maths, but in the past this method had been problematic due to the stigma attached to those in the lower group.

> [Group D] they'd got an 'O' Level or equivalent, but otherwise weren't as, weren't going to be taught at such an advanced level as the people in A, B and C. And that was known sort of half-jokingly amongst students and some staff as 'quantitative methods for dunces'... I make that point because you know we've got some issues here that actually go back a long way, sort of deep in the culture.

Students saw lectures as the least favourable method of delivery. The majority of negative comments regarding teaching methods were made about lectures rather than tutorials or computer workshops. Students mentioned lectures being restrictive in style and not lending themselves to class participation, group work, time for reflection or the opportunity to ask questions, all of which were seen as essential to fully engage with the topic:

> Scrap the whole lectures and have three tutorials a week.

Many participants mentioned that the sheer number of people being taught in lectures was an inhibiting factor and felt they would be better engaged if the lecture size was reduced.

> In a lecture of 200 people it's ridiculous to teach something that complicated ...

Students preferred techniques to be broken down into small steps and felt this helped their understanding by making it less confusing. They believed practice was the key to learning, suggesting they would be better able to get to grips with statistical techniques if there was greater use of practice examples in lectures.

> Like an old classroom situation ... teacher stands at front, or lecturer, they give you a 10-minute introduction, 'This is what we are going to be looking at today, this is how you do it,' and then she/he goes 'Right get into groups of three, here is your worksheet, go through it.'

The staff members agreed that it was important that students were able to work in groups on more challenging statistical exercises: encouraging team-work in this way would lower student anxiety and serve as good platform for learning.

> There is a lot of anxiety amongst some students about quantitative methods, that part of the solution is going to be team working ... if it's then an exercise where a group of say six come together ... you know that students have this emphatic 'Oh, I've got to grapple with this'. If it's 'We've got to grapple with this', then it may just take on a different complexion ... set up group activities rather than individual ones.

The smaller, more interactive learning that took place in the tutorials was welcomed by the students, helping to concretise knowledge gained in lectures and enabling them to acquire the skills necessary to apply their knowledge independently. Tutorials also increased confidence in the subject through the support and reassurance of the tutor and practice at techniques.

> There has been things I just never thought I'd understand and in the tutorial they have explained it so well and you suddenly go 'Oh!', and I just think they make it sound so difficult in a lecture.

It was considered possible that discipline specific tutorials might further integrate quantitative methods by using an increased number of examples on topics they were covering in substantive modules.

> Tutorials you could just split it up to like applied social scientists students, and then everything you had would be related, which would make maybe a bit more correlation.

Students felt the computer workshops were invaluable in helping them understand the methods taught in the lectures. They thought the skills learnt in these sessions were an asset to them, increasing their employability after gaining their degree. Overall, from a learner's point of view, tutorials and workshops functioned better than lectures because of the more practical forum, smaller class sizes and opportunities for actively participating in discussions.

Overcoming the barriers

Following the focus groups, the second phase of the project implemented a number of curriculum changes that directly addressed the issues raised by staff and students. To address the themes of relevance and integration we worked with substantive course lecturers to incorporate quantitative exemplars into their lectures. At the same time, we also worked with the quantitative methods lecturers to incorporate more subject exemplars into the statistics and research methods lecturers. The aim was to make these two curriculum reforms mutually reinforcing.

In order to choose the substantive modules that were most suitable for the inclusion of quantitative examples, a full audit of syllabuses in politics and international relations, sociology and social policy, social work, and applied social science was carried out. This revealed that the different disciplines included lectures around the same topics, for example lone parenthood, the labour market, immigration, asylum seekers, globalisation and poverty. This finding was interesting in that it indicated a 'bank' of examples could be developed around key topics that crossed discipline boundaries, in a similar manner to the Mathematics for Economics: enhancing Teaching And Learning project ('METAL'; see Chapter 9).

Working closely with the lecturers we sought to provide a consultancy service where they could ask us for information on a particular topic. We would then develop two or three slides displaying this information in different ways so they could choose which best fitted their needs. Our aim was to reduce the workload for teaching staff, rather than increase it. These slides took the form of graphs, tables, numbers, proportions and quotations. This process was successful and encouraged us to believe that a further integration of quantitative methods could be achieved with little extra work for staff in the different disciplines. Staff who were involved said:

> It is good to be able to make a point and then to follow this up with 'hard evidence' presented in an accessible way. This models the value of combining narrative and quantitative data to our students from the outset and we can now reinforce this approach throughout the degree programme.

> I think the project of integrating more quantitative material into sociology and social policy lectures is a very good idea ... I am sure that in the long run it will help [students] to get used to the interpretation and application of quantitative data during their study.

However, it is important to note that we were not successful in convincing all of the lecturers to participate in this innovation. *There was some resistance, with a few lecturers refusing to modify their lectures to incorporate the exemplars.* This relates to speculation elsewhere in this book that students' negative perceptions of quantitative methods may be a product of staff attitudes.

At the same time, the project team also worked with the first year quantitative methods lecturers. For each of the disciplines – politics/international relations, sociology/social policy, social work, demography, criminology, and anthropology – specific, weekly online practice questions for the first year quantitative methods unit were produced. Each discipline had six questions per week and ran for nine weeks during the autumn term of 2008 (324 questions in total). Each exercise comprised multiple choice questions with feedback explaining the correct answers. The exercises were made available both for use online and as downloadable Word documents. In addition, six 'study guides' were produced detailing the data sources and textbooks on quantitative methods that were especially relevant for that particular discipline.

Creating subject-specific practice quiz material was a vast undertaking. However, based on student take-up, we feel this was successful. At the end of all modules in the school, students were asked to fill out a course evaluation questionnaire; within the first year quantitative methods course evaluation we added questions that would allow us to assess the quiz material. Completion of a course evaluation by students is optional; for the project, 158 of the students attending the final lecture filled in the questionnaire, representing over half of those who had initially enrolled on the course (n = 269). Those who responded may have been different from those who did not, for example they may have had a particular interest in quantitative methods, had a specific comment they wanted to raise or may have been inclined to be more studious than the others (since they had attended the final lecture). Of those who filled out questionnaire (n = 158), the great majority of students (86%) reported either that they had found the material very or quite useful, or that they were intending to use it for revision. Indeed, monitoring website usage revealed that most of the use was in fact concentrated in the revision period.

We also worked with the second year quantitative methods lecturers to improve the relevance of examples, arranging for substantive lecturers to give seminars in the second year quantitative methods module about the use of quantitative methods in their research. It was hoped these seminars would inspire current students to use quantitative methods in the future.

In summary, creating quantitative examples for use by substantive subject lecturers opened up lines of communication between groups and worked well where lecturers were open to change. Creating subject-specific examples for students was time-consuming but succeeded in increasing the amount of practice students undertook, and helped them to perceive the relevance of quantitative methods for the rest of their degree. Producing subject-specific resource guides gave students a single point of reference for statistics that were relevant to their area of interest.

The sister project: increasing the use of quantitative methods in undergraduate dissertations

In addition to the work on integration, a sister pilot project addressed the use of quantitative methods in undergraduate dissertations, aiming to raise awareness and offer encouragement and support during the final year. Students who gained at least an upper second mark on the second year quantitative methods module in 2006–07 were invited to participate in the project during their final year. We set this eligibility criterion because we felt it was important that students did not become over-stretched on such an important piece of work. However, in the end we did enrol several students who had narrowly missed the 2:1 threshold as they were keen to participate and their research questions could be suitably answered using quantitative methods. Twenty-two students enrolled for a summer school held at the end of September 2007, immediately prior to the new academic year.

Our students had already been introduced to data-collection strategies, survey design and analysis, and research ethics as part of their (pre-modified) second year quantitative methods module. However, previous research by Williams et al. (2004a) suggests that a common problem is that modules in quantitative methods are often too ambitious, covering too many topics, too rapidly. The summer school was designed to revise and extend students' knowledge through a series of formal lectures, interactive tutorials and hands-on workshops in sampling, questionnaire design, interview skills and computer workshops. This experience would provide students with the skills, support and confidence to conduct their own survey and/or to carry out secondary analysis of large scale government surveys as part of their third year dissertation. They were expected to bring their own research proposals to the summer school and to work on these in the tutorials and workshops. A three-day winter school held in January 2008 continued the support and learning begun in the summer school. All those who took part in the summer school were eligible to take part; 19 of the 22 did so.

As the summer and winter schools were held in vacations when many students would have been in paid work, it was decided to reimburse them for loss of earnings. Students were paid approximately the minimum wage. Bursaries worth £150 were awarded on submission of a dissertation using quantitative methods, with a £250 prize for the best dissertation. Interestingly, although the financial incentives relative to student income were not insignificant, in the course evaluation only one summer school attendee said their main motivation for attending was money, while the rest said their main motivation was to improve their dissertation or to gain dissertation support. However, these were retrospective results, gleaned after students had already experienced the benefit of attending the school.

The intention of the two schools was to apply what we had learnt about teaching techniques from the earlier focus groups. We therefore afforded our students 'special' treatment as a means of changing the dynamics of the working situation and showing that we trusted them to act responsibly. We ran the schools in a separate campus building usually reserved for researchers and MSc/PhD students, and provided lunch and refreshments throughout the 9–5 working day. To build their confidence, staff treated the students as they would colleagues on a professional development course, which led to a relaxed atmosphere in which individuals could let go of some of their quantitative methods inhibitions and grow in confidence.

As well as statistical techniques, and finding/collecting/using primary and secondary data, we covered report writing and presentation. Teaching focused on revision and the development of ideas already presented in the first and second year quantitative methods units, as well as and signposting further information for the future, rather than attempting to cover every aspect. We encouraged interaction during the few lectures we delivered. Teaching concentrated on practical group tasks, interactive computer workshops, peer review, individual one-to-one tuition, worked examples and action learning. For example, rather than *lecturing* on questionnaire design we encouraged our students to get into groups, design a questionnaire, use it to go out and collect data, enter these data into SPSS, carry out some descriptive analysis, and discuss the issues and problems encountered. In this way, understanding the issues in data collection, the types of data produced and how they could be used was greater than what could be learned in a lecture format.

By the end of the schools, the majority of participants had developed their own research protocols, had drafts of their survey instruments and/or had sourced and downloaded datasets from ESDS or the Data Archive, and prepared draft data analysis plans. On the last day all the students gave a presentation to staff. They also received certificates to add to their curriculum vitae, acknowledging their hard work and achievements, valuable in their own right and distinct from the dissertation *per se*.

Drop-in clinics were held throughout the students' final year, to extend the support network for those carrying out quantitative methods dissertations and give them a point of contact where they could access information and advice. This was in addition to the standard tutorial support for their dissertation, because not all tutors were competent/confident supervising dissertations with quantitative methods. We originally intended that these weekly clinics should last one hour, but by the spring term much of our working week was being taken up with student queries. *It became apparent that students were overwhelmingly looking for reassurance.* Many came asking questions about things they seemingly already knew but gained confidence by discussing their ideas and thought processes with us.

Where students were confused or unclear about how they should go about their work, we were sensitive to the means of independent work and careful not to give them answers, but rather to point them in the right direction. The additional supervision time available to the project students, compared with the rest of their cohort, raised issues of equality. To go some way in redressing the balance we opened our drop-in sessions to those who had not attended the summer or winter schools.

Reflections on the project outcomes

The two pilot projects raised awareness of quantitative methods among both students and staff, not only for those who participated but also for those who did not. 'Talk' about the project quickly spread, with staff and students not directly involved in the project expressing interest. The work on exemplars increased communication between those teaching quantitative methods and staff in substantive disciplines. As word spread, staff not directly involved in these activities approached us for information to include in their lectures and their own research, or for help with advising their students.

Among the project students, we fostered a learning environment in which they were able to gain a deeper understanding of quantitative social research, its processes, techniques and implications. This brought students and staff together, and broke down pre-conceived ideas that QM staff were 'stuffy and boring'! Bringing together students from across the social sciences bridged discipline boundaries, with students forming strong bonds with one another through their shared experience.

We encouraged them to think realistically about data collection or indeed if they needed to collect primary data at all, given the wealth of secondary resources available they had previously not known about. Eighteen of our original 22 students went on to use an element of quantitative methods in their dissertations. Six students independently enrolled on an optional multivariate data analysis module in their final year. Four students have applied for an MSc in Social Statistics, all of whom have said they would not have thought this would have been open to them without the project activities. In addition, 24 students in the next cohort registered for our next summer school, which was held in September 2008. It is interesting to note that these students were *not* paid to attend. Their participation was motivated by the demonstration effect of the positive experience of the previous year's students. This reinforces our earlier finding that financial incentives were not the main motivating factor reported by students enrolled on the pilot summer school.

Key questions remain regarding the *generalisation* of the project lessons and experiences to other UK higher education institutions and the *sustainability* of the project activities in the university. Certainly some of the lessons have a broader relevance across the social sciences: the research highlighted the importance of ensuring that students can see the relevance of their disciplinary study. This involves making certain that the examples used relate to their chosen discipline and that quantitative materials do not only appear in quantitative methods lectures but are also used more broadly across the curriculum. Ensuring relevant, discipline-specific examples may be easier to achieve if quantitative methods is taught 'in-house'. However our experience shows that when attention is given to the selection of a range of examples, it is possible to achieve this on quantitative methods courses taken by a broad cross-section of social science students.

Moreover, our research highlights that there is potential for developing a 'bank' of examples around key topics that cross discipline boundaries. Monitoring the use of web-based quizzes highlighted that many students chose to take more than one quiz, i.e. they took their own subject-specific quiz and then delved into the quizzes for cognate disciplines. This had the benefit of increasing the number of worked examples for the students and of exposing them to concepts and issues in other cognate social science disciplines.

In our view the intensive quantitative methods schools and associated drop-in clinics were highly successful. However, the project highlighted that giving students both higher level tools and the confidence to use quantitative methods within an independent piece of work such as their dissertation was resource intensive. The summer school involved four academic staff for a week and the drop-in clinics expanded to become daily, all-day events in the run-up to dissertation submission. The University of Southampton decided to fund a repeat summer school in the year following the project and has made a commitment to do so in future. One option for the ESRC or HEFCE to consider is to fund an annual quantitative methods summer school that would be open to all final year undergraduates and for this to take place in a variety of venues across the UK. Our experience indicates that it would be important for this to be complemented by continued local support for students in order to back this up and provide students with the reassurance they needed to bolster their confidence. This may require offering training to tutors so that they in turn have the confidence to supervise dissertations involving quantitative methods. It is very clear that successful enhanced provision of the kind explored in these pilots cannot be produced from the present staffing resources for teaching in higher education institutions. Investment at all levels is needed if we are to overcome the critical deficit in quantitative skills within the UK.

References

Economic and Social Research Council (2005) *Demographic Review of the UK Social Scientists*. Available at: http://www.esrc.ac.uk/ESRCInfoCentre/PO/releases/2006/february/demographic_review.aspx? (accessed July 2008).

Economic and Social Research Council (2006) *Call for Proposals: The Development of the Undergraduate Curricula in Quantitative Methods*. Available at: http://www.esrcsocietytoday.ac.uk/ESRCInfoCentre/Images/Specification%20for%20Call%20for%20The%20Development%20of%20Undergraduate%20Curricula%20in%20Quantitative%20Methods%20PDF%20Version%20REVISED%20VERSION_tcm6-15643.pdf (accessed July 2008).

Higher Education Funding Council for England (2005) *Strategically Important and Vulnerable Subjects; Final Report of the Advisory Group*. Available at: http://www.hefce.ac.uk/pubs/hefce/2005/05_24/ (accessed July 2008).

The Royal Society (2008) *A Higher Degree of Concern*. RS Policy Document 02/08. Cardiff: The Clivedon Press. Available at: http://royalsociety.org/displaypagedoc.asp?id=28851 (accessed July 2008).

Williams M., Collett, T. and Rice, R. (2004a) *Baseline Study of Quantitative Methods in British Sociology*. Birmingham/Durham: C-SAP/BSA. Available at: http://www.britsoc.co.uk/Library/CSAP_BSA_Baseline_Study_of_ Quantitative_Methods_in_British_sociology_2004.pdf (accessed July 2008).

Williams, M., Hodgkinson, L. and Payne, G. (2004b) 'A crisis of number? Some recent research from British sociology', *Radical Statistics*, 85: 40–54. Available at: www.radstats.org.uk/no085/Williams85.pdf (accessed July 2008).

Increasing Secondary Analysis in Undergraduate Dissertations: A Pilot Project

Jo Wathan, Mark Brown and Lee Williamson

The UK has a world-leading data infrastructure. Individual-level data (or 'microdata') are readily available to teachers and learners, principally through the Economic and Social Data Service (ESDS). Although some effort has been made to re-purpose data for learning and provide appropriate learning and teaching materials, these data are still under-used. Using them in teaching, particularly undergraduate teaching, is an excellent way of exposing students to the problems and benefits encountered in real research. Students are rewarded with an increased understanding of the real world as they develop their quantitative skills; skills which are in short supply and very much sought after in both postgraduate research and many employment settings.

This chapter describes a project to increase the use of archived survey data in undergraduate research projects at a UK university. We refer to this throughout as 'secondary analysis' (Hakim, 1982; Dale et al., 1988): although it is of course recognised that secondary analysis of *qualitative* data is possible, this lies outside the remit of the present chapter. The scheme involved the development of an additional and optional programme of training based on workshops and drop-in tutorial support for a small group of volunteer students in sociology. This training recapped previously received quantitative training and focused on skills more specifically suited to secondary analysis of real data, such as deriving variables and weighting. Sessions were based around a set of bespoke workbooks based on the fear of crime using data from the British Crime Survey 2000 (University of Manchester, 2003). These, together with two other themed variants, are available via the ESDS website. An unusual feature was the use of financial incentives to encourage participation at all stages.

We describe the approach taken during the pilot project, the issues that were pertinent to its conduct, including students' prior expectations, the resources required, and the permanent module that was ultimately developed. We reflect on the lessons learned during the period, and how these have informed our thinking about the development of methods teaching within the undergraduate curricula. We also reflect more generally upon the issues facing teachers who wish to encourage the use of secondary data in teaching, and provide information about the resources available to them. While the pilot was aimed solely at sociology students, the issues discussed in this chapter have a wider applicability in the social sciences. The chapter may be of particular interest to criminologists as the materials produced relate to questions on the fear of crime asked in the British Crime Survey (BCS).

Background to the project

In common with other studies described in this volume, this project was part of a programme funded by the Economic and Social Research Council (ESRC) responding to the deficit of quantitative skills among undergraduates and the higher age of the social science community as compared with the natural sciences (Mills et al., 2005). It can be seen as having three key elements:

- The innovation was targeted at sociology students, a disciplinary group with a documented 'gap' in quantitative skills, and known anxieties about quantitative methods (Williams et al., 2004).
- The approach taken involved encouraging the use of pre-existing under-used data holdings, which have already been paid for by the ESRC, but which are seen to have obstacles to their use (Rice et al., 2001).
- Financial inducements were used to encourage student participation.

There continues to be considerable resistance to quantitative methods among sociology students. The problem has been well described by Williams et al. (2004) in their benchmark study of quantitative methods in UK sociology. Williams et al. found that students viewed quantitative research negatively, sometimes on the basis of negative accounts given by lecturers. However, their study also revealed a number of positive strategies by which students felt these negative views could be countered. These included greater use of contemporary examples as well as examples that related to students' own interests and more emphasis on data interpretation. Staff surveyed were keen for students to do their own primary research, although they also felt that there was a place for secondary analysis, even if this was currently limited by a lack of familiarity with the available datasets and how to access them. Frighteningly, participants in a survey conducted at the British Sociological Association annual conference, as part of the same study, felt that around three-quarters of students were not numerate and that they had actually chosen to study sociology in order to avoid working with numerical data. This research followed a previous content analysis of journals and British Sociological Association conference papers that showed that only 15% used quantitative methods and 7% used mixed methods, concluding that quantitative methods were currently under-used (Payne et al., 2004).

In a separate inquiry into the use of numerical data in learning and teaching (Rice et al., 2001) only one quarter of respondents to a national survey, who had used data in teaching, said that they considered using nationally funded academic data services provided by the UK Data Archive, MIMAS (at Manchester) or EDINA (at Edinburgh), although levels were somewhat higher among methods teachers. Obstacles to use included a lack of awareness of available materials, the resources (particularly teachers' time) required to prepare data, and the perceived complexity of registration requirements. Low levels of use of these data in learning and teaching are disappointing for several reasons:

- Making data available for teaching purposes represents a considerable investment of public funds and there is an understandable interest, on the part of the funders, to encourage maximum benefit to be obtained.
- The data are of exceptionally good quality and well documented.
- With thousands of datasets available covering a very wide range of topics, and increasingly well-developed systems for resource discovery it is often possible to locate a dataset which fits particular needs, or interests, well.
- Once past the initial barriers of learning an analysis package such as SPSS, students can quite quickly start enjoying exploring and deriving interesting results from the substantively rich resources of data available.
- An increasing amount of resources has been dedicated to easing the way for teachers, including 'cut-down' teaching datasets and accompanying learning resources designed to facilitate use by new and inexperienced users.

It should be noted that the data infrastructure has been subject to some reorganisation since Rice et al.'s study was conducted. Most noticeably work previously undertaken at the UK Data Archive and MIMAS has been brought together under the auspices of the new ESDS. The ESDS has a distributed structure, with the UK Data Archive holding many of its previous functions and a management oversight function, with specialist services in qualitative data (at Qualidata, Essex), international data (at Essex and Manchester), large continuous survey series (at Manchester and Essex) and longitudinal data (at Essex) (Cole et al., 2008). The new service has a wider role than was previously the case and has sought to respond to some of the obstacles to the use of numerical data in teaching identified by Rice et al.

The curriculum context of the Manchester project

The project was undertaken by staff at the Cathie Marsh Centre for Census and Survey Research (CCSR). The CCSR is an interdisciplinary research unit, focused on quantitative methods, and also home to two national data services: the government sub-service of the ESDS; and the support unit for the Samples of Anonymised Records. The CCSR typically has limited involvement in undergraduate teaching in the School of Social Science despite being active in postgraduate training. In this project, CCSR staff were employed to provide a small consultative input, while a research associate conversant with ESDS resources was employed to produce materials for the course.

The project captured sociology students in their second year at the University of Manchester in the academic year 2006–07 and continued through the year 2007–08. The timing was designed to fit with the students' normal dissertation training and supervision: students are provided with formal dissertation training in the second semester of their second year, before submitting a final proposal in the first semester of their final (third) year, with completed dissertations submitted in late spring. At the time of writing, students had completed their participation in the project and the project was moving into a period of evaluation and dissemination. An external evaluation report for the project is now available (Falkingham and McGowan, 2008).

Prior to the pilot project, second year sociology students at Manchester received research methods training in a series of separate five-week modules spread over the year, culminating in a 'research design' unit towards the end of the second semester. Quantitative methods were taught in a separate, five-week long module, but no specialist training in secondary analysis was provided in the existing degree programme. The project was offered as an optional extra to students taking sociology, or history and sociology degrees. It operated with features that were clearly atypical of much mainstream teaching (most notably the resources to produce bespoke training materials, and for inducement payments to students to encourage participation). However, the project has now spawned a secondary analysis module within the undergraduate programme, which provides a more sustainable legacy.

Structure of the project

Initial contact with students was made during the research training module in year two of their degrees. At this point students had already received some quantitative training, but were typically still some way from committing to a particular project or methodology for their dissertations. Given a climate where student interest, experience and confidence in using quantitative data were perceived to be low, recruitment onto an optional and non-credit bearing quantitative training programme was one of the project's major challenges. The strategy was to present the initiative within the context of pragmatic student concerns about final year dissertations. Thus permission was gained to talk directly to second year students as part of their formal dissertation research training, one session of which was devoted specifically to the use of quantitative methods.

This session was used to showcase the potential offered by the UK's rich survey resource, with exemplars chosen to map onto popular interests within the undergraduate sociology population. The training programme was presented as an opportunity to explore this further with 'hands-on' experience of working with real survey data. The focus was on the richness and variety of the data, the ease with which students could access the data and the potential of using survey analysis to address interesting and important research questions. Little emphasis at this stage was put on the statistical and technical SPSS skills required to undertake analysis, though the value to curriculum vitae of acquiring quantitative research skills over the course of the programme was stressed. Supported by the financial incentives offered through the project (£100 for participation in the training programme), this strategy resulted in almost half of the class applying to participate on the spot.

The first workshop (conducted in late May of the students' second year) provided an opportunity to discuss prior attitudes and experience, students' self-perceptions being seen elsewhere as a major determinant of success or failure (e.g. in Walters' (2007) discussion of meta-learning). This was undertaken by means of a group discussion and individual questionnaires that allowed us to produce baseline information about the group's perception of competence. The information enabled us to better target the content of the following workshops to the needs of the group.

A second aim of the first workshop was to provide participants with a clear sense of the potential of secondary analysis in research, focusing on how research questions can be approached using secondary data, and the associated tasks of searching for data and evaluating their fitness for purpose. This session therefore provided students' with insight into the types of project for which secondary analysis might be most appropriate. It was hoped that this intervention might be a timely one as students would be contemplating their dissertation topics during the summer preceding their final year.

On return to the university after the summer break, a further four three-hour workshops focused on the practical aspects of conducting secondary analysis with real data obtained from the ESDS. The content of these workshops was intended to build from students' existing competences and interests, and develop their skills and confidence in working independently on real datasets. A key learning resource was a workbook based on the BCS teaching dataset, which was relatively straightforward to use, while also satisfying the interests of many students as assessed in workshop 1. In terms of skills covered, the emphasis was on the data manipulation skills required to conduct meaningful work with a large scale dataset (such as selecting subpopulations, recoding and weighting) rather than higher level statistical skills (statistical testing related to inference was therefore omitted).

The financial incentive of £100 was offered to students who attended *all five* training sessions. Although no pressure was applied to persuade them to adopt secondary analysis for their actual dissertations, a further £100 was available to those students who submitted a dissertation with a secondary analysis component. For those who did opt for this route, a system of drop-in tutorial support (staffed by a PhD student) was made available on most Friday afternoons during the writing period. A final incentive payment was offered in the form of a prize for the best dissertation including a secondary analysis component.

The participants

A total of 14 students participated in the project. Given the subject of the training programme and the element of self-selection, one might expect the profile of participants to be more quantitatively experienced and confident compared with the wider cohort of sociology students. No conditions were stipulated beyond having attained a pass in a five-week quantitative methods course that was compulsory for all Second Year students. All the volunteer participants had GCSE or equivalent maths (a stipulation for all sociology undergraduates): three at grade A, eight at B (the modal grade), one at C and one at D. Only one student had A level maths or the equivalent, at grade C.

The students were asked to complete an initial self-evaluation of their experience and attitudes towards working with quantitative data (Table 8.1).

Table 8.1   Participants' views about quantitative methods at the start of the project (counts)

Views on quantitative methods	Agree	Neither agree or disagree	Disagree
Learning statistics makes me anxious	5	3	6
Sociology students should not have to study statistics	2	1	11
Qualitative methods tell you more about the social world	1	10	3
I'd rather write an essay than analyse data	5	6	3
Qualitative research is more interesting than quantitative work	3	9	4
Qualitative research is easier than quantitative work	1	8	5

Table 8.2 Participants' perceived barriers to secondary analysis at the start of the project (counts)

Barriers to a dissertation based on secondary analysis of a survey dataset	Agree	Not sure	Disagree
I lack knowledge about the datasets available to me	5	4	5
I lack the SPSS skills required	3	4	7
I would struggle with the interpretation of output	3	0	11
I do not find survey analysis interesting	2	2	10
Survey analysis will not answer my question of interest	5	5	4

None of the 14 said that they had particularly struggled with the prior quantitative methods course, though five expressed anxiety about learning statistics. Some stereotypes concerning sociology students were rejected, with only three of the 14 believing that qualitative research was 'more interesting' than quantitative work, and only one agreeing that qualitative work 'told you more about the social world'.

When specifically asked about barriers to undertaking a dissertation using secondary analysis, relatively few identified barriers relating to a lack of interest in, or perceived suitability of, the survey method (Table 8.2). Instead, 'a lack of knowledge about the available data' was the statement reporting the highest level of agreement (eight students). It was notable that the perceived barriers were not restricted to SPSS skills but extended to a lack of knowledge about which data were available and how to evaluate them. In this sense our students faced the same obstacles identified by Rice et al. (2001) in their evaluation.

However, when asked to rate their ability against specific competencies (Table 8.3) there was a widespread lack of confidence in fairly basic techniques that would be required for any independent secondary analysis (such as for a dissertation). Thus only a minority were confident about drawing sample subsets (four) and recoding (one), while none at all were confident about using a control variable in a three-way cross-tabulation.

In line with the project's conviction that the barrier to greater use of quantitative methods for most sociology students was not numerical competency but a more fundamental lack of awareness of what was available and its relevance to their fields of interest, the remit for the first 'initiation' workshop was explicitly about engaging and enthusing students in the potential of secondary data analysis, and the richness of the available data. Crucially the session was designed to enable students to discover and explore that potential themselves. Rather than getting them to work mechanically through pre-defined exemplars, students were shown the tools by which to

Table 8.3 Participants' self-reported competencies in quantitative research at the start of the project (counts, based on a five-point Likert scale)

Selected competency	1–2 (unable)	3 (neutral)	4–5 (able)
Locate social survey data for use in a secondary analysis	5	4	5
Evaluate suitability of a survey dataset to answer a research question	3	4	7
Open a dataset in SPSS and produce frequency tables and graphs for single variables	3	0	11
Derive simple summary statistics (mean, median, standard deviation)	2	2	10
Select a subset of a sample in SPSS (e.g. men aged <25)5	5	5	4
Carry out a simple recode	7	6	1
Use cross-tabulation to explore the association between two variables	2	4	8
Run a three-way cross-tabulation to explore the association between two variables while controlling for a third	9	5	0
Interpret output of basic exploratory analysis	2	5	7
Run a statistical test to see if an association was statistically significant	7	6	1

search for data that were relevant to their own topics or questions of interest. It was evident from the feedback forms that the overwhelming majority had been impressed by what they had found and were willing seriously to consider a dissertation based on secondary analysis.

Delivering appropriate content

As well as requiring the technical skills of data analysis, secondary analysis asks users to acquire an understanding of the origins of the datasets themselves.

This is essential in order to compensate for a lack of first-hand knowledge of the data collection procedures. Rice et al. (2001) argue that secondary analysts have to have information about the original methods, in order both to access data and to reinterpret them. As Arber (2001) simply states, secondary analysts need all the documentation they can get. Understanding the origins of data allows students to engage with the appropriateness of the data for a study (thus placing the onus on the student to determine whether these particular statistics will 'lie'). This is fundamental to interpretation and students' ability to assess whether procedures such as weighting are required or not. It follows that it is necessary for students to understand where to find documentation for themselves if they are to be empowered to carry out independent research. We therefore sought to show the students how to find this information by searching the archives and using the various tools of resource discovery now available.

Quantitative skills that are more likely to be important in secondary data analysis include selecting subsamples, recoding, computing new variables, dealing with missing data and weighting. The content of the year three workshops reflected this emphasis, as is indicated in Box 8.1.

Box 8.1   Workshops delivered

Workshop 2   Focusing in on your own dissertation topic
- Where does secondary analysis fit?
- Finding out about the potential datasets
  - Looking at questionnaires
  - Looking at documentation
  - Looking at frequencies

Registering for ESDS and ordering data (including licence conditions)

Workshop 3   Starting work with a dataset in SPSS
- Opening data in SPSS
- Running a 'frequencies'
- Things to look out for (variable distribution, missing values)

Workshop 4   Deriving new variables
Sample sub-sets
Understanding weights

Workshop 5   Moving on from one way frequencies
- Two-way tables
- Three-way tables
- Interval data
- Graphs

Reporting results

Some of these topics might be considered reasonably advanced issues, as only a bare knowledge of survey methods could be assumed. A thoroughly practical approach was taken to all topics using a combination of slides, demonstrations, group work and hands-on computer work based on prepared workbooks. An emphasis was placed on increasing students' confidence in correctly formulating and interpreting basic one-way and two-way tables of categorical data. A lecturer and teaching assistant were available during practical sections of work.

Weighting was a particularly challenging area for students who could only be assumed to have undertaken a five-week introduction to quantitative methods. A practical treatment of the topic was developed as follows:

1 This topic was introduced using graphics to show the different selection probabilities of individuals in smaller and larger households if only one person is interviewed per household.
2 Using a small artificial dataset, students were shown how (pre-prepared) weights could be applied, and how this affected the results.
3 The impact of weights, where the mean weight is greater than one, on n (as calculated by SPSS) was shown.
4 A new weight with a mean of one was computed, linking this area to that of deriving variables.
5 Students undertook an exercise applying weights to the BCS teaching dataset. They compared percentages with and without weights, and used prepared syntax to generate a new re-scaled weight.

Statistics theory and software skills were kept to a minimum. When describing weighting for example, the sole equation used was that for re-scaling the weight. However, students were provided with links to appropriate materials online to provide additional learning resources in these areas if required.

While staff presentations and demonstrations provided a structure to the workshops, the emphasis throughout was on active learning. This involved students in a variety of activities including, for example, interviewing each other about their research aims and working together to critique 'bad' report writing. However, a lot of student activity was in the form of hands-on sessions working with the data using workbooks. These workbooks are available for others to use or consult at the ESDS website (http://www.esds.ac.uk/government/resources/sass).

Producing the workbooks was a non-trivial task as we sought, from outside the discipline, to find material that would be considered relevant to the interests of the students. Time was necessary to identify research questions which would appear real and meaningful to students, to familiarise ourselves with the dataset, and to identify examples within the data that were suitable to the particular learning objective. The workbooks sought to provide step-by-step guidance, followed by questions with less guidance, in an attempt to move students towards working more independently. Each workbook

Getting ready for EDA using the BCS 2000 Teaching Dataset

Before exploring the dataset it is useful to know about the *Variables* tool 🔲 which opens up the *Variables* window which displays all the information on the variables including| how the variable has been coded (including information on missing values).

→   **To display this information either click on the 🔲 icon in the tool bar or by going to the menu: Utilities > Variables.**

The *Variable* window is shown below for the variable 'HomeAlon'

What is the value label for value 9?

Are higher valid (i.e. non-missing) values associated with more or less fear

Figure 8.1   Students were introduced to new material in a manner suited to self-learning

adhered to a limited number of related research questions in order to ensure consistency.

Greater emphasis on the workbooks' ability to stand alone as a self-learning resource meant that this work was more time-consuming than might be necessary in most teaching and learning settings. While workbooks in most practical sessions can be supplemented by teacher interventions, this is not the case where materials are to be deposited for others to use. This, together with our need to research the substantive material, meant that each workbook took several weeks to put together. This is considerably longer than we would expect a lecturer familiar with their area to spend. Some illustrative images from the workbooks are given in Figures 8.1 and 8.2.

Student participation and outcomes

The project had been designed, at the outset, to be a small one targeted at no more than 20 sociology specialists. We actually started with 14 participants, which we felt to be a satisfactory, although sub-maximal, number. Following the summer break a request was made by the students' discipline area that empty places be offered to students who were not currently on the project. Accordingly a small number of new entrants were taken at this point, on the understanding that if they attended all four remaining sessions they would be entitled to a reduced incentive payment. Figure 8.3 shows the attendance patterns among the students.

Secondary Analysis in Undergraduate Dissertations

You've got a dataset and research question.
You've identified some variables that are useful.
You can work with these variables to make them more appropriate.

Check your documentation to see where the variables have come from.

Check the values and value labels for your variables. Be particularly aware of the presence of missing values.

If a variable has too many categories, think hard about how you would like the categories to look before you attempt to recode it.

If you want to do some sort of calculation you can use the Compute command.

Remember that its possible to do recodes and computes for some of the cases (as defined by some criterion).

Microdata gives you a lot of flexibility – keep your research question in mind, and work out what you'd like to be able to show with your graphs and tables. This will help you to work out what you would like your data to look like!

Figure 8.2   Sections were concluded with a summary of the skills that students should have gained and be able to apply in their independent study

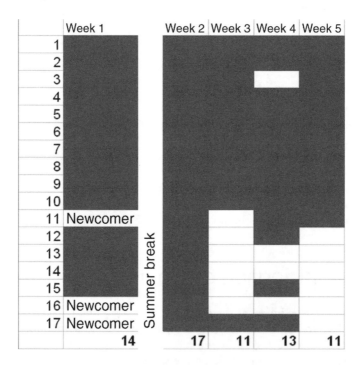

Figure 8.3   Student participation levels and attendance during the project

Each row in Figure 8.3 represents a student, each column represents one of the five workshops, with a shaded cell indicating that the student was in attendance. Nine students attended all workshops, although one other student missed just one and gave acceptable reasons for non–attendance. A notable feature of the attendance patterns was the large number that dropped out after workshop two. The most likely explanation for this was that this was the point at which students were required to commit to a particular dissertation project. It is likely that those who dropped out at this point decided not to pursue secondary analysis. This drop-out pattern suggests that the timing of the course may have been too late in the degree programme. Had we been able to finish the training workshops, a greater proportion of students might have stayed the course.

Four students returned to the project workshops despite having missed at least one session and consequently having ceased to be eligible for the workshop attendance incentive payment. Although it is undoubtedly the case that some students attended the workshops solely for pecuniary reasons, this suggests that the returnees continued to attend for other reasons. This is reassuring for the majority of teachers who do not have the luxury of being able to pay students to attend secondary analysis sessions.

Our discussion of project outcomes focused on two key areas: the measured improvement in students' confidence in skills taught on the project, and dissertations submitted. Students were given a questionnaire at the final workshop. We asked students whether they had found the workshops useful. Seven of the 11 present said that they had found these very useful, and three said that the project has been of some use (there was one non-respondent).

An indication of improved confidence was measured by repeating some of the questions asked in the initial skills inventory undertaken at the start of the project. It should be noted that the questionnaire was completed confidentially; it is therefore not possible to look at before and after reports for individual students. We provide, as before, the results in the form of counts because we need to be cautious about the results on two grounds. First, the data relate to those who were present at the last workshop: this excludes five students who dropped out of the project and includes one newcomer who joined in year three. Second, the data relate to very small numbers. The results in Table 8.4 are best understood by contrasting them

Table 8.4 Participants' self-reported competencies in quantitative research at the end of the project (counts)

Competence	1–2 (unable)	3 (neutral)	4–5 (able)
Locate data	0	0	11
Evaluate a dataset	0	2	9
Open a dataset and run some frequencies/graphs	0	0	11
Produce summary statistics	0	2	9
Sample sub-setting	0	1	10
Carry out a simple recode	1	6	4
Interpret a cross-tabulation	2	1	8

with those reported in Table 8.3. Reassuringly, Table 8.4 shows that students were more confident in all areas after the project than before. We are unable to assess the full extent of the improvement due to compositional effects; however it is clear that the increase cannot be solely due to attrition. Improvements appear to be related to the amount of emphasis in the course given to particular topics. Two-way tables were undertaken only briefly during the course (having already been taught on the quantitative methods course) and show only some improvement. The greatest improvement was seen in the area of finding a dataset. This was the area in which students had reported least confidence during the first workshop.

So did students undertake secondary analysis in their dissertations? The answer is a qualified yes. Five students submitted dissertations at the end of the project with a secondary analysis component. This is in part a reflection of the subject matter students were researching in their independent study, and partly a methodological preference on the part of the students for mixed methods. A list of dissertation topics that students were following during the workshops is given in Table 8.5. While some of these topics readily lent themselves to quantitative secondary analysis it is clear that for some other topics, different methods are more appropriate at least as a primary method. Those students who submitted dissertations as part of the project typically required at least limited help in approaching their datasets to get them into a workable format. However, the students' needs were not extensive: little use was made of the drop-in sessions, despite email reminders to participants. No more than a total of approximately five hours in total was spent in student contact with participants during the independent study period.

We found that students' expectations about what they could do with secondary analysis did decline over the period of the project. At the start of the third year most of those on the project expected to use secondary analysis in their dissertations. By the end of the workshops six students expected to do mixed methods research, another three expected a small component (e.g. a table or two). Only one student expected to do no

Table 8.5 Planned dissertation topics and associated data-sets in Semester 1, Year 3

Dissertation topic	Dataset
Attitudes to crime	British Crime Survey (BCS)
Background to gender differences in labour markets	Labour Force Survey (LFS)
Background to study into the Girl Guide movement	Young Peoples' Social Attitudes Survey
Relationship between poverty and crime	BCS
Sexual health (especially young)	Sexual attitudes and behaviour
Class homogamy	Samples of Anonymised Records (SARs)
Intergenerational differences in attitudes	British/Young Peoples' Social Attitudes Survey (BSAS /YPSAS)

secondary research at that point. Overall it appears there was a general scaling down of aspirations during this time.

Although one dissertation was based around a secondary analysis of administrative data, most dissertations were primary research using only a small secondary analysis component. As such, the analyses were typically located in the background or literature review sections. Analyses typically involved one- and two-way tables for the whole sample or named subset. These simple analyses nevertheless required skills in locating, assessing and working with major datasets, which the students obtained from the ESDS itself, and the limited role that the tables played in their research belies the skills the students' obtained to produce them. *We would advocate that the marking scheme for dissertations should explicitly give extra rewards for these achievements.*

What do we learn from the project?

A particular pleasure of the project was the enthusiasm of the participants. It was clear that they understood that the skills that they were learning were useful and marketable, and potentially of considerable use in their dissertations.

Although our understanding of the role of the financial rewards is currently limited, our impression is that the financial rewards became less important to students as they became more interested in the material; however, this was not the case for all.

Students informally fed back that they felt that the project was not optimally timed. The project occurred at a point when they were deciding on their research projects for their dissertation. It was felt that it would have been better to have learned the material in their second year, so that they had the tools in place well before the decision about dissertations needed to be made. Students did not undertake assessment during the course of the project; this might have been a shortcoming. By including the material within the standard degree structure it would be possible to substitute financial incentives for assessed credits. In such a format, the use of suitable and well-formulated formative and evaluative assessment might have provided an opportunity for the clearly defined challenges and formal feedback which can assist deep learning (see Norton, 2007).

Although project evaluation centred on the experience of participants in the pilot training programme, the real value of the project depended on the extent to which it could make a sustainable impact in the longer term. The key task here was to consider how the training provided could be incorporated more directly into the undergraduate curriculum. Without the financial inducements available in the pilot, efforts to recruit students onto anything extra-curricular and non-credit-bearing are unlikely to be successful.

Rolling forward ...

With this is mind, the pilot was used as a basis for designing a credit-baring module to be introduced as part of the suite of methods training courses offered to all second year sociology students. Specifically it was designed as a follow-up to the compulsory introductory course on quantitative methods. The new module was marketed as a way of building on basic quantitative skills to equip students with the additional knowledge and skills required to undertake a dissertation based on secondary data analysis.

This five-week course was designed very closely around the pilot workshop model, with each weekly session modelled on one of the project workshops. Thus students were guided through the stages of a secondary analysis project from question formulation to data analysis – in contrast to quantitative courses built around the learning of statistical techniques in SPSS, this course sought to incorporate these techniques within a more holistic framework with a strong emphasis on the process of operationalising questions, and searching and evaluating data sources. Without these skills many students are left unable to relate their training to the demands of a real research project.

The new module was formally put on the books for the second semester in 2007–08, attracting an initial intake of five students (the objective was to pilot the course with a small group prior to undertaking a concerted effort to recruit students for the 2008–09 year). Incorporating the format and pedagogic approach of the project workshops, the course was strongly practical and supported personalised student-led learning wherever possible. As an example, the learning objective relating to the identification and evaluation of datasets was met by students searching for data with which to address their own research questions. Formative assessment involved students completing weekly question sheets that required them to reflect on their completed tasks, with formal assessment centred on a 2,000-word write-up of a secondary analysis project for which the data and brief were provided.

Performance in class, the quality of assessed work and formal and informal student feedback were all positive. The students who enrolled were diverse and again defied expectations that they would only include those with strong quantitative backgrounds. All five passed the course well (with two first class grades), and had acquired and demonstrated the skills and knowledge to be able to undertake a final year dissertation based on secondary analysis of survey data, should they have elected to do so.

Resources for learning and teaching with secondary data

In this final section we discuss some general issues for teachers interested in encouraging learners to use real datasets in their learning and teaching. The resources listed are of use in both teacher-led situations and in supporting independent learning. Being aware of the scope of secondary data, and how to locate and evaluate these, is a key skill for learners and teachers alike. Finding data that capture the imagination of students with very specific interests is fundamental to demonstrating the relevance of secondary analysis.

The range of datasets available for secondary analysis is very wide, and many of these are available for teaching and independent learning. Data sources range from large collaborative comparative projects such as the European Social Survey, to national surveys such as the UK's General Household Survey. Both of these surveys have merit as teaching datasets. The European Social Survey deals with interesting methodological issues that are well documented in the data and metadata. The General Household Survey was used as the basis of older sociology teaching guides (the 'Surrey' files: for a broader description of data availability see Dale et al., 2008, or Arber, 2001). Increasingly datasets are re-purposed for teaching purposes. In the UK, teaching datasets are now available for a range of large cross-sectional surveys as well as the British Household Panel Study. Each teaching dataset is a cut-down version of the greater dataset, enabling students to engage with real data, without the effort of navigating a large file.

As data archives have become increasingly reliant on web-based dissemination (Cole et al., 2008) it has in principle become simpler to locate, interrogate and access data subsets for independent and teacher-led study (although many users still find the websites user-unfriendly). Dale et al. (2008: 521) suggest a five-point strategy for finding suitable data, as indicated by Box 8.2. It is also often possible to draw upon the experience and knowledge of librarians, or specialist data librarians within one's own institution. Using resources such as these, including helpdesks where available, can provide some shortcuts in the form of handouts and prepared teaching data. Data services may also have helpdesks to provide support should advice be needed. Box 8.3 gives an indication of the key sources for data access.

Box 8.2   Tips for locating data

1 **Search major data archives in your country.** Most countries now have one or more major data archives from which major data-sets can be obtained. In the UK, for example, the first port of call will be the Economic and Social Data Service. This service provides access to many of the data housed in the UK Data Archive as well as international time series data. Lists of other major European archives can be found on the website of the Council of European Social Science Data Archives (CESSDA). For archives outside Europe the websites of the International Federation of Data Organisations (IFDO) and International Association of Social Science Information Service and Technology (IASSIST) can provide links to relevant national and other major archives. These archives will at minimum allow you to see online lists of their holdings,

usually in the form of keyword searchable catalogues. Users, including teachers and learners, may also be able to directly download data.

2 **Look for data from data collectors.** If you are unable to find a dataset you know exists, the organisation that collected the data may be able to provide access or point you towards another organisation which can do so.

3 **Establish whether a dataset exists.** In addition to helping you to pin down a research question, your literature review will also help you to work out where data exist in your area of interest.

4 **Information sources and portals may be of help.** Some online data resources are provided in Box 8.3.

Box 8.3 Some data discovery resources for teachers of secondary analysis

Economic and Social Data Service (ESDS)
http://www.esds.ac.uk
This UK data service provides access to tens of thousands of datasets most of which are available for student use, including a number of teaching datasets for surveys such as the British Crime Survey, Labour Force Survey, General Household Survey and British Household Panel Study. Students can register individually online, or in class situations; a sign-up sheet is available to enable registered teachers to share data with students. Value-added documentation such as topic guides, SPSS and Stata workbooks is also available.

Council of European Social Science Archives (CESSDA)
http://www.cessda.org
In addition to providing lists of European data archives, CESSDA has a search facility that allows users to search across European data archives to locate key datasets.

Inter-university Consortium for Political and Social Research (ICPSR)
http://www.icpsr.umich.edu/
ICPSR is a US membership organisation. Outside the USA many countries have national memberships enabling students from outside the USA to access data. ICPSR has a broad catalogue and provides online study modules, for example a guide to analysing social capital based on Robert Putnam's *Bowling Alone* (2000) as well as data-based instruction material. Teachers have access to a batch account creation tool to enable teachers to deal with registration.

International Association of Social Science Information Service and Technology (IASSIST)
http://www.iassistdata.org/
The main benefit of this website for learners and teachers will be the extensive list of members' organisations, which provides useful leads when looking for data.

Data are not the only resource available to teachers interested in pursuing secondary analysis with their students. Resources for teaching are available online, varying from the class notes of individual lecturers to nationally funded learning and teaching resources. Teachers are unlikely to find that any resource fits their needs perfectly, but some resources (for example the materials produced as part of the Collection of Historical and Contemporary Censuses) are designed to be broken down into learning objects which can be disassembled and reused in small chunks (See et al., 2004). Box 8.4 provides some examples of learning and teaching materials that have been developed in the UK for reuse and are relevant to secondary analysis.

Box 8.4 – Learning and teaching resources for secondary analysis – some UK exemplars

Economic and Social Data Service (ESDS) Teaching Resources includes a learning and teaching page with links to relevant materials, guides and registration information at http://www.esds.ac.uk/findingdata/learning.asp. Teaching datasets have been produced for a range of datasets. In most cases these stand-alone cut-down datasets will offer a limited number of variables based around a theme, and a codebook. Links to teaching data based on the large cross-sectional government datasets (such as the BCS and Labour Force Survey) can be found at http://www.esds.ac.uk/government/resources/teachingdatasets.asp. Sampler data from the British Household Panel study are available for online exploration in Nesstar; a guide to this is available at http://www.esds.ac.uk/longitudinal/support/L1.asp. The X4L materials are a more ambitious attempt to produce a suite of teaching materials based around the BCS. These can be found at http://x4l.data-archive.ac.uk/. Teachers and learners may also find other ESDS guides, such as the guide to weighting, of use.

The Collection of Historical and Contemporary Censuses (CHCC) was a project undertaken in 2000 to produce a range of teaching materials that could be used online or offline based on the full range of UK census data. Materials include slides, notes and exercises for aggregate, historical and contemporary microdata. See et al. (2004) give an account of the production of the materials, many of which are now located in Jorum (see below).

Practical Exemplars in Analysing Surveys (PEAS) is a web resource available at http://www2.napier.ac.uk/depts/fhls/peas/index.htm containing learning and teaching material relating to the impact of survey design on analysis. Issues such as sample design (and the effect of deviating from simple random sampling) and weighting are well explained using examples from surveys such as the Family Resources Survey and Scottish Household Survey for users of statistical packages R, SAS, Stata and SPSS (using the complex samples module).

Jorum is an online repository of learning and teaching materials, from a simple object containing material relating to one learning object, to more developed complex materials. The Jorum repository contains the resources listed above as well as a range of others contributed and shared by teachers. Users can deposit as well as download materials. The Jorum website is at: http://www.jorum.ac.uk/.

References

Arber, S. (2001) 'Secondary analysis of survey data', in N. Gilbert (ed.), *Researching Social Life*. London: Sage.

Cole, K., Wathan, J. and Corti, L. (2008) 'The provision of access to quantitative data for secondary analysis', in N. Fielding, R. Lee and G. Blank (eds), *Sage Handbook of Online Research Methods*. London: Sage.

Dale, A., Arber, S., and Procter, M. (1988) *Doing Secondary Analysis*. London: Allen and Unwin.

Dale, A., Wathan, J., and Higgins, V. (2008) 'Secondary analysis of quantitative data sources', in P. Alasuutari, L. Bickman and J. Brannen (eds), *The Sage Handbook of Social Research Methods*. London: Sage.

Falkingham, J. and McGowan, T. (2008) *Increasing the Use of Large Scale Social Surveys in Undergraduate Dissertations in the Social Sciences: External Evaluation Report*. Available at: http://www.esds.ac.uk/government/resources/SASS/evalutionreport.pdf.

Hakim, C. (1982) *Secondary Analysis in Social Research*. London: Allen and Unwin.

Mills, D., Jepson, A., Coxon, T, Easterby-Smith, M., Hawkins, P. and Spencer, J. (2005) *Demographic Review of the UK Social Sciences*. Swindon: ESRC. Available at: http://www.esrc.ac.uk/ESRCInfoCentre/Images/Demographic_Review_tcm6-13872.pdf (accessed 20 May 2008).

Norton, L. (2007) 'Using assessment to promote quality learning in higher education', in A. Campbell and L. Norton (eds), *Learning, Teaching and Assessing in Higher Education*. Exeter: Learning Matters.

Payne, G., Williams, M. and Chamberlain, S. (2004) 'Methodological pluralism in British sociology', *Sociology*, 38 (1): 153–64.

Putnam, R. (2000) *Bowling Alane: The Collapse and Revival of American Community*. New York: Simon and Schuster.

Rice, R., Burnhill, P., Wright, M. and Townsend, S. (2001) *An Enquiry Into the Use of Numeric Data in Learning and Teaching*. Edinburgh: Edina. Available at: http://datalib.ed.ac.uk/projects/datateach/DataReport.pdf (accessed 20 May 2008).

See, L., Gould, M.I., Carter, J., Durham, H., Brown, M., Russell, L. and Wathan, J. (2004) 'Learning and teaching online with the UK census', *Journal of Geography in Higher Education*, 28 (2): 229–45.

University of Manchester (2003) *British Crime Survey, 2000: Teaching Dataset* [computer file]. Manchester: Cathie Marsh Centre for Census and Survey Research, and Colchester, Essex: ESDS Government, Home Office; Research, Development and Statistics Directorate, National Centre for Social Research, [original data producer(s)] distributed by UK Data Archive November 2003. SN: 4740.

Walters, D. (2007) 'Who do they think they are? Students perceptions of themselves as learners', in A. Campbell and L. Norton (eds), *Learning, Teaching and Assessing in Higher Education*. Exeter: Learning Matters.

Williams, M. Collet, T. and Rice, R. (2004) *Baseline Study of Quantitative Methods in British Sociology*. C-SAP: Available at: http://www.britsoc.co.uk/library/ C-SAP_Baseline_Study of Quantitative_Medhods_in_British_Sociology_ 2004.pdf (accessed 20 May 2008).

This chapter has been funded by the ESRC.

Mathematics for Economics: Enhancing Teaching and Learning

Rebecca Taylor and Angela Scott

The development and delivery of resources in the METAL project (Mathematics for Economics: enhancing Teaching And Learning; www.ntu. ac.uk/METAL/index.html) originated from a specific academic need encountered by lecturers in economics and related disciplines. Although universities vary in the emphasis they place on mathematical content in their economics degrees, almost all economics programmes expect students to study maths and statistics in their first year. However, since 1990, it has been increasingly the case that, in any given cohort of first year economics students, maths skills will vary widely and lecturers are no longer able to expect all students to have comparable depth of mathematical ability, or indeed confidence in their own maths skills.

This is largely the result of university expansion and the move to admit students from more diverse backgrounds. One consequence is that first year economics students may have a maths ability ranging widely from GSCE to A level standard (and their equivalents). Lecturers in economics, and on economics related programmes, frequently find that many students now need to refresh and improve their mathematical skills in order to comprehend the key concepts being taught in stage one modules. Without specific support that recognises and fills this skills gap, students lose confidence and the motivation to continue their undergraduate programme of study. Furthermore, stage one economics students often perceive themselves as having poorly developed mathematical skills in relation to their peers. Engaging students in learning and understanding maths concepts therefore often demands additional time and effort by lecturers. The lecturers' task becomes one of breaking down predefined fears, preconceptions and learning preferences, in addition to introducing the necessary concepts and helping students to identify why they are learning mathematics as part of their programmes of study. This in turn presents an additional problem for lecturers, who, having identified those students most in need of support, need to locate sufficient practice materials and illustrative examples to use in class. Lecturers have individual teaching styles and preferred approaches, and many 'off the shelf' resources such as course texts assume and dictate a programme of study that is not suited to the kinds of teaching and learning needed to plug the specific knowledge gaps encountered at undergraduate level.

The key problems become:

- identifying students' learning needs;
- locating discrete, flexible materials and resources that address these needs;
- finding sufficient examples to help students apply the mathematical concepts to key economic issues;
- applying them usefully in small and large group teaching sessions;
- using them to contextualise mathematics concepts in relation to the field of economics;
- developing students' interest and understanding of the subject;
- coordinating all of these elements into each lecturer's unique personal approach to effective module design and delivery.

The identification of these key problems led to the establishment of the METAL project consortium. The breadth of the consortium's activities requires a fuller account of the contributors and their working processes than a smaller scale project. Whereas most of the other chapters in this book focus on the diagnosis of numeracy problems, this chapter concentrates on a series of concrete aids to learning quantitative methods developed in the METAL project. Although we address the learning issues in economics and related subjects, many of the examples provide a model that could at least in part be transposed to tackle the quantitative methods deficit in a wider range of social science disciplines.

The project's rationale and structure

National concerns about providing interactive, student-focused, and inclusive learning enabled the METAL project consortium to obtain funding through the Higher Education Funding Council for England's Fund for the Development of Teaching and Learning Phase 5 (FDTL5) initiative. The project was specifically designed to produce innovative and interactive materials that addressed the changing needs of economics students, and maximised student attendance, engagement and participation with the subject of mathematics for economics. It was the goal of the METAL consortium to develop a range of materials that specifically highlighted the relevance and importance of comprehending the application of mathematical concepts by making clear their relevance for topics in economics.

The METAL project's materials were designed to be used by lecturers in both small and large group teaching sessions. These resources are presented on the project website as 'bite size' elements and can be used in a variety of teaching settings on a 'pick and mix' basis according to the lecturer's own needs and teaching preferences. All resources are also available to students in a format that can facilitate distance learning and/or can foster students' autonomy and ownership of the learning process.

In order to achieve the above mentioned ambitious goals, a consortium was established that drew together a breadth of expertise that would be able to provide a broad and rich set of resources. Major contributors to the work of the consortium include Rebecca Taylor, Director of the METAL project and Head of the Economics Department at Nottingham Business School, who specialises in the teaching of mathematics and statistics to students studying for a degree in economics or a related discipline. She is also Associate Director of the Economics Network, one of the 24 subject centres of the Higher Education Academy. Rebecca focuses on developing and delivering resources that specifically concentrate on engaging both students and lecturers more fully in the teaching and learning of mathematics. Martin Greenhow is a senior lecturer at Brunel University with an academic interest in mathematics education, especially computer-aided assessment and the accessibility of teaching software. With a team of his students he had already developed the computer-aided assessment package 'Mathletics' prior to being involved in METAL, and was engaged to produce a downloadable programme offering tests and assessment material. Ken Heather, a University of Portsmouth microeconomist specialising in business and industrial economics, joined the project to write and produce a set of video clips and animations showing mathematical issues in real world settings. With significant publishing experience in introducing economics to non-specialists, he has an interest in distance learning: prior to his involvement in METAL he and a team at Portsmouth had produced teaching materials that had been streamed online.

During the course of the project, support and feedback were provided by several professional teams and organisations, including:

- The Economics Network – which provides support specifically to university lecturers in economics. Its mission is to enhance the quality of teaching and learning in the higher education economics community by providing resources, running events, offering funding, contributing to national policy initiatives in economics, and also providing guidance to economics professionals (http://www.economicsnetwork.ac.uk).
- The **math**centre – based at Loughborough University, this was created to deliver mathematics support materials, free of charge, to students, teachers, lecturers and everyone looking for post-16 maths help. **math**centre gives students an opportunity to study important areas of pre-university mathematics (http://www.mathcentre.ac.uk).

- The Educational Broadcasting Services Trust ('EBST') – established in 1987 to spread specialist learning through broadcast and new media, the trust has its roots in the BBC and public service broadcasting. EBST online is now the access point for the best of EBST video for learning, with a focus on mathematics, science and skills development. EBST maintains the high academic and production standards set by its founder Jim Stevenson, former BBC Education Secretary and Open University Head of Programmes. EBST video is the result of a collaboration with consortia of university and college academics and media departments, supported by input from business and industry (http://www.ebst.co.uk/shop/).
- The University of Birmingham – which has extensive experience of the development and dissemination of teaching and learning projects and has contributed to the METAL project team's successful dissemination strategy. The project outcomes have been demonstrated to lecturers in mathematics for economics in over 40 departments of economics across the UK (http://www.bham.ac.uk).

The METAL project materials

The METAL project has produced four types of learning material, which are available through a common website. The four outputs are: the online question bank; videos and animations; teaching and learning guides; and real world case studies. In the following section we discuss each in turn.

The online question bank of mathematics teaching and assessment materials specifically applied to concepts in economics was created by Brunel University. This resource is presented as a set of executable (.exe) files which can be readily downloaded and launched. At each runtime the software launches a newly realised set of questions based on a specific question style, incorporating several random parameters whose values range over specified values or words or question scenarios; thus each question style generates millions of *question realisations* that can be delivered to the student. The question bank is divided into five key subject categories: algebra; economics applications; calculus; matrices; and numbers. It uses a range of *question types*, mainly: multiple choice, multiple response, numerical input, responsive numerical input; and true/false/undecidable. The random parameters generate question wording, correct answers, distracters, (usually extensive) feedback, and the appropriate question-description metadata and outcome metadata (both primarily used in the answer files).

Students enter their responses into the fields provided, and once submitted, the software generates feedback based on the answer given. The distracters are based on mal rules and are therefore able to generate targeted analysis and feedback to students. An 'additional materials' function allows students to source further reading and practice materials. This function also

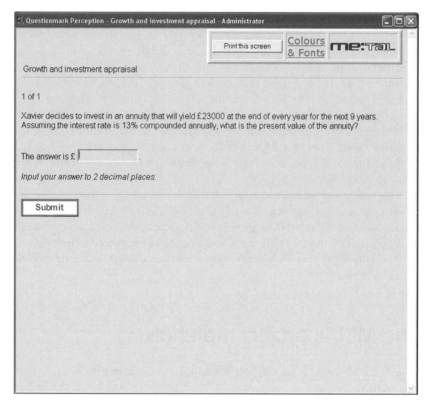

Figure 9.1 An example of one type of question screen

Reproduced with permission.

links back to additional METAL resources, including the videos described below, proposing selected films for background study and information.

An example of one type of question and answer is illustrated in Figure 9.1, and the associated feedback to students is presented in Figure 9.2. Mathematical expressions that carry through the random parameters are generated at runtime using MathML. Graphs and diagrams that carry through the random parameters are generated at runtime using Scalable Vector Graphics (SVG). The display of all elements is under the control of the individual student, who can set his/her own preferences for font size and family, and font and background colours.

The second group of materials was created by the University of Portsmouth and consists of over 50 video clips (see Figure 9.3) and flash animation files that can be streamed online or can be downloaded. The high-quality, 'mini documentary' videos utilise an on-screen presenter who discusses economics-based problems by applying them to real world situations. The videos present a range of intriguing economics problems to consider, and examples are drawn from a wide variety of settings designed to inspire the student. For instance, the calculation of percentages is illustrated

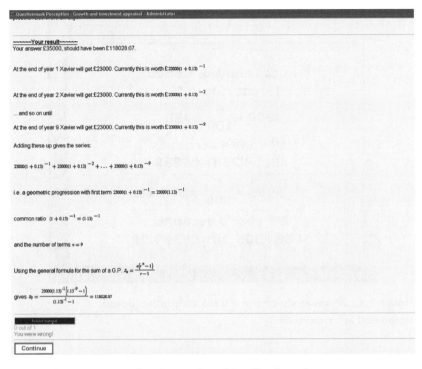

~~~~~~~Your result~~~~~~~
Your answer £35000, should have been £118028.07.

At the end of year 1 Xavier will get £23000. Currently this is worth £$23000(1 + 0.13)^{-1}$

At the end of year 2 Xavier will get £23000. Currently this is worth £$23000(1 + 0.13)^{-2}$

... and so on until

At the end of year 9 Xavier will get £23000. Currently this is worth £$23000(1 + 0.13)^{-9}$

Adding these up gives the series:

$23000(1 + 0.13)^{-1} + 23000(1 + 0.13)^{-2} + \ldots + 23000(1 + 0.13)^{-9}$

i.e. a geometric progression with first term $23000(1 + 0.13)^{-1} = 23000(1.13)^{-1}$

common ratio $(1 + 0.13)^{-1} = (1.13)^{-1}$

and the number of terms $x = 9$

Using the general formula for the sum of a G.P. $S_n = \frac{a(r^n - 1)}{r - 1}$

gives $S_9 = \frac{23000(1.13)^{-1}[(1.13)^{-9} - 1]}{(1.13)^{-1} - 1} = 118028.07$

Related material

0 out of 1
You were wrong!

Continue

Figure 9.2 An example of associated feedback and answer screen
Reproduced with permission.

Figure 9.3 A still from a video

through international comparisons in the price of consumer goods, the consideration of risk and uncertainty is set against the gambling towns of

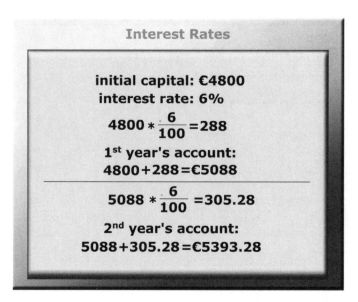

Interest Rates

initial capital: €4800
interest rate: 6%

$$4800 * \frac{6}{100} = 288$$

1st year's account:
4800+288=€5088

$$5088 * \frac{6}{100} = 305.28$$

2nd year's account:
5088+305.28=€5393.28

Figure 9.4   A screenshot from a flash animation board
Reproduced with permission.

Colorado, and the production and sale of French wine is used to illustrate simultaneous and linear equations. This is in addition to the many examples of more domestic economic issues, such as student loans, travel cards, and acquiring a mortgage. A typical film lasts approximately five to 10 minutes.

Each video presents a problem or concept, and the subsequent animation demonstrates the mathematical principles that can help solve or explore the problem. Thus the videos manage to place a variety of mathematical concepts into a real and pertinent context in a concise and effective manner, which is engaging and allows further class discussion where desired. Flash-based animation boards (see Figure 9.4) follow most films, and a voice-over examines the mathematical applications that can help resolve the issues raised in the relevant video. It is possible to view the animation boards independent of the films, as they can be streamed separately. The film pages also link back to specific question bank materials, encouraging users to practise the concepts introduced by the animation boards.

Nottingham Trent University was responsible for the development and delivery of the teaching and learning guides, and for developing the guide specifications and activities, which were then contracted out for authorship by economics lecturers at five UK universities in order to engage more end-users in the development process. The 10 guides cover the following topics:

1 mathematical review;
2 linear equations;
3 linear equations – further topics;
4 linear programming;

5   finance and growth;
6   non-linear equations;
7   differentiation;
8   partial differentiation;
9   integration;
10 matrices.

These subjects progress via a fairly basic reintroduction of key mathematics concepts through to more advanced topics. By allowing downloads of the resultant materials in both Microsoft Word (.doc) and PDF (.pdf) formats, tutors are invited to edit the guides for their own use.

The METAL teaching and learning guides are written primarily for lecturers and tutors, and present innovative and interactive approaches to teaching mathematical concepts to economics students. The guides include:

- the presentation of specific mathematical concepts;
- top tips;
- teaching and learning suggestions;
- seminar activities, which are also available as separate files in a PDF or Microsoft Word format.

The teaching and learning guides have been popular with initial users of the METAL project resources. We have also had strong positive feedback from students on the use of activities and best practice in large and small group teaching sessions. Each concept in the guides is linked to a related video unit and the relevant section of the online question bank (Figure 9.5). This useful design feature of the METAL website means that all resources have links and references to the other related resources on the site, thereby enabling users to provide students with a more complete and inclusive learning experience.

The Nottingham Trent University team then created an additional resource in the form of 15 case studies funded by a Joint Information Systems Committee Distributed e-Learning II (JISC Del II) project. These brief case studies (see Figure 9.6), available to download in a PDF format, identify and present mathematical concepts related to real world economic issues such as household credit, public funding, and competition in sport. The project team at Nottingham has also developed, and maintains and manages, the core METAL project website though which the case studies together with the other three types of resources discussed (above) are made available (Figure 9.7).

Employability

The principal and most direct benefit of the METAL resources is to allow lecturers to select from a diverse range of tools which can help enhance the

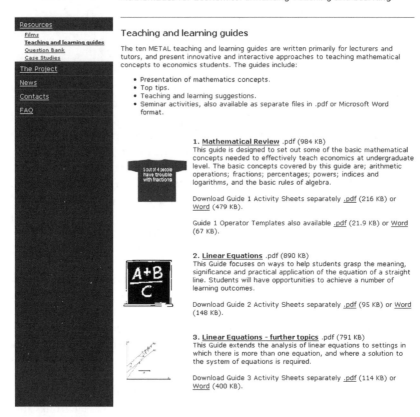

Resources
  Films
  Teaching and learning guides
  Question Bank
  Case Studies
The Project
News
Contacts
FAQ

Teaching and learning guides

The ten METAL teaching and learning guides are written primarily for lecturers and tutors, and present innovative and interactive approaches to teaching mathematical concepts to economics students. The guides include:

- Presentation of mathematics concepts.
- Top tips.
- Teaching and learning suggestions.
- Seminar activities, also available as separate files in .pdf or Microsoft Word format.

1. Mathematical Review .pdf (984 KB)
This guide is designed to set out some of the basic mathematical concepts needed to effectively teach economics at undergraduate level. The basic concepts covered by this guide are; arithmetic operations; fractions; percentages; powers; indices and logarithms, and the basic rules of algebra.

Download Guide 1 Activity Sheets separately .pdf (216 KB) or Word (479 KB).

Guide 1 Operator Templates also available .pdf (21.9 KB) or Word (67 KB).

2. Linear Equations .pdf (890 KB)
This Guide focuses on ways to help students grasp the meaning, significance and practical application of the equation of a straight line. Students will have opportunities to achieve a number of learning outcomes.

Download Guide 2 Activity Sheets separately .pdf (95 KB) or Word (148 KB).

3. Linear Equations - further topics .pdf (791 KB)
This Guide extends the analysis of linear equations to settings in which there is more than one equation, and where a solution to the system of equations is required.

Download Guide 3 Activity Sheets separately .pdf (114 KB) or Word (400 KB).

Figure 9.5   A screenshot from the teaching and learning guide landing page
Reproduced with permission.

student learning experience in mathematics for economics in year one. A better understanding of the application of mathematics to a wide selection of economic issues in their first year of undergraduate study then enables students to better understand and apply mathematics in the later stages of their degree programmes. Not only should this facilitate improved student achievement, but it will also provide them with a depth of understanding and confidence in their subject that can only help them to respond to the needs of future employment.

In other words, the project resources and their integration into the curriculum not only have a direct benefit, but can also contribute towards equipping students with the 'transferable skills' that increase student employment opportunities at the end of their degree programme. For example, the METAL resources promote the acquisition of presentation skills by students. Discussion/presentation questions are provided for each mathematical concept featured in the teaching and learning guides. Lecturers can

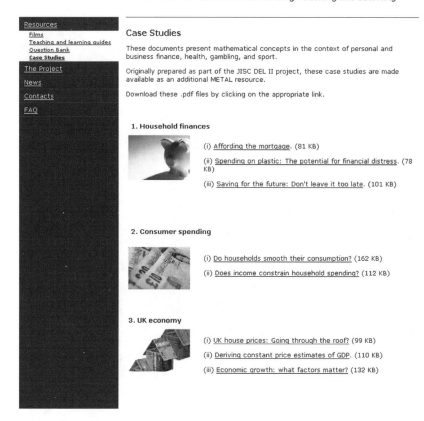

Figure 9.6   A screenshot of the case studies 'landing page'

Reproduced with permission.

easily adapt the materials, or use questions from the online question bank to assign quick and relevant presentation topics to individuals or groups of students. The resources offer flexibility in how, when and where they are used. This enables lecturers to integrate a video clip into a lecture or seminar session and so encourage students to discuss the content, reflect on how the mathematics concepts relate to other aspects of economics, and develop a deeper understanding of economics and its relevance to employers.

Transferable skills are now an essential feature of undergraduate programmes. However, opportunities to develop these work-related capabilities in the more quantitative aspects of the economics degree have, to date, been scarce. The METAL project resources enable lecturers to embed the development of these skills into the mathematics curriculum, which will, in turn, build a foundation for subsequent employment-related learning, both quantitative and qualitative, throughout an undergraduate's studies.

The METAL project

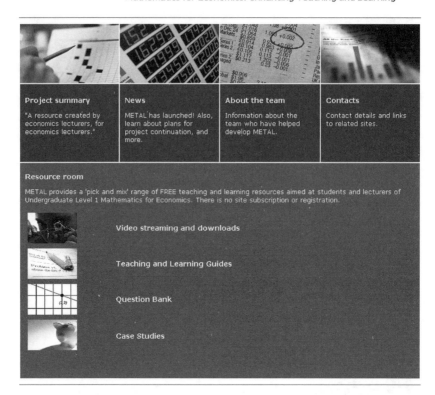

Figure 9.7   The METAL Project homepage
Reproduced with permission.

According to Andy Ross, (2007), Deputy Director of the Government Economic Service, the largest employer of economists in the UK:

> Most of the things that economists do don't even look like economics: adoption policy; money laundering (detecting!) ...

> The range of topics is truly astonishing.

The Government Economic Service receives over 500 applications for posts from more than 50 universities each year and the majority of candidates fail because they do not understand the fundamental principles, concepts and analyses of economics, and hence find them difficult to apply and easy to forget. The key weaknesses that graduates demonstrate have been identified as a lack of:

- communication skills;
- ability to work effectively in teams/groups;

Teaching Quantitative Methods

- capability to apply theory to real world situations;
- understanding of the requirements of employers;
- deep understanding of, and the ability to apply, key economic concepts.

There is no doubt that the pressure on staff workloads caused by more students, larger/fewer classes, a crowded curriculum, modularity and choice, and the demand to balance academic standards with maintaining student progression rates contributes to the number of economics graduates who lack the transferable skills that are most in demand by key employers of economics graduates. While no single solution will be found to solve this issue, the METAL project's resources were developed to promote greater engagement by students in mathematics for economics, while at the same time enabling lecturers to encourage the development of transferable skills in students studying their subject. The feedback to date suggests a positive move towards the integration of transferable skills development into the more quantitative modules at undergraduate level.

Dissemination and evaluation

A distinctive feature of the METAL project was the way the team developed and implemented a very intensive campaign to disseminate and embed the project resources into the economics community. These activities included conferences, seminars, promotional materials, advertising and departmental meetings. The team also delivered a series of 16 workshops to demonstrate the resources directly to the end-users and to talk them through different ways to incorporate the resources into their teaching sessions. The purpose of these sessions was two-fold; to disseminate the project outcomes to potential end users, and for lecturers of mathematics for economics to gain first-hand experience of the four types of resource. Each workshop was hosted by a different institution and included participants from the host institution and lecturers of mathematics for economics from the institutions in that region. Subsequent sessions with individual lecturers provided the project consortium with an insight into how the resources were being used in small and large group teaching sessions.

Project evaluation was conducted at key stages throughout the development process. The team engaged internal and external evaluators who participated in a number of events, including the Project Workshop at Kingston in September 2007 and the Lecturer Feedback Session in London in April 2007, the outcomes of which helped to inform and guide the development of the final project resources. The project team also commissioned an independent evaluation in January 2008, which involved a survey and individual interviews with a number of lecturers of mathematics for economics. A striking feature of the survey was the unanimous and positive support which respondents gave to the METAL project. All participants thought that the project was creative and innovative. While most suggested that METAL had set itself ambitious targets, all the respondents thought the project achieved these goals. Respondents independently identified different contexts and applications for the METAL resources. This confirmed that the materials can be flexibly used in a wide range of settings and can achieve a significant and positive impact on students' learning. Much of the project's success was attributed to working with a clear brief, good project management, and the proactive approach, which informed lecturers and supported them in trialling the new materials. Among the key strengths identified in the project were:

- the high quality of the resources and their wide applicability to the teaching and learning of mathematics in economics courses;
- that the resources and materials could have a wider application beyond undergraduate economics, e.g. accounting, business;
- that the applied nature of the resources was seen to directly address the issue of making mathematics easier to understand;
- that the resources could be used to meet a wide range of teaching and learning needs;
- that the materials were well written and offered interesting and engaging activities which accommodated different learning styles, e.g. kinaesthetic, auditory and visual.

An additional feature of METAL resources is that each resource is available to end-users under a separate Creative Commons license, mainly under the attribution – non-commercial – version of the licence. This allows users to freely copy and redistribute the resources, including uploading the resources to their virtual learning portals. In the case of the Teaching and Learning Guides, and the Question Bank, users are also able to make derivative works of their own. This is subject to the condition that they are not sold commercially, and that the source is acknowledged. This feature of METAL ensures that the project's key objective, to make available fully accessible and flexible learning materials, is made explicit and legally enabled. It also encourages end-users to treat the METAL resources creatively to inspire their own teaching and learning practices.

Conclusion

Economics is not the study of money, but is about choice and scarcity. Armed with an understanding of how individuals, industries, organisations and governments structure themselves and make decisions, graduates have the abilities and transferable skills which make them highly employable. A critical understanding of economic forces and structures, and the confident application of the insights that the study of economics offers, along with the ability to break down and analyse complex problems using both creative and logical principles, can be applied to a vast number of careers.

The reluctance shown by level one students to study mathematics as part of a economics degree will often date back to their GCSE or pre-GCSE learning experiences. There seems to be an acceptance that students will decide at an early stage that they are either 'maths' or 'non-maths' people, in a way that is less common in other subjects – for example, one hears fewer students claiming that their innate abilities make them either 'English' or 'non-English' people. Thus typically in the social sciences, lecturers will experience a particular challenge when teaching students who must learn mathematics in subject areas that are not strongly mathematical subjects in their own right. The lecturers' task then becomes focused on breaking down predefined conceptions/fears/preferences, in addition to teaching the necessary concepts for the chosen field of study. This makes the task considerably more difficult and accentuates the need to help students come to an understanding about why they are learning mathematics and statistics as part of their programme of study.

Lecturers often find it onerous to guide students through the process of learning key mathematical concepts and apply them to relevant economic issues. However, one of the key requirements of the undergraduate degree in economics is the need for a constant highlighting of the relevance of the mathematical concepts learned. This is an important strength of the METAL project resources in that they present maths concepts in the context of real world situations. Our project evaluation showed that both new and more experienced lecturers were enthusiastic about the availability of a set of resources that could enable them to focus student learning, so fostering independent study and encouraging a deeper understanding of the relevance of the mathematical concepts essential to the study of economics.

The METAL project outputs, while of specific interest to economics undergraduates, present mathematical concepts and offer resources that are of general interest to anyone wishing to improve their skills and understanding of mathematics. This extends not only to the more obvious areas of accountancy and business studies, but also to social policy and sociology, disciplines which traditionally have relied less heavily on mathematics but whose students need to re-learn some of the basic techniques. However, in economics, the confidence and ability of students to apply maths skills to different aspects of their chosen field of study are of critical importance both in terms of their deeper understanding of the subject area and their ability to provide employers with essential skills and understanding. The METAL resources, with their built-in flexibility and concrete exemplification, encourage lecturers to make the study of mathematics more interactive and inclusive, and help to incorporate the application of mathematics into the broader study and understanding of economics.

Reference

Ross, A. (2007) *Educating Economists for Government*. Paper presented to the Developments in Economics Education Conference, Cambridge, 6–7 September, http://www.economicsnetwork.ac.uk/dee2007/

Jorum: A National Service for Learning and Teaching

Jackie Carter

The best hope for development in the teaching of quantitative research methods is to pool our limited resources. The internet is now offering ways of sharing and exchanging knowledge, and this chapter explores the components of one collaborative scheme in some detail. 'Jorum' is a national service which provides a means of sharing electronic materials for use in learning and teaching in the UK's further and higher education. Its primary aim is to support 'communities' of lecturers who can share, reuse and re-purpose the materials provided (which cover all discipline areas). The name Jorum refers to a sharing or drinking bowl, 'a large drinking vessel or its contents', with probable biblical origins. The Jorum model is that its content, which can be thought of as learning resources, is made available for others to discover. The resources are intended to be downloaded and integrated into a learning activity within a user's local environment, perhaps for delivery via a learning platform, such as a virtual learning environment.

The service has developed, and continues to develop, against a backdrop of well-recognised commercial ventures that provide a space into which users can put their content to share with others. Examples include YouTube (video sharing; http://www.youtube.com/) Flickr (photos: http://www.flickr.com/) and Slideshare (presentations: http://www.slideshare.net/). However, the sharing of content is only one aspect of these types of service. What makes them interesting to participants are the 'conversations' or 'participatory activities' that take place around the content, and which justify the use of the term 'virtual communities' for those who engage with these sites. These interactive services are examples of what are widely referred to as Web2.0 or social media services, and usually provide access to 'single object types': video, or photos, or presentations. Jorum, on the other hand, extends this by providing a place where teaching and support staff can locate learning and teaching content of a *variety* of types developed for use in post-16 education.

To explain how this works, we begin by describing the context of the project, before introducing the component parts of the service – people; the website; the technical infrastructure; collections of resources; the creation of descriptive records ('metadata') to enable the discovery of the resource content; licensing frameworks to support sharing; and the communities of users. However, as we shall see, the potential of Jorum to assist in the teaching of quantitative methods in the social sciences is, at the time of writing, still under development. Indeed Jorum has undergone significant changes since this chapter was initially written in response to changing user requirements, in turn due to a changing external environment in which more content is being shared more openly in more online spaces. It follows that as well as the activities that were undertaken in Jorum's earlier days, we need to consider current steps to make Jorum a more user-focused organisation in its continuing stages of work, if it is to support future community engagement in the teaching of quantitative methods. This chapter therefore also describes several early experiences to date in collecting learning resources, and some of the subject areas that have engaged with the service. A brief case study of learning materials developed around international socio-economic data resources provides an example of how materials can be applied across a wide range of social science disciplines. Finally the chapter outlines the challenges that Jorum has identified in its initial phase, and is working to overcome in its continuation activity, if it is to be taken up by new virtual communities, including social science methods teachers.

Jorum: a service in development

Jorum started in 2002 as a Joint Information Systems Committee (JISC; www.jisc.ac.uk) development project. JISC's mission is to provide world-class leadership in the innovative use of information and communication technology to support education, research and institutional effectiveness. The project's remit was to develop a national repository that was capable of storing the outputs of national (primarily JISC) funded learning and teaching resources. It was initially funded under a programme called X4L (Exchange for Learning). The X4L website notes that:

> X4L has been motivated by the imperative to make the most of the considerable investment that has taken place in a range of content which has high potential value for use in learning. X4L was led by 31 projects from across the UK and involves more than 140 institutions and teams from colleges, universities, libraries, JISC services, local authorities and commercial companies

> It is clear that colleagues in the classroom wish to actively take a role in defining the kinds of content that would best fit their learning aims, and for national agencies and support services to work to provide the tools and infrastructure to allow exchange of learning to take place. (JISC, 2008)

X4L was thus a national venture, with widespread engagement, and Jorum was tasked with providing the national infrastructure required for sharing the learning content that the projects were creating.

Following a series of wide-ranging activities since the completion of the X4L programme, Jorum has now received continued financial support from JISC, with an associated plan for further development of the service until at least July 2011. A number of lessons have been learned during the period from its inception to the end of what can be regarded as its Phase One (to July 2008) and subsequently into its second phase (beyond August 2008). Because enhancements of the service are ongoing, this section necessarily describes a snapshot in time (in October 2010). The Jorum website was rebranded in September 2010 based on user feedback, but the future look of Jorum is likely to be different to its current form, the one described here. Such is the nature of changing online services.

Jorum was jointly established and is now managed by the two national data centres, Mimas and EDINA. Mimas (www.mimas.ac.uk), based at the University of Manchester, is a JISC and Economic and Social Research Council (ESRC)-supported centre of expertise and nationally designated data centre hosting a significant number of the UK's research information assets and building applications to help people make the most of this rich resource to support teaching, learning and research. EDINA is the JISC national academic data centre based at the University of Edinburgh: EDINA's mission and purpose is to 'enhance the productivity, quality and cost-effectiveness of research and education in the UK and beyond' (www.edina.ac.uk). The data centres provide support for networked access to key data and information resources to learners, teachers and researchers, primarily in UK post-compulsory education.

As the scope of Jorum is so wide – currently supporting all discipline areas in UK further and higher education and aimed at teaching and support staff – Jorum has aimed to work with intermediaries. Consequently the team also has links with bodies such as the Higher Education Academy and its 24 subject centres. The Higher Education Academy seeks 'to help institutions, discipline groups and all staff to provide the best possible learning experience for their students' (http://www.heacademy.ac.uk/ and http://www.heacademy.ac.uk/ourwork/networks/subjectcentres). Jorum also works with the 13 JISC-funded regional support centres (http://www.jisc.ac.uk/whatwedo/services/as_rsc/rsc_home.aspx), and provides training and support for nationally funded projects such as those of the Higher Education Funding Council for England (HEFCE)-funded Centres for Excellence in Teaching and Learning (http://www.hefce.ac.uk/Learning/TInits/cetl/) (until summer 2010) and the JISC/Higher Education Academy Open Educational Resources programmes (phase 1 http://www.jisc.ac.uk/whatwedo/programmes/elearning/oer and phase 2 http://www.jisc.ac.uk/oer) involved in developing learning resources. In short, the Jorum team engages with a wide range of people and organisations tasked with supporting the learner experience. Jorum continues to review its method of user engagement, with a view to adapting the existing model if necessary.

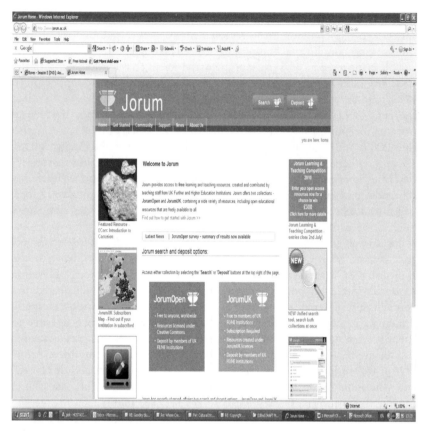

Figure 10.1   Screenshot of Jorum web page 2008

Reproduced with permission.

Jorum comprises a team of people, a website, a software system – called the repository – that holds the content and supports the searching of it, two collections of resources (JorumOpen and JorumUK), associated descriptions about those resources (the metadata), a licensing framework to support sharing of content, and a number of 'users'. The Jorum team has two co-directors, a service manager, a project manager, and a number of staff whose roles cover technical support and development, web development, communications, training and outreach, and user support, although not all staff are employed full-time on Jorum. Our website provides information about Jorum services and activities (www.jorum.ac. uk). Note this has developed as Jorum has responded to user feedback. Two screenshots are shown in Figures 10.1 (August 2008) and 10.2 (October 2010).

The website is an information resource in its own right. In Jorum's earlier days (phase one) the distinction between those who contributed content (depositors) and those who searched for or downloaded content (users) was more stark, partly due to the different and more complex licensing, and associated logging in, mechanisms associated with each of these functions. The website launch in September 2010 brought to the fore the key benefits for all users of the service; thus the *Find*, *Share* and *Discuss* actions associated with Jorum can now be clearly seen on the homepage. Featured resources chosen by the Jorum team and the community can also be viewed from the homepage, putting the content in Jorum at the heart of its online presence. Information on 'How to' is available from each of the context-specific areas of the website. Further user support is provided through a helpdesk and support team (http://www.jorum.ac.uk/support/index.html) by email or by phone. The Jorum mailing list supplies regular updates about development activities, new content, training events and so on (http://www.jiscmail.ac.uk/lists/jorum-update.html). Finally an electronic newsletter is distributed to the jorum-update distribution list on a quarterly basis, with monthly updates of bitesize news made available on the Jorum news blog (http://jorumnews.blogspot.com/).

In phase one, when institutions signed up to use Jorum, they were asked to nominate two people – typically located in the institution's library – to assist in local support. These individuals accepted a responsibility to make themselves known to their local users. Since Jorum has moved towards supporting open access to its materials this institutional sign-up is no longer required for content deposit, and so a supporting link with institutions has been lost. Working out how Jorum is supported at an institutional level is not easy, given the differences in support at a local level for learning and teaching across the sector. Jorum's work with intermediary organisations as noted above is therefore paramount to its success in this regard.

One of the lessons learned during the first phase of activity is that Jorum is more complex than it appears to its members, not least because it has two communities (depositors and users). The national data centres have traditionally provided access to services that have collections of content licensed for use by academics (so the deposit side has been attended to), whereas the aim of Jorum is to gather content developed at an institutional or cross-institutional level, and licence it back for use to the entire UK higher and further education community (for JorumUK) or globally (for JorumOpen). This is challenging from a licensing perspective, and also raises difficulties for the Jorum team in managing expectations. A common comment especially in Jorum's early days was that there was little or nothing in the repository on a particular subject. Our usual response cannot be other than to say that Jorum's role is not to *generate* content itself, but to be the *medium* through which academics can share content with others. It is a repository for other people's materials, and a means for others to access its content, and not a producer in its own right. In order to explain this position, and encourage participation, members of the Jorum team attend and give training events, and run workshops and awareness-raising sessions, give presentations at conferences and so on.

The Heery and Anderson (2005) report attempted to provide a typology of repositories, when they were in their infancy in academic institutions, defining a repository as 'a mechanism for storing and managing digital content' and identifying Jorum as a 'learning objects' repository. Jorum prefers to use the term 'learning resources' when it talks generically about the materials that can be deposited in the system, as learning objects can be a rather ambiguous (and now an out-moded) term. Repositories have been in vogue since the start of the twenty-first century, with much of the attention focused on access to research papers and publications, and a move towards establishing open access to content, both arguably driven by the post Research Assessment Exercise (RAE) 2008 agenda. Several publicly funded activities have run in parallel with Jorum, to open up access, under a variety of licensing models, to digital content for research and teaching and to provide the infrastructure (locally or nationally) to support this; JISC investments in this area are described under the banner of programmes on digital repositories (http://www.jisc.ac.uk/whatwedo/topics/digitalrepositories.aspx) and learning resources (http://www.jisc.ac.uk/whatwedo/topics/learningresources.aspx). The UK is fortunate to have had access to national initiatives of this nature to support the sharing of resources for the common good.

The Jorum repository is the software system and infrastructure that underpins the Jorum service. It can be regarded as a database which stores learning and teaching resources and the associated descriptions of that content, and supports a number of contribution options for depositors. The repository should be hidden from the user as far as possible, with their experience of engaging with Jorum being through the website. Significant work has been undertaken to achieve this, and the Jorum website launched in September 2010 hides the complexity of the underlying software from the user. More work remains to be done to improve the user experience; this is at the heart of Jorum's on-going development activity.

Anyone can search Jorum's content holdings at http://www.jorum.ac.uk/searchOptions.html but only authorised depositors can contribute content to the repository. The method for depositing content in Jorum has been streamlined (to make it easier for lecturers to share content quickly with their peers). Usually a depositor:

- logs onto the system;
- chooses a licence scheme under which to deposit their content;
- chooses a collection in the repository (via a subject classification) where their content will be located;
- uploads their materials;
- provides some descriptive information (title, keywords);
- saves and publishes the material on the system.

Further details of the steps to deposit content are available at http://www.jorum.ac.uk/deposit/deposit.htm with user guides for depositors at http://www.jorum.ac.uk/support/jorumopen_guides.html (for JorumOpen) and http://www.jorum.ac.uk/docs/pdf/jorumContributorQuickguide.pdf (for JorumUK). A later section discusses the matter of metadata, which will enable the resources to be discovered by others, describing how Jorum's approach has changed in line with social media services as they increasingly move towards 'user-generated' metadata rather than relying on qualified professionals to assist with this process. Institutions may require a 'quality assurance' step to support the sign-off of resources before they are published to the service; this can be carried out locally and requires a procedure to be set up at the depositing institution.

Jorum users

Jorum has two types of users. One type – the depositors – contribute content into Jorum for use under well-defined licensing arrangements by the others – the users – who access, download, reuse and re-purpose those resources. Informally these two groups can be thought of as 'putters' and 'getters', the first being a much smaller group than the second. The key verbs that Jorum uses in its web presence are 'Find', 'Share' and 'Discuss' in support of the actions these two constituent groups undertake. One of the original aims of Jorum was to provide a 'keepsafe' for learning and teaching resources that had been created under national, publicly funded projects, so naturally its initial content came from these sources. However, project teams will frequently disband at the end of the funding period and move on to other ventures, so some of the initial contributors are unlikely to remain active in this role. On the other hand, the user groups for these materials have grown, and often increased in size as a direct result of training and outreach work.

It is interesting to note how Jorum's use has changed with its development in the wider landscape; so under phase one of Jorum's activity when an institutional licence was required both to deposit and to use Jorum, at the end of May 2008 the number of institutions that had signed up to *contribute* content in Jorum was 93: 39 from higher education (23 per cent of all higher education institutions), and 54 from further education (12 per cent of the total possible). However, the number of institutions who signed up to be *users* of the service was 405: 135 (or 80 per cent of all higher education) and 270 (60 per cent) from further education. The total number of registered contributors and users was 5,200. In its earlier phase, Jorum therefore fared better as a user service than as a contributor service.

However, this is in part a natural outcome for a contributor/user scheme. By definition, a contribution can count only once, whereas it can then be – and is intended to be – utilised by an unlimited number of users. Arguably, users have more to gain than contributors because their effort costs are lower and their benefits are greater.

This participation inequality, well known in participatory services, is often referred to as the '90–9–1' rule.

> In most online communities, 90 percent of users are lurkers who never
> contribute, 9 percent of users contribute a little, and 1 percent of users
> account for almost all of the action.

> All large-scale, multi-user communities and online social networks that
> rely on users to contribute content or build services share one property:
> **most users don't** participate very much. Often they simply **lurk** in the
> background. In contrast, a tiny minority of users usually accounts for a
> disproportionately large amount of the content and other system activity.
> (Neilsen, 2006)

These earlier participation figures indicated room for improvement. The
team undertook an evaluation exercise in 2007, and has since implemented
the recommendations that arose from this. Also the external culture of sharing resources has changed in response to more widespread sharing on social
media websites, and funding councils recognising the need to provide access
to suitably licensed content for teaching and learning. Thus while the first
phase of Jorum required both an institutional and user sign-up, the second
phase requires only a user sign-up for the deposit of content, and some content is made available on open access. Work in hand will produce improved
information about the most popular resources (as viewed and downloaded).
The changes follow Eigen's five principles for making participatory services
a success:

- make it easier to contribute;
- make participation a side effect;
- edit, don't create content;
- reward – but don't over reward – participants;
- promote quality contributors.

   The Jorum team's experience indicates that the service is a 'recognised
brand', but as yet mostly in the area of learning technology and library staff.
The challenge for taking Jorum forward into the mainstream – for both
contributors and users – is not an easy one and the team recruited a community enhancement officer to assist with this remit and invested effort in
rebranding the Jorum website in line with user feedback. Where strong
academic communities already exist Jorum would wish to work with them
to support the sharing of materials, and conversations (the 'discuss' part of
Jorum) around the use of those materials. New lecturing staff and graduate
teaching assistants are a prime example of where exciting and innovative
teaching practice is developing; Jorum provides an opportunity for them to
share resources and ideas, and in this role can assist those new to teaching to
become reflective practitioners.
   There are several references throughout this section of initiatives such as
Jorum needing to be responsive to the changing environment; in Jorum's
case two key factors have affected its development. The first is the changing
culture and acceptance of sharing (so sites such as YouTube, Flickr and

Slideshare have met with phenomenal success); the second is the open access agenda, which has developed in the early twenty-first century alongside government initiatives to promote more open and widespread sharing of publicly funded data and resources for the public good. JorumOpen (the collection of resources in Jorum available under Creative Commons open licenses) had over 10,000 resources deposited within six months of it becoming available. This success, compared with the first phase of Jorum as discussed above, indicates the community's willingness to engage with an initiative to make teaching resources available under clear, open licensing arrangements for the benefit of others.

Jorum learning resources

The resources accepted for deposit in Jorum are described in the Collections Development Policy (http://www.jorum.ac.uk/docs/pdf/CollectionDev Policy2010.pdf), which has changed as the collection has developed. The policy refers throughout to learning and teaching resources (in contrast to the previous policy which made reference to learning objects, a rather laden and out-moded term).

Learning and teaching resources may be from any subject area, with a focus on the disciplinary content and skills in higher and further education. These resources range from well-defined learning and teaching resources (that may be contained within a 'wrapper' that describes the order in which the resources should be displayed in, for example, a virtual learning environment) to individual files and stand-alone digital assets. For example, Jorum accepts for deposit: documents; presentations; images; audio files; video and film; weblinks; links to resources held elsewhere; content packages; and courseware. The Jorum team can assist depositors by providing further information about the resources that can be accepted, as well as how they can be deposited into the service.

Examples of learning resources that have been deposited include many of those described on the 'featured resources' section of the website (http://www.jorum.ac.uk), such as the Social Care Institute for Excellence (SCIE) resources on teaching law for social workers; macro and micro data: the basics (featured in the case study section below); and the Integration by Parts materials. The featured resources at the time of writing include materials that were entered in the annual Jorum Learning and Teaching competition (http://jorumnews.blogspot.com/2010/09/top-three-announced-in-jorum-learning.html). Materials can be deposited into Jorum for 'keepsafe' or be linked to from Jorum and made available on an external website. This simply means that contributors can submit descriptions of resources that are contained elsewhere on the internet. A catalogued record is then held in the repository system which describes the external resource, and potentially its use in learning and teaching.

Single file objects that can be used in learning and teaching but are presented in themselves without any learning objectives can also be stored in – or be linked to from – Jorum. Examples would be video clips or short podcasts, audio files of classical music, an animation of a biological function, a set of PowerPoint slides or a PDF document. Indeed some of these materials have been among the most popular in terms of downloads from Jorum. Examples include a Flash resource for teaching shorthand; an interactive diagram of a direct cold water system; and a set of assets from the REHASH (Re-purposing Existing Healthcare Assets to Share) project to support student progression from further to higher education in medicine and healthcare; as well as images of artefacts from a digital collection such as the Betty Smithers Design Collection at Staffordhsire University (http://open.jorum.ac.uk/xmlui/handle/123456789/7376).

Information about the contribution processes in a quick reference and step-by-step format is available at http://www.jorum.ac.uk/docs/pdf/jorumContributorQuickguide.pdf (JorumUK) and http://open.jorum.ac.uk/xmlui/handle/123456789/7376 (JorumOpen). The uploading – or depositing – of single asset and web-based resources is extremely straightforward and requires no specialist skills. Depositing learning resources known as content packages, a collection of files that need to be structured in such a way that both the Jorum repository system and the Jorum users' local learning management system can interpret them, requires a little more expertise, but the Jorum training and support team can assist in this process as requested.

As we noted earlier, accessing contributions also necessitates information about the nature and location of the content in the form of 'metadata'. Metadata are not usually the most gripping of topics for academics! Fortunately Jorum has reduced the amount of descriptive information it requires from its contributors to a minimum. So a title, brief description and top level classification of the resource are all that is required, in addition to attaching a licence to the resource to make clear information about the rightholders of the content. The metadata in phase one of Jorum were enhanced by a team of information professionals who had been contracted to undertake this work; however, this practice has been replaced by the production of metadata purely by depositors.

The issue of 'discoverability' of resources is one that is still being debated as social media websites develop. This affects Jorum similarly. Previously, like Jorum, other repository ventures such as the Learning Exchange (a digital library for learning resources for social services and social work education in Scotland: http://www.iriss.ac.uk/learnx) have emphasised creating high quality metadata and effectively organising information. The Higher Level Skills For Industry project encapsulated the issue thus:

If you cannot search for an educational resource because it does not have metadata, or a search returns several hundred or thousand results, you either cannot re-use the resource because you cannot locate it or decide which resource is relevant to your needs because of the time required to assess the results of the search. (Ryan and Walmsley, 2003)

Jorum previously worked with Intute (www.intute.ac.uk) which, as well as assisting with a quality assurance of the metadata in the repository, also generated descriptions on its website about useful resources, or the 'Best of the Web', for users to browse at subject level. So, for example, the Intute editor for sociology created a description of Jorum that was both searchable through Intute's catalogue, or browsable through the Sociological Methodology structure, and provided information about the Jorum-update mailing list. Methods resources in Jorum were also described in Intute's Social Science Research Tools and Methods section to support the external discovery of resources (http://www.intute.ac.uk/socialsciences/researchtools/). Unfortunately, Intute was wound down from mid 2010 (http://www.intute. ac.uk/blog/ 2010/07/02/intute-end-of-an-era/) and this previously valuable activity will no longer support the discovery of methods (or other) resources in Jorum. However, JorumOpen resources are searchable through Google to assist in their discoverability.

Jorum licensing framework

During phase one, access for teaching and support staff (students were not included in the first phase) was arranged by their institutions signing up with the Jorum User Service through the Jorum Repository Licence. At login, users were required to agree to terms and conditions, reflecting those that had already been agreed to by the contributors. The permissions granted to use the materials, which are much wider than those granted by the Copyright Act, include permissions to aggregate, annotate, excerpt and modify; search, retrieve, display and download; save and print; incorporate into learning environments and compile into study packs; and use for promotional purposes (workshops, seminars, and conferences). Users' institutions are not allowed to sell or re-sell materials, or use them for commercial purposes; remove, modify or obscure copyright notices; or display or distribute the materials on externally facing websites or networks.

This clarity of conditions at login attracted welcome commentary in the Jorum External User Evaluation study conducted in 2006:

Focus group participants value Jorum simply for providing a facility for sharing content on clear terms and conditions. Content in Jorum may be used under the terms specified in the licence without seeking permission directly from the creator or rights-holder; the terms and conditions of use are clear. It is also valuable as a home for content created by projects which otherwise may be (and has previously been) lost. (Jorum External User Evaluation, 2007, section 5.1)

On the other hand, the complexity of the licensing regime during phase one, and the Jorum deposit licence, attracted widespread criticism. Again, comments from the evaluation study showed there was a perceived mistrust by Jorum of those it was attempting to attract to deposit content:

the relationship between the licences is presented on the Jorum website in a manner that may suggest a gross imbalance in trust. The webpage addresses depositors with information about what they 'cannot' do unless they sign the user licence ... it appears that Jorum secures promises and in return refuses to trust the depositor institution. (Jorum External User Evaluation 2007, section 7.1)

The news of Jorum relaxing its early licensing regime, or at least addressing the concerns caused by it, was generally met with considerable bonhomie; the result was that Jorum was able to support the JISC/Higher Education Academy Open Educational Resources programme (http://www.jisc.ac.uk/ whatwedo/programmes/elearning/oer Phase 1 and http://www.jisc.ac.uk/ oer Phase 2), and indeed share open resources beyond this programme.

The challenge for Jorum in its developing activity is to get the balance right between contributors and users, while retaining clear terms that protect rights-holders. The open licensing framework introduced in early 2010 concentrates on use of an established model used in the Open Educational Resources community; that is, the use of Creative Commons and its variants. The OpenLearn (http://www.open.ac.uk/openlearn/home.php) initiative through the Open University has employed this framework successfully. Jorum has thus been able to move to a more open model, which it calls 'JorumOpen'. However the service will also continue to offer a place where content can be shared specifically *within* the UK education domain; this will be known as 'JorumUK' (and includes the collection in Jorum's phase one). Where institutions or third party rights-holders wish to share with restricted communities, this will be supported through 'JorumPlus'.

Thus at the point of sharing resources, Jorum depositors have a choice of which community to share with, and are asked to assign a licence to the resources they deposit to make this intention clear (http://www.jorum.ac. uk/deposit/deposit.htm).

Jorum and the social sciences

Jorum's subject coverage is wide ranging, potentially covering all subject areas. In reality the subject areas which deposit content for sharing in the repository are likely to be those that:

- are active in eLearning;
- can see the benefits of Jorum as a place for sharing content and ideas about teaching;
- and/or have been mandated to deposit their content – or pointers to content held elsewhere on the internet – as a keepsafe activity.

To indicate the kinds of content currently available, three examples are briefly described here. All the resources described were deposited in Jorum's phase one (and so are available at JorumUK) and it is anticipated they will be made available at JorumOpen. The first example identifies resources developed around the issue of crime for the purpose of teaching and learning about variables and cross-tabulation. The second focuses on a prize-winning learning object developed for use in social work courses, while the third forms a case study for the remainder of this chapter, showing how social scientists could use the service to support quantitative methods teaching.

The first illustration is a simple case that gives a direct example of material that could be taken and re-purposed for other disciplines or themes and hence become highly relevant to the reader. Searching the Jorum repository for 'statistics' finds 147 hits; refining this by searching for 'social AND statistics' finds 30 hits. One of these resources is 'X4L SDiT Module 4: Examining Evidence: how to integrate crime statistics' with the associated metadata:

> This module looks at linking variables and constructing and analysing tables. Contains exercises using the British Crime Survey. The appendix to this module looks at statistical significance and shows how to use NSDstat to investigate this. (http://search.jorum.ac.uk/?q=Statistical+AND+Analysis)

The description links to a resource that is actually held at the University of Essex (http://x4l.data-archive.ac.uk/learning/module4/), one of a set that was developed under the X4L Programme, with the following learning objectives:

- you learn how to alter data;
- you learn how to examine associations between two variables;
- you learn how to present and analyse data in tables.

The second example is included not because of its relevance for quantitative methods, but because it illustrates the way clear learning resources and the associated metadata can enhance the utility of the core content. One of a series of 12 learning resources contributed to Jorum initially, with more to be placed in the service as they are developed, the resource was developed by SCIE for social work teaching. The example, 'All in a day's work' (see Figure 10.2), won an Association for Learning Technology prize for best learning object in 2007; indeed SCIE went on to win awards in the Jorum Learning and Teaching competitions in 2009 and 2010. The description below is taken from its metadata:

169

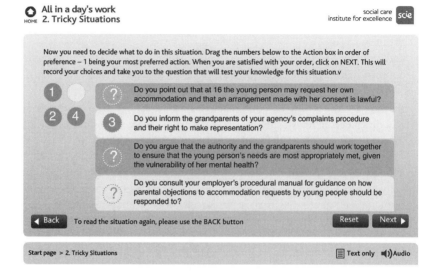

Now you need to decide what to do in this situation. Drag the numbers below to the Action box in order of preference – 1 being your most preferred action. When you are satisfied with your order, click on NEXT. This will record your choices and take you to the question that will test your knowledge for this situation.v

1 ◯ **?** Do you point out that at 16 the young person may request her own accommodation and that an arrangement made with her consent is lawful?

2 **4** **3** Do you inform the grandparents of your agency's complaints procedure and their right to make representation?

? Do you argue that the authority and the grandparents should work together to ensure that the young person's needs are most appropriately met, given the vulnerability of her mental health?

? Do you consult your employer's procedural manual for guidance on how parental objections to accommodation requests by young people should be responded to?

◀ Back   To read the situation again, please use the BACK button   Reset   Next ▶

Start page > 2. Tricky Situations   📄 Text only 🔊 Audio

Figure 10.2   Screenshot of SCIE page
Reproduced with permission.

This exercise forms part of a series on social work and the law. The object presents a series of interactive questions relating to a number of "tricky situations" that a social work practitioner may have to deal with. Users have to decide what action they would take and answer questions on the law as it relates to each situation. The aim is to enable users to assess their knowledge of social work law. There is a text only version of this learning object available. (http://search.jorum.ac.uk./?q=Social+AND+Work)

The SCIE (2008) website gives further details:

Who's it for?

SCIE's e-learning activities are designed to be used in a number of ways:

- as interactive self-study materials for students taking the Social Work degree;
- as e-learning materials that can be integrated by HE academic staff into their curriculum and/or their virtual learning environment (VLEs);
- as presentation material that academic staff can use with students in plenary mode through use of a multimedia projector or interactive whiteboard;
- as interactive self-study materials for Social Care practitioners;
- as e-learning materials that can be integrated by Social Care trainers into their training programs.

Figure 10.3   Screenshot of Jorum webpage October 2010
Reproduced with permission.

Learning aims

All in a day's work will:

- help you to reflect on what approach, or combination of strategies, you adopt to being a social work law practitioner;
- enable you to undertake an assessment of your social work law knowledge (SCIE, 2008).

While the SCIE resources are not aimed at quantitative methods teachers, they provide excellent examples of good learning materials whose design ideas are transferable to teaching substantive issues. In other words the objects are *re-purposeable*. In fact the objects could be redesigned to teach quantitative methods, though a certain level of technical skills would be required to achieve this.

Our third example was part of the ESRC-funded Researcher Development Initiative 2006–07, the materials being developed in the Linking International Macro and Micro Data project, later renamed 'Countries and Citizens' (http://www.esds.ac.uk/international/elearning/limmd/index.html or see the Jorum repository). The aims of the project were two-fold: to raise awareness of international data resources; and to increase understanding of the linkages between the macro and micro data (in this case provided through the Economic and Social Data Service (ESDS) International Service: http://www.esds.ac.uk/international). The content was made available both as learning resources in Jorum (through phase one so in JorumUK) and on open access on the ESDS International Service's website. It constitutes an interactive training resource developed for postgraduate and researchers (though they can be used by undergraduates) with online tutorials, activities, study guides and videos, designed to show how to combine socio-economic data from country level aggregate databanks (macro data) with individual level survey datasets (micro data).

The resources are presented as five self-learning units, each of which has been written by a subject specialist:

- Linking international macro and micro data – the basics (Celia Russell);
- Making cross-national comparisons using macro data (Dave Fysh);
- Making cross-national comparisons using micro data (Siobhan Carey);
- Combining macro and micro data (Steve Fisher);
- Using multilevel modelling (Mark Tranmer).

Unit One, by far the most popular, covers basic material (its learning objectives are outlined in Box 10.1).

Box 10.1   Unit One Learning Objectives

By the end of this unit you should:

- Understand the basic conceptual differences between aggregate and survey data
- Know how international data is produced and disseminated, and the role of ESDS International
- Know more about the organisations that produce the international databanks
- Outline the content of the major international aggregate databases
- Access, subset and chart data from the World Development Indicators
- Outline the content of the major international survey datasets
- Search for specific data using the ESDS International resources
- Look up original sources and definitions

The exercises presented in this unit require no specialist software or skills. All the analysis can be carried out on freely available data (the World Bank's World Development Indicators) using Microsoft tools (Excel). Later units require access to statistical processing software, and in some cases logging on to the databases in the ESDS International Portfolio. Indeed, the simplicity of Unit One has resulted in a request to translate the unit into Spanish for Latin American countries.

Unfortunately, as the website does not currently provide a feedback mechanism directly (though there is the option to email the ESDS International support team via the website), there is a paucity of information about how the resources are being used and by whom. Nonetheless, in terms of wider access Countries and Citizens has been a clear success story. Between May 2007 (when the website was launched) and August 2008, there were over 52,500 pages viewed by more than 33,300 unique visitors (as measured by IP addresses). The most popular unit is the introductory one, with 27,000 accesses to the PowerPoint slides for Unit One alone in that period. Interestingly the other units have received more hits for the online webpages than their PowerPoint slides. A crude analysis of the origin of those website visits shows that 13 per cent come from the USA, 10 per cent from China, 9 per cent from the UK, 6 per cent from India and Russian Federation, respectively, and 5 per cent from Korea.

However, in contrast to this wider open access take-up, the Countries and Citizens resources deposited in Jorum during its phase one have not been so well used and this in part is likely to be due to the fact that Jorum required a login which is clearly a barrier to use. Jorum could be used to best effect in this situation to initiate or signpost *discussions around the use* of the materials. In order for Jorum to engage with a full discussion of how and where the resources are being utilised, they would also need to be available on open access, through JorumOpen. An excellent opportunity therefore exists in taking the Countries and Citizens materials and experimenting with feedback around their use. Whether this discussion takes place in Jorum (for example in the Community Bay; http://community.jorum.ac.uk/) or elsewhere (for example in subject community areas where they exist, such as SAGE's MethodSpace; http://www.methodspace.com/) remains to be explored. There is nonetheless an opportunity for rich discussions and a sharing of information between teachers about the use of these valuable resources.

Exploration about the best way to support community evaluation of materials contained in Jorum is underway. Jorum (phase one) supported two mechanisms for evaluating resources; one was the facility to 'star rate' the material, the other was to provide comments on a resource, or its deployment. This enabled users of the resources to participate by adding value to them but this has not been widely used (as users needed to log in to leave comments/star ratings). Other mechanisms that are more akin to social software solutions (for example blogs and wikis) are being explored by the Jorum team, in consultation with their user community. A further function that could be introduced is 'really simple syndication' (RSS) feeds which would provide an immediate direct computer connection without having to visit the Jorum website whenever new materials, comments or updates are added. Many sites already provide this functionality including the BBC for 'news feeds'. In academia this technique is being used by some of the Higher Education Academy subject centres to pull back resources to a location that can be displayed as a resource list. For example, the Engineering Subject Centre does this and provides a searchable catalogue of learning and teaching resources for engineering students and teachers. This mechanism is under further investigation by Jorum and the aforementioned Open Educational Resources (OER) projects.

Jorum working with subject communities

An internal report commissioned for Jorum noted that:

> Users will only come to Jorum if they believe that it will offer a sufficiently good return on the effort they expend in using it. ... for web services ease-of-use is a pre-condition in offering a good return. Jorum will be used if it fulfils real user needs. (van Harmelen, 2007)

Associated with this is the requirement to support subject communities' needs. The growth of services in the Web2.0 world is proving that communities can develop around good content. Van Harmelen comments that:

> Powazek, who is a noted expert on community building and who was previously very active in community building, recommends that one way to get communities to form is to give the nascent and forming community great content. (2007)

The recommendation that follows on from this is to acquire great content, make it easy to get to, and advertise it widely and in a targeted manner. Individuals and departments can be targeted in order to reap success in sharing and reusing the content. Some of the responsibility for this falls on the Jorum team (make it easy to get to) and some on the contributors (great content), while there are also dependencies on other agencies to get the message across to those communities that could benefit from deploying the content. The chicken-and-egg nature of Jorum is a problem that remains to be solved but understanding the problem and its possible solutions is being explored through the JISC/academy OER programmes.

The content in Jorum can be regarded as 'social objects' around which communities can form. Engestrom links social software systems to their having social objects. He says:

> Objects are interesting as such. Yet it's even more in interesting what other people say about an object and what they do with it. (http://www.zengestrom.com/)

One way of providing opportunities for conversation to form around the content deposited in Jorum is to add social software techniques into the service or point users from Jorum towards the places where this conversation is occurring. Developing of such tools and techniques should assist in the ease of use of the service which has responded well to the changing environment, but Jorum is aware that more could be done to improve the user experience and support an easier sharing of content (the Jorum Roadmap at http://community.jorum.ac.uk/course/view.php?id=61 shows the plans for further development). The real issue is how to acquire good content in the first place. The Higher Education Academy subject centres could be instrumental in this regard. Working with professional associations and learned societies to assist in supporting their subject communities is another avenue that remains to be further explored.

Jorum's future role in developing learning and teaching

This chapter has discussed a national, innovative, exciting and *developing* resource that can assist teachers and learners of quantitative methods to share content, experiences and a network of like-minded contacts. The service could be used in the early stages of a teaching career and provides an opportunity for all those developing materials for the learner experience to become reflective practitioners. Until now Jorum has focused on building a framework and infrastructure (technical and legal) to support the collection of content. It has matured against a background of exciting initiatives that have taken this a step further by developing communities around good content. The focus of future work will be to engage contributors and users in conversations around content sharing and, importantly, teaching. In other words, Jorum is in a position to embrace 'social software' methods in its mission to support a community for sharing. The social science communities would appear to be well placed to embrace this step change in direction, with Jorum providing an opportunity for this enhancement of learning and teaching.

There are nonetheless many unanswered questions. Even though Jorum has becomes a more open place to share content, there are significant cultural and economic barriers to be overcome before the sharing of learning and teaching materials becomes widespread. Probably the key issue is 'Why share?'. The Jorum team is currently involved in opening up the debate in this area, challenging practitioners to reflect on their own (and their institutional) practices. Vast amounts of both public funding and also personal time, ingenuity and effort on the part of lecturers have been spent in developing content for learning and teaching. The challenge for Jorum is to support and encourage these people, to save them from unnecessarily reinventing the wheel, and at a system level to improve the educational effectiveness and product. Quantitative methods teaching is a prime example of an area which ought to be able to benefit from the Jorum initiative; here success will depend not only on the organisation and performance of Jorum but also crucially on the willingness of the community to contribute. Critically, quantitative methods teachers form part of this challenge. In order to facilitate engagement and growth, their – your – involvement in Jorum can help shape the direction it takes. Questions to be answered include:

- What types of resources are useful, and at what level?
- Do they already exist; how can they be released into sharing; or do they need to be created?
- What skills do lecturers need to develop interactive eLearning content?
- Who is best placed to carry this forward, and how will it be resourced?

The Countries and Citizens materials provide an exemplar of well-designed learning resources that have attracted significant use. The next steps are to build on this type of activity and use the lessons learned through the first phase of Jorum to aspire to reach the next level. Jorum has the potential to be a truly participatory service; social scientists can be part of that endeavour and they and their students will be the ultimate beneficiaries.

(All web addresses in this chapter were accessed between 10 and 18 October 2010.)

References

Engeström, J. (2010) Available at: http://www.zengestrom.com.

Heery, R. and Anderson, S. (2005) *Digital Repositories Review*, UKOLN and AHDS, 2005. Available at: http://www.jisc.ac.uk/uploaded_documents/digital-repositories-review-2005.pdf.

JISC (2008) *Exchange for Learning Programme (X4L) Programme: X4L Staff Development Resources.* Available at: http://www.jisc.ac.uk/whatwedo/programmes/x4l.aspx.

Jorum External User Evaluation Study (2007) Available at: http://www.jorum.ac.uk/docs/pdf/070717_JorumExternalUserEvalFinalJC.pdf.

Neilsen, J. (2006) Participation Inequality: Encouraging More Users to Contribute. Available at: http://www.useit.com/alertbox/participation_inequality.html.

Ryan, B. and Walmsley, S. (2003) 'Metadata collection: a project's problems and solutions', *Learning Technology*, 5 Available at: http://www.ieeetclt.org/issues/january2003/index.html#3.

Social Care Institute for Excellence (2008) *All in a Day's Work.* Available at: http://www.scie.org.uk/publications/elearning/law/law10/index.asp.

Van Harmelen, M. (2007) Enhancing Jorum's Use (internal project report).

The Problem, Strategies and Resources in Teaching Quantitative Methods: The Way Forward

Matthew David

The danger in outlining a problem lies in the risk that it has of disheartening those who would seek to tackle it. It is essential that any such account should not only attend to the processes that have led to things being as they are, and which keep them that way, but should also attend to the potentials for change that exist within any given state of affairs. The value of the contributions contained in this volume lies in striking that balance between the reality of the problem of relative weakness in social scientific training in quantitative methods and the array of strategies and resources that already offer the scope to address it. The problem is real, but not intractable. The solutions are available, but will not implement themselves. Far from fitting the common, if mutually contradictory, stereotypes of quantitative social scientists as either objectifiers of the way things are ('positivists') or objectifiers of inevitable changes through underlying mechanisms beneath the feet of living actors ('reductionists'), the authors in this collection highlight both patterns and possibilities.

The problem

The core problem takes a variety of forms across the social science disciplines, and the solutions will always require working within the traditions of each discipline. It is not possible to generate one single blueprint for a generic social science curriculum for quantitative methods teaching. It is one of the key observations of this book that such a 'one size fits all' approach, often delivered on grounds of cost saving or staff shortages, alienates students and staff not deemed experts in such a mythical 'generic' quantification. Rather it is essential to make quantitative training subject specific. The act of building teaching programmes that explore what is relevant and what is not, is one important way of building bridges between those badged as quantitative experts and those whose expertise is deemed field and content specific. In building such targeted teaching programmes, those labelled as technical experts can learn how to communicate with particular student audiences, just as those with other forms of substantive expertise may find it easier to develop their own technical competence and confidence.

In rejecting the fatalism of beleaguered zealots, triumphant in their own righteousness, but resigned in the face of their inability to get everyone else to see things their way, the authors in this collection also reject the inverted snobbery of the snubbed. It is not a question of returning to a golden age where all students and their teachers shared a knowledge and passion for quantitative methods of research design, data collection and analysis. This is a fictional past for the most part and in most places. Rather, this collection highlights the need, and the potential, for a future in social science where mixed methods means a genuine scope to choose and combine methods (quantitative and qualitative) to suit the problem being addressed. This bright future is far more attractive than the current state of affairs, where most practitioners are bound to a limited either/or choice between quantitative and qualitative, a choice often made, consciously or otherwise, at the very start of their social scientific training, and one which many feel unable to reverse once a sufficient amount of time has gone by.

It should be noted that the opening chapters in this work are as much concerned with outlining the nature of the problem of limited training in quantitative methods as they are with challenging the sense that such limits cannot be undone. The impasse in pre-university education, between a path that values language skills and one that emphasises numeracy, can be plotted back through the whole history of (at least Western) schooling, with the 'two cultures' divide very much favouring the former over the latter. This same division manifests itself in universities – and in social science departments in particular – with quantitative training being typically detached from substantive topic areas in a way that theory is not. The evidence put forward in this book repeatedly highlights that this state of affairs is not only problematic, but also seen as problematic by all parties to its continued existence. Universities, funding councils, employers, teaching staff and students all agree that things are not as they should be. There are no ardent defenders of the status quo.

Strategies

Even those who promote qualitative challenges to quantification in the social sciences tend to do so as a corrective to deterministic readings of statistical analysis rather than as an absolute rejection of numbers. Those truly and ideologically hostile to quantitative social science are relatively few.

An overwhelmingly non-quantitative teaching body tends to reproduce an overwhelmingly non-quantitative student body, from which the next generation of teachers will be selected. However, this reproduction is rather by default than from ideological commitment or design.

Students recognise the problem. Teaching staff recognise the problem. Perhaps the most significant empirical evidence presented in this work is the twin findings that 75 per cent of social science teaching staff believe students choose social science to avoid numbers, while 75 per cent of social science students claimed that they did not choose social science degrees to avoid numbers, but rather that the staff do not teach numbers as an integrated part of their degree programmes. Staff blame the students and students blame the staff. Each side expresses the view that things should change, but both claim they are constrained by an external reality they imagine is represented by the other.

While objective levels of innumeracy are problematic in staff and students alike, the above two statistics suggest the fundamental problem is not innumeracy itself but the belief that innumeracy is an ingrained and immovable property of 'other' social scientists, whether this be staff views of students or student perceptions of staff. Added to this mix of misperceptions are social statisticians' views of non-technical colleagues and of non-technical colleagues attitudes towards 'techies' and themselves. As such, having demonstrated how the problems in quantitative methods teaching in the social sciences are relatively open to change, this book devotes greater attention to the strategies and resources that can move beyond the present situation.

In seeking to debunk any sense that today's innumeracy is intractable, this text adopts a very inclusive conception of 'we'. 'We' includes those badged quantitative methods teachers, those who do a little quantitative teaching, those who have one foot in the water, those who are thinking about having a go, and also those who wonder whether they could or should find out more. 'We' also extends to all those social science students who are so often mis-labelled as number phobic. While the inner layer of this onion is rather small, the outer layers make up the vast majority of staff and students in the social sciences. While there are many who remain defensive on the question of their relationship with quantitative methods, this book offers useful avenues for engagement.

The array of strategies set out in Chapters 5–8 all aim to make numbers fit within substantive subjects, such that students and other staff can engage with numbers on their own terms rather than as an oblique exercise in technical proficiency. These four chapters, with their case studies of training for students in social research, politics, sociology, social work and social policy students, used a variety of techniques to make quantitative social science come alive. While each project was made to fit the disciplinary interests of the students concerned, all shared the common approach of building confidence and interest through sufficient time, practical engagement and tutor support. In particular it was noted throughout that numeracy can be learnt. It is not a prior quality that students either have or do not have in a fixed measure.

Resources

One growing possibility in teaching quantitative methods is to include fieldwork exercises where students can spend a protracted period focused on the actual business of doing a survey as part of a professional research team. Whether or not this be linked to academic researchers, government funded research projects or market research, the scope for fieldwork and placement-based learning is large. Within the curriculum, scope also exists for both improving the delivery of methods courses and for the integration of data collection and analysis components into theoretical and topic-centred modules. Both these approaches offer scope to engage not only students but also staff who can thereby escape the all too common binary opposition of either being a methods person or a non-methods person. In addition, the increased availability of secondary quantitative data through online access to ever-expanding data archives offers staff and students the opportunity to generate robust results with relatively limited time and resources. While time and resource limitations have encouraged anti-quantitative research specialisation because theoretical and qualitative research were seen as more feasible in the absence of a large grant or time-window, it is now possible to mine huge longitudinal and cross-sectional databases relatively quickly and with very little financial outlay. Getting students and colleagues to a level where they can engage with such material, and improving the ease of access to raw data, is a key strategy that itself chimes with the rise of a number of other key resources.

As well as increased online access to huge quantitative data archives for secondary analysis, other resources are becoming available to enable those seeking to teach quantitative research methods to do so better and more easily. Chapters 9 and 10 highlight just some of these resources: all the chapters indicate materials of value to anyone embarking on the task of delivering quantitative methods training in their respective social scientific field. While the Mathematics for Economics enhancing Teaching and Learning (METAL) project is focused on one particular social science, Jorum has created a web forum for sharing useful teaching resources for a range of subject areas. Cambridge University's Statistical Laboratory's website provides lots of useful examples of risk and probability examples from all aspects of life to be used as the basis for teaching formal calculation. Shared learning materials are being collected and posted online in increasing profusion, with a particular emphasis on the pooling of small, teaching-friendly datasets. Local, national and international networks of support and resources are developing apace.

In the UK, the funding councils and charitable foundations such as the Nuffield Trust are looking to invest heavily in the development of quantitative methods training capacity. The Royal Statistical Society now offers a part-time/online training programme, which can be taken either to gain a formal qualification in quantitative methods or on a more pick and mix basis for those wanting more specific training. The biennial Economic and

Social Research Council (ESRC) Research Methods Festival at Oxford University is an opportunity to learn and share ideas face to face. Information about all of the above was circulated through the Quantitative Methods Teaching network, which can be jointed by sending a blank email to quantitative_methods_teaching-join@ncrm.ac.uk. For those wanting to get into the loop, this is one very good place to start.

A way forward: enabling and encouraging mixed methods

The value of quantitative methods in social science is not because they are seen to be intrinsically superior to qualitative approaches. Rather it is the value of a genuinely open and mixed methods approach to the study of society that is called for, and it is simply the current weakness of quantitative methods training that is highlighted as the Achilles' heel in attempts to achieve such a balanced approach to research. In highlighting this weakness, as well as in showing the ways beyond the current difficulties, this book is of value not only to those currently teaching quantitative methods, but also to those who are not. As such it is a call for action and a presentation of the means by which an inclusive social scientific 'we' can choose to act.

INDEX

A level mathematics 19–20, 112, 142
access to staff training 23, 24
active citizenship 2–3
active participation 76
American Mathematics Association 41
antipathy 23
anxiety 86–7, 102–3
archived survey data *see* secondary analysis
assessment
  and assignments 90–4
  secondary analysis project 136
attitudes of students and staff 69–73, 86–7,
    97, 102–4, 155, 178–9
Australia 38–9

barriers/blockages 23, 177–8
  attitudes of students and staff 69–73,
    86–7, 97, 102–4, 155, 178–9
  'crisis of number'/numeracy 1–4,
    11–12, 14–18, 177–8
  integration *vs* isolation 107–11
  outcomes 117–19
  overcoming 26–9, 75–7, 178–9
    curriculum 113–15
    dissertations 115–17
  perceptions of relevance 104–7
  perceptions of secondary analysis 127
  technical language, pace and mode of
    delivery 111–13
benchmarks 9
best practice 32–3
  degree programmes 33–5
  identifying 40–2
  integrated approach 41, 42–3, 44, 45
  international comparison 35–7
  national patterns 37–40
  recommendations 44–5
  resources 46
  rigorous methods training 41
  undergraduate research 42–4
British Crime Survey 121, 122, 169
British Household Panel Study 137
British Sociological Association (BSA) 53,
    68–9, 69–70, 99, 122–3

Brown, G.W. 54
Brunel University 144, 145
Bulmer, M. 51, 52, 60
  et al. 61
business studies 38–9

Cambridge University Statistical
  Laboratory 180
Canada 39, 43
Cathie Marsh Centre for Census and
  Survey Research (CCSR) 124
Cicourel, A.V. 52–3, 54
Clawson, R. et al. 93
Cole, K. et al. 123, 137
Collection of Historical and
  Contemporary Censuses
  (CHCC) 139
Commission on the Social Sciences
  15, 16
communication 109–10, 118
competencies 11
  self-reported 127–8, 133–4
consultancy service 114
Council of European Social Science
  Archives (CESSDA) 138
Countries and Citizens project 171–3,
  176
Creative Commons license 154,
  165, 168
credits 135, 136
'crisis of number'/numeracy 1–4, 11–12,
  14–18, 177–8
Crompton, R. 54

Dale, A. et al. 121, 137
data collection and analysis 92–4, 96
  see also secondary analysis
data services 123
Department for Education and Science
  (DfES) 14, 67
disciplinary challenge 67–9
discipline(s) 10–11, 13
  -based research 76
  interdisciplinary approach 59, 80

dissertations 10, 42–4, 100, 101, 115–17
  optional statistics 96
  requirements 39–40
  see also secondary analysis
drop-in clinics/tutorials 117, 119, 126

Economic and Social Data Service
    (ESDS) 123, 124, 125, 130, 135, 138
  International Service 171–2, 173
  teaching resources 139
Economic and Social Research Council
    (ESRC) 1, 3, 10–11, 14–15, 17, 18,
    22, 24
  data 121
  'deficit' 99, 100
  funding 119, 122
  *International Benchmarking Review of
    Best Practice* 35
  postgraduate research 62
  promotion of quantitative methods
    74, 85
  Question Bank (Qb) 61
  Research Methods Festival 180–1
  Researcher Development Initiative 171
  Survey Link Scheme 59–61
  training and awards 58–9
  undergraduate student attitudes
    survey 70–3
economics 38–9
  see also mathematics for economics
    (METAL) project
Economics Network 144
EDINA 159
Educational Broadcasting Services Trust
    (EBEST) 145
employment issues 20–1, 67, 85–6, 94,
    149–53
enabling resources 23
Engestrom, J. 174
European Social Survey 137
Excel 100
Exchange for Learning (X4L) 158–9, 169
expertise, limits of staff 110–11

feedback 95–6
fieldwork 77
  case study: Belfast, Northern Ireland
    77–82
financial incentives 116, 118, 125,
    126, 135

Finland 43
focus groups 101, 102–3, 109
Fry, H. et al. 76–7

GCSE mathematics 19, 20, 21, 67, 85,
    126, 142, 155
General Household Survey 137
general research methods
  requirements 38–9
government censuses and surveys
    55–7, 68
Greenhow, M. 144

Heather, K. 144
Heery, R. and Anderson, S. 161–2
Higher Education Academy 24
  Open Educational Resources
    programme 168
  subject network/centres 69–70, 144,
    159, 173–4, 175
Higher Education Funding Council 15,
    99, 119
  FDTL5 initiative 143
Higher Level Skills for Industry
    project 166–7
Howery, C. and Rodriguez, H. 41, 42, 43
Husbands, C.T. 52, 53

integrated approach 41, 42–3, 44,
    45, 100–1
  balanced 13–14
  vs isolation 107–11
Integrating Data Analysis (IDA) project,
    USA 41, 42
Inter-university Consortium for Political
    and Social Research (ICPSR) 138
interdisciplinary approach 59, 80
international approaches
  comparison 35–7, 58
  Countries and Citizens project
    171–3, 176
  see also specific countries
International Association of Social
    Science Information Service and
    Technology (IASSIST) 138
internet resources 22–3, 114–15, 118–19,
    137–40, 180–1
  see also Jorum; Mathematics for
    Economics (METAL) project
Intute 167

Joint Information Systems Committee
(JISC) 158–9, 162
Distributed e-Learning II (JISC Del II)
project 149
Higher Education Academy Open
Educational Resources
programme 168
Jorum 140, 157–8
External User Evaluation study 167–8
future role 175–6
licensing framework 167–8
metadata 162–3, 166–7
resources 165–7
service in development 158–63
social sciences content 168–74
users and contributors 163–5
working with subject communities
174–5
JorumOpen 160, 161, 162, 165, 167, 168,
169, 173
JorumUK 160, 161, 162, 168, 169

'language brain' and 'maths brain'
103–4, 111
Levine, F. et al. 41, 42, 43, 44
Lewis-Beck, M. 86–7, 88
Linking International Macro and Micro
Data see Countries and Citizens
project
London School of Economics (LSE)
50–1, 52, 53, 54, 56, 57, 58, 59
Lonergan, N. and Andreson, L.W. 77
Lynch, R. et al. 13, 15

MacInnes, J. 9, 17–18, 21
McVie, S. et al. 13, 15, 23, 24
mandatory statistics 88–90
Marsh, C. 53–4, 55, 73
Cathie Marsh Centre for Census and
Survey Research (CCSR) 124
mathcentre 144
mathematics
A level 19–20, 112, 142
GSCE 19, 20, 21, 67, 85, 126, 142, 155
and science, school standards in
19–20, 21
mathematics for economics (METAL)
project 142–3, 154–5
dissemination and evaluation 153–4
employability 149–53

mathematics for economics (METAL)
project cont.
key problems 143
materials 145–9
rationale and structure 143–5
team development 153
MIMAS 123, 159
Minority Opportunities through School
Transformation (MOST) programme,
USA 41, 42
mixed methods 13–14, 181
Moser, C. 50, 52, 55–6

National Science Foundation, USA 35, 36,
41, 42
Netherlands 38–9, 43
Norway 43
Nottingham Trent University 148–9
numeracy/'crisis of number' 1–4, 11–12,
14–18, 177–8

Office of Population Censuses and Survey
(OPCS) 55–6, 57
optional statistics 96

Payne, G. 16, 74
et al. 10, 12, 123
pilot studies 92
Platt, J. 53, 68
political science 38, 39, 73, 86, 106
Political Analysis: Approaches and
Methods project 88–96
'positivism' 51, 53, 69, 83
postgraduate research 62
postgraduate training 58–9
Practical Exemplars in Analysing Surveys
(PEAS) 139
presentation problems 89
problem-based learning 76, 78, 79
professional challenge 73–5
professional training
accessibility 23, 24
contemporary and future challenges
62–3
early years 49–51
government and academic survey
research 55–9
interdisciplinary approach 59
international approach 58
LSE 50–1, 52, 53, 54, 56, 57, 58, 59

professional training *cont.*
  postgraduate training 58–9
  research methods teaching (1979–1981)
    51–5
  research resources 59–61
psychology 37–8, 39, 42

quantitative methods
  definitions 10–14
  and non-quantitative methods
    12–13, 106
  mixed methods 13–14, 181
Question Bank (Qb) 61

relevance, perceptions of 104–7
repositories 161–2
Research Methods Festival 180–1
Researcher Development Initiative 171
resources 46, 59–61, 180–1
  enabling 23
  internet 22–3, 114–15, 118–19, 137–40,
    180–1
  see also Jorum; Mathematics for
    Economics (METAL) project
  secondary analysis 136–40
Rice, R. et al. 122, 123, 127, 129
rigorous methods training 41
role models 110
Ross, A. 152
Royal Statistical Society 180
Ryan, B. and Walmsley, S. 166–7

schools
  MOST programme, USA 41, 42
  standards in mathematics and science
    19–20, 21
  summer and winter 116–17, 119
SCIE *see* Social Care Institute for
  Excellence
'scientific method' 88–9
Scottish Funding Council 15
secondary analysis 121–2
  appropriate content delivery 128–31
  curriculum context of Manchester
    project 124
  dissertation topics 134
  new module design and assessment 136
  participants 126–8
  participation, attendance and outcomes
    131–5

secondary analysis *cont.*
  project background 122–3
  project evaluation 135
  project structure 124–6
  resources 136–40
self-evaluation 126
self-reported competencies 127–8, 133–4
small group learning/tutorials 96, 112–13,
  117, 121
Social Care Institute for Excellence
  (SCIE) 165, 169–71
social work 106, 165, 169–71
sociology 37–8, 39, 42, 68–9
  presentation of material 26–9
  see also professional training
SPSS software 90, 93–4, 100, 127, 130,
  136
staff
  attitudes of students and 69–73, 86–7,
    97, 102–4, 155, 178–9
  communication 109–10, 118
  limits of expertise 110–11
  teaching assistants 95–6, 130
  see also entries beginning professional
statistics
  mandatory 88–90
  optional 96
  SPSS software 90, 93–4, 100, 127,
    130, 136
streaming 112
students
  attitudes of staff and 69–73, 86–7, 97,
    102–4, 155, 178–9
  engagement 75–7
  as victims 18–22
subject communities 174–5
subject-specific approach 114–15,
  118, 177–8
summer and winter schools
  116–17, 119
Survey Link Scheme 59–61
survey method 53–4
survey research 55–9, 68
Survey Resources Network 61
Sweden 38, 43

targets and tactics 22–6
Taylor, R. 144
teaching assistants 95–6, 130
transferable skills 150–1, 153

UK Data Archive 123
University of Birmingham 145
University of Edinburgh 159
University of Essex 169
University of Manchester 121, 124, 159
University of Plymouth 76, 77, 78, 81
University of Portsmouth 144, 146
University of Sheffield 88
University of Southampton 100–1
USA 37, 39–40, 41–2, 43
    National Science Foundation 35, 36, 41, 42
    social survey research 56–7, 58, 68

van Harmelen, M. 174
videos 146–8
virtual learning environment (VLE) 95

Wakeford, J. 51–2, 53
Williams, M. 67, 69, 75
    and Cheal, B. 74
    et al. 14, 26, 68–70, 86, 99, 116, 122
winter and summer schools 116–17, 119
Wooding, D. 85
Woolcock, N. 85
work-based learning 76–7
workbooks 130–1

X4L (Exchange for Learning) 158–9, 169